BECKHAM

WAYNE BARTON

BECKHAM

THE MAKING OF A MEGASTAR

First published by Pitch Publishing, 2020

Pitch Publishing
A2 Yeoman Gate
Yeoman Way
Worthing
Sussex
BN13 3QZ
www.pitchpublishing.co.uk
info@pitchpublishing.co.uk

A CIP catalogue record is available for this book
from the British Library.

ISBN 978 1 78531 676 0

Typesetting and origination by Pitch Publishing
Printed and bound in India by Replika Press Pvt. Ltd.

Contents

Too Good to be True

MOST STORIES about a player signing for a club as a youngster follow a similar pattern: a young lad is spotted by a scout whilst playing for a local team; there is possibly some competition for his signature and a decision to make. Maybe the story has a little more flavour if some skulduggery is involved – incentives that would be frowned upon today, and indeed would have been back then if they had been made official or public. Sometimes it is the identity of the scout, a legendary talent spotter – and goodness knows, Manchester United had a few – who finds and identifies a rare gem destined for greatness. David Beckham was not so much discovered as he was served up by himself on a silver platter, donned in the red, white and black of Manchester United.

This is not to say that his path to professional football was remarkably different to that of any other aspiring young boy. The things that in hindsight are seen as fated are probably not so exceptional when considering what was normal at the time. David Robert Joseph Beckham was born in Leytonstone, north-east London, to Sandra and Ted on 2 May 1975 – his middle name after one Bobby Charlton, the then-recently retired Manchester United legend. This was because his father was a huge United fan.

According to Ted, young David was almost too good to be true: never in trouble at school, the best at every ball sport. To the thrill of his father, the son excelled at football, and loved it from the second he was introduced to it. He also shared his love for Manchester United, and the pair would go to see their team whenever they were in the capital. When he was six, David went on a summer course organised by Spurs legend Cliff Jones (Jones, incidentally, had been one player the former Manchester United assistant manager Jimmy Murphy had tried to sign when he was interim manager after the Munich air disaster). He showed tremendous promise, earning the 'top badge' award for completing various drills better than other young players who were ten years older.

David would accompany his father when he was playing for semi-professional side Kingfisher. They trained at Wadham Lodge, and the waif-like child found that the adults were happy to allow him to play in five-a-sides – so long as he could take the bumps that came with it.

The following year, Beckham was spotted playing on the park across the road from his house – Chase Lane Park – by Stuart Underwood, the coach of local youth team Ridgeway Rovers. Ted recalled his son running home excitedly to tell him that a man wanted him to try out for a youth team. An alternative recollection of this story, presented here for completeness, was that David attended a trial after an advertisement had been placed in the local newspaper, the *Walthamstow Guardian*. It is long enough ago for the specifics of the arrangement to be lost from memory, although the coach was clearly left with a vivid impression.

'He was a football nutcase,' Underwood remembered in 2003. 'His life was football. He wanted to be a pro aged seven … he looked a professional from day one … he could hit the ball from every corner of the pitch. His timing was incredible.'

Underwood was regarded as a 'sergeant major' type: a hard but fair leader who was not shy in telling children as young as Beckham was that they needed to improve, or that they'd had a bad game. Ted was sometimes hesitant – like most reasonable parents, he was not always comfortable with his son, who could be sensitive to criticism, being scolded in front of other kids – but David was in fact very responsive to the leadership. Perhaps that's because, despite the generation gap, there was a kindred spirit between him and Underwood. David was a very tidy child, according to his parents, and liked everything to be neat. Underwood was also a stickler for the perfect preparation, be it ensuring the pitches were good, or even demanding that the young players wear a shirt and tie when turning up for an important game like a cup final. The coach also instilled discipline: if a youngster was late for training during the week, they wouldn't be able to play at the weekend. The high calibre of organisation provided the perfect platform for young players to shine.

Ridgeway's talented side were winning games handsomely; it was a regular occurrence to hit double figures. Ted had joined the coaching staff there, working alongside Underwood and assistant coach Steve Kirby.

In the summer of 1985, after Manchester United had won the FA Cup, David enrolled in the Bobby Charlton Soccer and Sports Academy, attending for the residential summer classes after seeing a feature for it on the television programme *Blue Peter*. The boy who had grown up in a red-and-white kit did not initially take to life in Manchester University's halls of residence.

'Mum and Dad came up and stayed with relatives near Liverpool, and I was on the phone to them every evening,' Beckham admitted. 'I had toothache. I was homesick. And the week just passed me by a little.'

Many children might have given up after such a setback. David might not get his dream of playing for United, but getting a chance to become a professional footballer was at least something within the realms of possibility.

Local professional clubs like West Ham were sniffing around the Ridgeway Rovers players, though the coaches such as Underwood were advising that it was best for their collective development to stay where they were to improve for the time being. They did just that, but there was no doubting even at that stage that there was one name which stood out. The present day Ridgeway Rovers website boasts that over two years, Beckham scored around 100 goals.

Ted and Sandra had been sufficiently tempted by the prospect of West Ham to take David to watch a game there; however, they too were sensible enough to not bite the first offer, taking Stuart's advice that offers would continue to be forthcoming. The Hammers had offered ten-year-old David a trial.

No concrete decision was taken on his future, so Ridgeway were blessed to retain his talents, but the talented young midfielder did enjoy some training sessions at top London clubs like Arsenal, and his maternal grandfather's club, Tottenham Hotspur. With David approaching his 11th birthday, it was decided that the time was right to commit to a professional club, and so the names of the fierce north London rivals were put into a hat. Thankfully for the sake of family relations, Spurs were picked out, and he joined their school of excellence.

In the summer after he turned 11, David went back to the Bobby Charlton school in Manchester, desperate to make a better impression. He did, excelling on all the skills courses through his week, and advancing to the 'Grand Final' which was to be held in Manchester in December 1986.

Ironically enough, on the weekend of this final, United were entertaining Tottenham. In the morning, David had to go to The Cliff, United's famous training facility in Lower Broughton, Salford. There was a competition in the indoor sports hall and David won through, impressing with his short passing, ball-juggling and target shooting.

'In addition to his natural ability, David displayed a fantastic work ethic and a great deal of determination, which meant he was continually practising his individual skills,' recalled Bryn Cooper, the director of the courses. 'It was clearly evident to the coaches that David was completely focused on becoming a professional footballer.'

The second part of the final was to be staged before the game at Old Trafford, which was being aired live on the BBC.

Almost 36,000 supporters were in attendance to witness a moment that would forever be remembered by the Beckham family, although it passed without any significance to most who were there.

'He looked so tiny and the stadium seemed so enormous around him,' Ted recalls of seeing his son walk on to the Old Trafford pitch for the very first time. Not for the last time, there was a sense of occasion and dramatic tension, although on this introductory stage, it came with the traditional pantomime feel that football 'banter' often carries. Young David was introduced as hailing from Leytonstone – cue cheers from the Tottenham fans – before being revealed as a 'massive United fan' – prompting a retaliatory roar from the home crowd.

What a galvanising lift for the young boy, who had already shown such confidence in the morning's event. The drills in this portion of the event were dribbling and long passing. Of course, in years to come, both of these skills would often be used in different evaluations of David's ability, but here he excelled at both, winning the competition. The first reward seemed more for Ted – the presentation of the award in the Europa Suite at Old Trafford was by none other than Sir Bobby Charlton himself. The prize, however, was definitely for David – two weeks training with Barcelona at the Nou Camp, to take place in early 1987. The youngster was more interested in watching his team play, however, and settled down to witness a frenetic 3–3 draw, as the first few weeks of Alex Ferguson's era as manager continued to be bumpy. David's heroes were Gordon Strachan – he modelled his hairstyle after him – and Bryan Robson. Both were influential as the home team stormed to a 2–0 lead, but Spurs turned it around in the second period, and looked set to win 3–2 before Peter Davenport levelled with two minutes left. (Incidentally, on the Spurs team that afternoon was one Glenn Hoddle.)

Barcelona were capturing the attention of the British press due to the fact they had Terry Venables and Gary Lineker as manager and star striker respectively. They also had the attention of the Beckham family thanks to the presence of former United striker Mark Hughes. David travelled with two other winners – aged 15 and 19 – and Ray Whelan, from the soccer school. They stayed in a converted farmhouse in the Catalan club's La Masia complex. It was an education on and off the pitch for the young Londoner, who described the training as 'amazing', but also recalled some of the older boys whistling at prostitutes who were walking around the other side of the railings on the training ground. 'The football was an experience,' Beckham later said. 'And so was the rest of it.'

Despite this heady experience, the youngster did not forget his roots, and initially had reservations about going to Spain at all. Ridgeway Rovers had a cup final against Forest United on the middle Saturday of the planned trip. To top it off, the game was being played at White Hart Lane. David was desperate to play in it. His grandfather, Joe, the Spurs fanatic, was as well. So much so that he paid for a flight to get his grandson from and back to Spain to play in the game. (Incidentally, Joe had also paid the £130 registration fee for the Charlton soccer school.) Ridgeway lost 2–1: no fairy-tale ending this time.

The mid-trip break did nothing to make his Spanish hosts think any less of him. Venables, in fact, could not have sung David's praises any higher. 'I knew from the first time I saw him that David Beckham would be something special,' Venables said. 'The way he looked, the way he played and the way he conducted himself on the training pitch around international stars. Becks, then ten, came over to our training ground as part of his prize for winning a competition run by Bobby's soccer school. He had apparently been his star pupil in the half-term and summer holidays training camp – and when he arrived at our training base it was not difficult to see why. A quiet lad, we showed him around and posed for the usual photos. Then he watched us train and we invited him to take part in a couple of sessions. Blimey. He raised a few eyebrows that day. I must have watched thousands of kids in my time but as we said goodbye I made sure I would not forget his name.'

The same could be said for Manchester United, who had apparently now got the hint, and had their London scout Malcolm Fidgeon watching Beckham more closely. United would invite the Beckham family to attend some of their London games, and to spend time around the squad at the hotel. David would arrive with gifts for his heroes – hair gel for Gordon Strachan, a pen for Alex Ferguson. Ferguson took the pen and informed the boy he would one day use it to sign him for the club. David had been invited to train in Manchester during school holidays.

In late October 1987, United were down in London at West Ham. Fidgeon informed the Beckham family that they had been invited to dinner with Alex Ferguson the night before the game at the team hotel. The manager told the boy to go and get the autographs of his heroes, who were all eating on nearby tables. David was invited to be the team mascot for the game and was even able to kick the ball around with the likes of Bryan Robson and Gordon Strachan. When the game started, Ferguson insisted that the young boy should sit next to him for the duration of the game. The game was live on ITV, a fine memory for the family to look back on.

Now his name was becoming more prominently known around the soccer circuit. The precocious 12-year-old was coveted by many clubs, with some more keen than others to take a chance and snap him up before someone else came in. Norwich City were one. Then-Canaries manager Kit Carson recalled observing the young midfielder at close quarters, describing him as 'highly professional'. 'We all thought he was a brilliant person and polite and thoughtful,' Carson said. 'He was always clean and smart on and off the ball and asked questions and listened. At the end of the week I knew that David was exactly the type of boy we wanted in our very successful youth policy at Norwich City.'

David, however, said no to going back. He rejected a trial at Nottingham Forest, concerned that it took place during a week when he was supposed to be training at United. He was still able to play for Ridgeway, and his school team at Chingford High, and consequently for the district side for Waltham Forest, also representing the Essex county side. David likened being selected for Waltham Forest to being picked for England.

At county level, David was coached by a man by the name of Martin Heather, a contrasting character: well-spoken and studious, so when he was stern, you knew he meant it. It was with Heather that a young David went over to play in the Dallas Cup, a prestigious but rarely acknowledged world youth competition in Texas which had recently seen former Queens Park Rangers and Millwall boss Gordon Jago join its board. The Dallas Cup welcomed teams from all over the world, and in later years, clubs like Manchester United would send junior sides over and introduce them to working with the media as part of some early-stage development in the early 1990s. This was a unique tournament: the organising committee also operated a homestay programme where visiting players could stay with volunteer families whilst they were in Dallas. David stayed with a Mexican family and enjoyed McDonald's 'for breakfast every morning'.

He returned from the US with a renewed focus to sign schoolboy terms with a professional club. The dream remained to sign for United, but there was a realistic alternative in Spurs. It would not have been a dreadful scenario. David enjoyed training there and had a good relationship with the youth development officer, John Moncur. When new Tottenham boss Terry Venables was discussing prospects with Moncur, he was delighted to discover that the boy who had impressed him in Spain was a candidate.

David remembered John introducing him and his parents to Terry for a meeting just before his birthday, where it was more or less straightforward that Spurs would offer terms. First impressions clearly count for a lot: Terry asked John what he 'had to say about this young lad', and the Beckhams got the distinct impression that the Spurs manager was not as familiar with the youngster as they had hoped. And definitely not as familiar with him as Alex Ferguson at Manchester United seemed to be.

'I got the impression that, although I'd been training at Spurs for a couple of years, the manager didn't really have any idea who I was,' Beckham recalled. 'I couldn't help thinking about the times I'd been up to Manchester. Alex Ferguson knew all about me. He knew all about every single boy. He knew their parents, he knew their brothers and sisters. That seemed important to me. Important for my future. It always felt like you were part of a family at United.'

If Venables seemed aloof, well, that certainly was not the case when it came to the offer on the table from the club. It was, in effect, a six-year proposal offered by Tottenham. Two years as a schoolboy, two years on the Youth Training Scheme apprentice programme and two years on a professional contract. There was also the promise of a signing-on fee of at least £70,000. 'I could buy a Porsche,' Beckham remembered thinking, but he showed a calmness that belied the situation by asking for time to think about it.

His head had been turned by the promise from Ferguson that he would be signed for United, and there was a meeting scheduled for around three weeks later at Old Trafford. That meeting took place on 9 May 1988, one week after David turned 13.

In his first full season, Ferguson had steered United to second place in the First Division. A comfortable second – not close enough to challenge Liverpool, but too far in front of Nottingham Forest to be frightened about dropping down a position. A run of eight draws from the first 15 games had really hampered serious talk of title ambitions, but United had finished with seven wins from their last eight, including the end-of-season game that the Beckham family attended against Wimbledon.

When they arrived at Old Trafford, Ferguson left the team, who were having lunch, to greet the family and to tell them he would see them after the match. Who is to know how events might have transpired if Spurs had shown the sort of personal touch that United showed? On the drive to Manchester, Ted had discussed with his son the various options, and urged him to think long and hard about the security of the offer in London.

He needn't have worried. United showed just as much commitment to his son's future as Spurs were willing to. In addition to the red carpet, it made for a memorable day. At 5.30pm, around half an hour after the game had ended, Joe Brown, United's youth development officer, took the family to the manager's office. Also present was Malcolm Fidgeon, the London headteacher and United scout who had driven David to and from his training sessions in Manchester. Les Kershaw, one of the senior scouts, was there. To make the boy feel more at ease, Ferguson remarked that he felt David had enjoyed a growth spurt since they'd last met, though he joked that he didn't like his new spiky haircut. The discussion became more formal as Ferguson sat at his desk.

'He has everything it takes to become a United player,' he said to Sandra and Ted, 'and everything it takes to become a United legend. We've kept a dossier on him for the last couple of years. He's an incredible player who we believe is getting better and better. He's a credit to you. He has everything we're looking for and we want him to become a Manchester United player.'

The manager then said he was offering 'two, two and two': the same structure as Spurs. Ted asked his son what he wanted to do. 'I want to sign,' David said. And, using the same pen he had given Ferguson as a gift, he did just that.

Fated

THERE ARE incidents and moments to come – as there are some already discussed – where it feels safe to assume that there was some gentle manipulation by David Beckham when it came to the way his career seemed to be carved by destiny. There were some moments that were, no matter which way you want to look at it, purely and simply coincidence. Take ending up with the room which Mark Hughes used to lodge in as an apprentice, for example.

David was such a fanatic of Manchester United that almost any player could have been described as his hero. But some stood out more than others. There was Bryan Robson in the number 7 shirt. Gordon Strachan with his clever wing-play. And then there was Hughes, who the youngster had not only idolised at Old Trafford, but had managed to share some time in Barcelona with, too. In his own teenage years, Hughes had stayed with Annie and Tommy Kay, who lived in Lower Broughton – in fact, across from The Cliff training ground.

It took a short while for David to settle there. In his first digs, he was upset when the dad clipped him around the ear for getting home late. The club moved him into another residence, where he roomed with another youngster who had been making cross-country trips to Manchester. That boy was defender John O'Kane, an equally gifted footballer, who shared with David a cultured style that the club were keen to see in the youngsters on their books.

O'Kane was from Nottingham – much more local than London, but far enough south to strike up a kinship with the Leytonstone lad.

'Me and him came up a lot earlier to train than most of the other players at United,' O'Kane recalls. 'We soon became attached to each other, as we both were from down south so we sort of got each other. He seemed shy until he was on the field. He was switched on from an early age. As a person he wasn't very outgoing, which is strange because of his exterior. The clothes, the good looks, the fame which eventually came … we spent every day together, for the best part of four years in digs and then a few more whilst we were at United. I think I can say I knew him pretty well, warts and all. Watching him closely, I knew there was something special … he just had this desire I wish I had. I was a very natural player, and so was he, but the desire and determination was what set him apart from most players.'

Perhaps the extra on top was Beckham's fanatical obsession with being at Old Trafford. There are a number of contrasts between him and O'Kane, one of them being the fact that Beckham was not only a paid-up member of United's supporters' club, but so obviously so as to make him the butt of early jokes.

'Becks came with the reputation of being a Bobby Charlton soccer school winner, which he was teased a lot about by the Manchester-based lads and some of the older pros,' O'Kane remembers. 'He didn't care about that – he was just focused on the bigger goal, which obviously turned out OK for him.'

Beckham's visibility made him something of a special case. His pathway to Old Trafford was, of course, the result of an intensive and extensive recruitment drive by Alex Ferguson, who had instructed his scouts to find the best young players in the country. His presence, be it in newspapers or on the bench alongside Ferguson at games, was almost a deliberate ploy in itself to emphasise the success of the new regime, at least when it came to attracting the talent. It left an impression inside the club, too.

'He was a very exciting young player,' former United owner Martin Edwards wrote in his autobiography. 'The main parts of his game were his energy and dead ball skills, his vision and his supreme passing ability ... Everyone knew who Beckham was in the dressing room because Alex, when he was courting David and making sure he signed for us, used to bring him to home matches. I always used to see this little blond kid in the dressing room and wonder who it was – it turned out to be the young Beckham.'

There were easier elements of Beckham's make-up to make him the butt of the joke inside the dressing room of young lads than just his – perhaps – over-the-top love of the club he had just joined.

'Becks was the only one who didn't come from around Manchester, and I remember a lot of us taking the piss out of him because he lost his Cockney accent so quickly,' Ryan Giggs said. 'We know that didn't last, but he didn't start talking like a southerner again until Teddy Sheringham joined us. Becks never got treated differently because he was from London, but he did get a lot of stick. He coped with that well, though – he was always a confident lad.'

The confidence came from his football ability. Beckham played in midfield, both in the centre and out wide. Those endless hours spent driving crosses into his father's hands, and evenings staying behind after Ted's football training to work on his own free kicks, had created a level of accuracy rarely seen in one so young. When it came to the factors he could control, he worked as hard as possible to maximise his capability or potential for success.

Alongside the likes of O'Kane, Gary Neville, Giggs/Wilson, and others like Ben Thornley, Keith Gillespie, Nicky Butt and Paul Scholes, Beckham was part of a group that was getting rave reviews and regularly attracting fairly generous crowds to games at The Cliff and Littleton Road, where the junior sides would play.

Before the word got out, though, legendary football writer Paddy Barclay remembered watching the junior side play in front of an audience of two, against Morecambe reserves at The Cliff. 'The one who enthralled me,' Barclay recounted in *Football – Bloody Hell!* (his biography of Sir Alex Ferguson), 'was Beckham. He epitomised the style. Lean and upright, with floppy hair, he exuded a calm you seldom found in English footballers of even the highest class.'

Barclay was so taken, he was compelled to 'share the excitement' of his discovery, and so he told the other man in attendance that 'I felt certain that boy wearing number 8 would get 50 caps for England'.

'I hope so,' came the reply from Ted Beckham. 'He's my son.'

In his formative years in the youth team, David played in the middle of the park. 'David Beckham was my captain and central midfielder,' said coach Nobby Stiles, 'because of the natural creativity of his passing.'

He was competitive, but not a natural tackler. His diminutive frame – the one thing Mother Nature controlled that he could not – counted against him, and, although he was a player of supreme class and intelligence, there were some concerns that he might be susceptible to being bullied out of a game.

'He was so slim, he looked like he'd be blown over in a gale,' Neville recalled. 'At first glance, you wondered what could be so special, but when we started training he could deliver a ball better than anyone I'd seen. His technique was straight out of a textbook: the body angle, the grace, the spin on the ball. He looked stylish.'

Competition was fierce, and whilst players such as Neville, John O'Kane and Nicky Butt were given a decent chance in the team which played in the Lancashire League Division Two in the 1990/91 season, Beckham had to be satisfied with just two appearances, both from the bench: first as a replacement for Colin Telford in a 2–1 win over Blackburn Rovers 'B' on 11 October, and then as a substitute for Simon Davies against Oldham 'B' in a 1–0 defeat on 23 February. Whilst acknowledging the reservations about his size at that stage, it is important to address the fact that in the footballing pyramid of the time, these teams would comprise a real mixture, just as the reserves did. Depending on the day and the situation, it would not be uncommon to see a few seasoned veterans in the 'A' or 'B' sides; so, far from this quiet introduction being an indication of reticence, it was in fact quite the opposite, and a big pat on the back for a 15-year-old lad. The spring, summer and autumn of 1991 was a time when things began to feel a little more serious.

First of all, having just turned 16, he was made captain of the United team which played in the Milk Cup in Northern Ireland in May 1991 under the guardianship of Stiles. It was an eventful tournament.

Against Motherwell, the youngster both infuriated and impressed his coach.

'He couldn't get truly involved in the game, and to make matters worse, when we won a penalty near the end of the match, he claimed it and missed it, which meant that we had to go into extra time,' Stiles recalled. 'I wanted more bite down the middle of the pitch, something David just hadn't been providing, so I pushed him out wide right and brought Paul Scholes inside. Beckham put on a massive sulk. It was infuriating to see such a talented player letting himself down like that, but when extra time was over and we were still level and had to go to penalties, I saw something in him that I liked very much and almost made me forget what had gone before. Gary Neville claimed the first penalty, but Beckham, who had missed from the spot earlier, did not hesitate to follow him. He smashed the ball into the back of the net with great power and, I thought, quite a bit of anger. Before the next game, I told him I was putting him back into the centre of midfield, but at no stage did I want to see any signs that he might get another "cob" on if the game didn't quite go how he wanted. I told him he had behaved like a naughty boy who had had a sweet taken away. You didn't win matches, you didn't become a big player, like that.'

Beckham scored another penalty in the shoot-out of the final which helped United win the trophy; a test of character had been passed, and a lesson learned, perhaps, for the precocious talent. When he returned for the 1991/92 season, things were already beginning to change for him.

'David had to be nursed along a bit between the ages of 16 to 17 because his physique was changing dramatically,' Eric Harrison remembered. 'He literally shot up in size. The stamina was still there – believe you me, David can run all day – but the strength was not. He was frustrated at not progressing as fast as some of the other lads. As always, I was constantly talking to the boys, one-to-one, and I think that these chats helped David. He has always been a little sensitive but a brilliant lad to work with. When David started getting stronger, he really blossomed. We now had a midfield player who had all the skill in the world, who could run for fun and had the physique to go with it. Quickly he had been transformed from a small, skinny kid to a six-footer with broad shoulders. We were now seeing the David Beckham that I had always visualised.'

In the midst of this growth spurt, the midfielder seemed to covet attention. Given a run of games in the 'B' team, Beckham, wearing the number 7 shirt, would often try the audacious. This would range from the 'normal' – the so-called 'Hollywood' passes which would occasionally make Eric Harrison apoplectic with rage – to the downright obscene: Beckham would not only try to shoot from his own half – on more than one or two occasions he attempted to score directly from the kick-off. It was not uncommon for the junior sides to register tallies of four, five, six or even seven goals. In the autumn, Beckham was regularly among the scorers, with an impressive record of eight goals in eight consecutive appearances.

It was the first of these – in a game at Bury on 5 October 1991 – which is worth remarking upon. On the coach going there, the players had watched a video of a remarkable goal from Uruguayan midfielder José Luis Zalazar, who played for Albacete in Spain, and had scored from his own half in a September game at Tenerife.

'After we'd watched it, Becks turned round to the lads and said he was going to do that today,' Kevin Pilkington remembers. 'And he did.'

Bury were a rare side able to give United a good competition, and were 1–0 up heading into the last ten minutes. Searching for a late goal, Beckham, from his orchestrator's position in the centre circle, demanded the ball and surveyed his options. A five-yard pass wouldn't do. A 50-yard pass wasn't on. Rather than keep the ball moving, or waiting, Beckham decided he would go for the extravagant again. Just inside his own half, he struck the ball with precision and power; it sailed over the goalkeeper like a chipped effort from much closer range, and into the top corner for a late winner. Naturally, the parents on the sidelines – David's included – could barely believe what they had seen. His team-mates, though, were barely even surprised. (Incidentally, Zalazar would repeat the trick the following season. David would too, to much greater acclaim, almost five years later.)

Those exploits were enough to accelerate him into the 'A' team. Neville, O'Kane, Gillespie, Butt, Thornley, Chris Casper and Robbie Savage had already been playing regularly. The promotion coincided with the commencement of the FA Youth Cup. The side was brimming with creative midfield talent; less so with natural strikers. Colin McKee led the line, but would be accompanied by either Savage, Thornley or Ryan Giggs, who made the occasional return from his first-team duties to turn out for the youth side. Harrison's choice for the midfield would read something like Gillespie, Butt, Davies and Thornley; with Davies, a natural left-sided player, possibly getting a sympathy vote due to the deluge of left-sided players in that team.

It meant Beckham had to make do with substitute appearances as United progressed through the early rounds of the competition – coming on for Butt against Sunderland, for Gillespie against Manchester City, and then for McKee against Tranmere. By the time the semi-final against Tottenham had come around, though, David had done enough to convince that the team were in greater need of his creative abilities, to better complement and facilitate the gift of penetration which they had in bucketloads. He still had to make do with an appearance from the bench for the first leg, but made his first start in the competition at White Hart Lane, a fitting arena considering his background. There, he lined up against Darren Caskey, Nicky Barmby and Sol Campbell, three young lads he had trained with when he still lived in London.

With a 3–0 advantage from the first leg, the second meeting was something of a formality but still called for a professional job, which Beckham and his team-mates provided in a comfortable 2–1 win. On 4 April, he scored the only goal in the Manchester 'A' team derby, and ten days later he was named in the number 6 shirt to start the first leg of the Youth Cup Final against Crystal Palace at Selhurst Park.

It was another competent and mature job by Harrison's boys. Nicky Butt gave United a 17th-minute lead, and on the half-hour, Ben Thornley pulled the ball back for Beckham 'to shoot inside the far corner from eighteen yards for a spectacular goal', according to David Groves of the *Croydon Advertiser*. (Incidentally, the goalkeeper Beckham beat was a youngster by the name of Jimmy Glass, who would have his own career highlight in May 1999, albeit in remarkably different circumstances to those of his opponents in the spring of 1992. Glass, on loan from Swindon Town, scored a last-minute goal on the last day of the season to keep Carlisle United in the Football League.)

Palace pulled a goal back five minutes from time, but United responded immediately, this time with Beckham turning provider for Butt to convert a third goal. The first team were celebrating winning the League Cup the previous weekend, but were about to embark upon an end-of-season capitulation of form which would wreck their chances of winning a first league title for 26 years. The wait for a Youth Cup had been even longer – 28 years – and the nature of the collapse at senior level brought the need for concentration into sharper focus for the youngsters, who could ill-afford to take their lead for granted.

Somewhat anxiety-inducing for most of the near-15,000 crowd who were in Old Trafford, the kids indulged in another aspect of their make-up which they would become renowned for almost as much as their terrific skill: a tendency to make things difficult for themselves. One would surely attribute Palace's first-minute goal more to nervousness than complacency.

In the 33rd minute, a superb Thornley equaliser settled the nerves, and Simon Davies added a second just after half-time to make it 5–2 on aggregate and just about settle the tie – although both teams managed to get another goal each. There was no statement contribution from Beckham in the second leg, and the headlines were stolen by a spotlight-hogging Ryan Giggs, who had returned to the youth team for the second leg; Giggs was the focus for photographers as he held the trophy aloft, with Beckham standing in the shadows holding the base. Like the rest of his team-mates, though, the time for standing in the shadows was most definitely over.

Education

IN THE general order of proceedings, David Beckham's introduction into the Manchester United first team is remembered as one of the later ones from the class of '92. It's true to say that Ryan Giggs was already a first-team player. Gary Neville made a place his own when Paul Parker picked up an ankle injury in the summer of 1994 and new signing David May was ill-suited to full-back. Nicky Butt was thrown into the general mix of rotation following Bryan Robson's exit that summer, too. Some would say that the slight frame of the 17-year-old was the reason for a more staggered introduction; though, to be fair, Beckham was among the earliest of the famed academy group to get a debut.

United had just drawn at Tottenham Hotspur in September 1992, with Giggs scoring a wonderful solo goal. The start to the season had not been great for Alex Ferguson's team, but there were some indications of a brighter future. With a League Cup trip to Brighton coming up in midweek, the manager called up some of the younger players to train with the first team. David Beckham was among the contingent for the first time.

'To be honest,' Paul Parker recalls, 'even with the success they'd had, whenever young lads were brought up through the youth team into first-team training, they'd just be skinny little fresh-faced kids and you didn't know too much about them. David was just one of them. I had a bit of a connection with Nicky Butt as he was my boot boy, and also a little bit in your face. When I was introduced to David and found out we were from the same corner of the world, I did build a decent relationship with him. He was quiet, shy in certain ways, but give him a football – give any of them a football – and their confidence shone. You might say that their personalities were reflective of how soon they were all introduced. Gary always had something to say. Nicky wasn't shy. Paul Scholes was streetwise. Ryan was just streets ahead of any young player in the country and was a little bit older.'

Another difficulty for the youngster at the time was his preferred position. Ferguson had a clear profile in mind for the battle tanks he wanted in the middle of the pitch. Bryan Robson and Paul Ince were the senior custodians. Nicky Butt was being groomed into that sort of role and, of course, Roy Keane would later come into the reckoning.

Beckham not only wasn't a natural tackler, but was an awkward one: an element of his technique that he would carry throughout his career was the way he would plant a standing foot and swivel his body in a protective manner to shield against a tackle and protect the ball. The timing of this trick was, of course, perfected throughout the course of the coming years. Doing this in the middle of the park in games against players of his own age was fine, as he had the superior technical ability to compensate and a competitive body size.

'He seemed to model himself on Glenn Hoddle,' remembers Parker, 'but there wasn't room for a Glenn Hoddle-type in an Alex Ferguson team of the time. It wasn't the way Manchester United played. The boss saw his strength as a wide midfielder, though of course the difficulty there was having Andrei Kanchelskis and Ryan Giggs and then Keith Gillespie and Lee Sharpe. In basketball you have players who specialise in scoring three-pointers. I would use that comparison for David; you knew that if he had the space he could deliver, that much was clear from a very early age. I don't think it's an exaggeration to say that if he did have the space to cross, nine times out of ten he would give you a good delivery. He was exceptional. So the emphasis on the players around him was creating the space and opportunity for him to do that.'

United were leading at Brighton through Danny Wallace's first-half goal until the Seagulls equalised in the 72nd minute. Ferguson decided to see if Beckham's supply line was in working order and, tellingly, brought him on for Andrei Kanchelskis. Beckham was so excited to be told he was going to get on that he jumped up and banged his head on the roof of the dugout. It was an unspectacular 18-minute cameo from the youngster, who couldn't remember doing anything wrong, but still found himself the target of a hairdryer from his manager after the game.

For perhaps the first (and if so, certainly the only) time so far in David Beckham's career, there was a sense of stalling, a backward step. He had started the season playing reserve-team football in the Pontins League, with games against Leicester City and Nottingham Forest in early September, hinting at his imminent promotion and opportunity. United had a packed squad, though. In the reserves, there were Keith Gillespie and Russell Beardsmore vying for a right-hand slot. There was the pair of Mick Phelan and Clayton Blackmore, now veteran midfielders, and Darren Ferguson, son of the manager, all demanding opportunities in midfield in the second string. So Beckham returned to earth with a bump, dropping back into the 'A' team. He also represented the academy side in the Youth Cup. The idea was to give him a long run in his preferred position in the middle, wearing the number 8 shirt, in the hope that experience would help bring on the physicality and robustness which was missing from his game.

He was back in the 'A' team for his long run on 14 November against Blackpool, scoring in a 5–2 win. The high score was typical of that side, which would usually include the likes of Butt, Scholes and Savage. Take these results over the following two-and-a-half months of winter: 6–1 against Liverpool, 5–3 against Tranmere, 4–1 versus Chester, 4–1 versus Everton, 4–3 at home to Blackpool, 5–1 against Morecambe, 7–1 against Tranmere in the return and 6–2 at The Cliff against Bolton. Beckham helped himself to a few goals along the way, but was flourishing in his orchestrator role in the middle.

By now, Beckham was four years into the six he had been promised; but when the time finally arrived, as it did in January 1993, to trigger the professional contract option in his agreement, that was extended to four years instead of two, just as it was for all of the other youngsters who had so impressed in making their own mark in history. For a while, it seemed as if United were destined to repeat their FA Youth Cup success. In the fourth round, Beckham scored in a 3–0 win against Wimbledon, beating the offside trap to net. He scored in the next round, too: 'another spectacular goal with a shot which flew into the roof of the net from fifteen yards', as described by Malcolm Huntington of the *Yorkshire Evening Press* of the youngster's effort in a 5–0 win over York City.

The kids were hitting their stride as the season reached its climax. Division One of the Lancashire League was being won with some comfort, as emphasised by an astonishing 10–0 win over Marine on 3 April, in which Beckham netted his first and only hat-trick wearing United colours at any level. It should have been ideal preparation for a game against Millwall in the first leg of the semi-final of the Youth Cup at Old Trafford. The travelling Lions were only too aware of the reputation of their illustrious opponents and decided to enhance their own; their young collective took it upon themselves to all shave their heads to attempt to intimidate the opposition. It worked. Beckham was just one who confessed to being unnerved by the unusual sight.

After an anxious opening, United actually managed to go into half-time a goal up when Ben Thornley scored a great goal; but Millwall capitalised on second-half jitters to turn the score around and inflict a 2–1 defeat on the holders.

Eric Harrison confessed he had never seen that group of players so 'shaken', but insisted they would play better at The Den, Millwall's imposing home ground. They did. Inspired by a necessary calm and professional job by Butt and Beckham in the middle, United scored twice in the second half to overturn that deficit and qualify for the final.

Ten days later, United also qualified for the Lancashire Youth Cup Final; there, they met Blackburn, and won at a canter, with Beckham netting in a 3–0 win.

Perfect preparation for the FA Youth Cup Final against Leeds, then, with the first leg played at Old Trafford. But Leeds had a growing reputation of their own when it came to a production line of young talent. Playing in the Northern Intermediate League, Noel Whelan had scored over 20 times. Just behind him was Jamie Forrester on 17 goals; Forrester and Kevin Sharp had actually been due to play alongside Beckham at United a couple of years prior. They had provisionally agreed to go to Old Trafford from the FA's School of Excellence, but French club Auxerre nipped in and offered lucrative deals to both. The pair grew homesick very quickly and agreed a deal to move to Yorkshire.

For the second home game in a row in this competition, United's young starlets were struck by a strange anxiety. A week earlier, Old Trafford had played host to the first league title party since 1967. Just over 40,000 had packed into the ground. Now, 30,562 were at the Theatre of Dreams to see these prodigies. That was more than, for example, the number that had turned up to see the first team play the return leg against Brighton in the League Cup tie where Beckham had made his senior bow.

Faltering under the weight of expectation, United stuttered, and their visitors claimed a 2–0 win. 'I think the lads were shocked to find 30,000 had come to watch them at Old Trafford and the expectations after the championship success got to them,' Harrison said afterwards. 'I had never seen so many white faces before. They were overwhelmed, but it was a priceless experience and I'm sure they will have learned from it.'

This time, however, they didn't. Nicky Butt and John O'Kane were missing through injury, making it an even tougher ask. Despite these setbacks, Paul Scholes did reduce the aggregate deficit when he scored a penalty, but Leeds took the wind out of their opponents' sails by equalising within a minute. They eventually won 2–1.

Continuing the end-of-season deflation for Beckham was exclusion from the England under-18 squad for the European Championship that summer. Gary Neville, Paul Scholes and Nicky Butt were selected. The likes of Darren Caskey, Forrester and Mark Tinkler were preferred as midfielders.

There was some consolation when Beckham was taken with the United first-team squad to South Africa for their pre-season preparations.

He was even given an opportunity from the bench in a friendly against Kaizer Chiefs – a 1–1 draw in front of 65,000. It seemed clear, though, that he was there to bulk out the squad and benefit from the experience rather than to travel with a genuine hope of being integrated into the first team.

Now 18 years old, in the second full season after winning the FA Youth Cup, and seeing many of his colleagues get increasing opportunities to be around the first team, one would have forgiven Beckham if he was growing frustrated or even wondering whether he was in the club's long-term plans. It was a sign of his professionalism and maturity, even at this young age, that he took it all in his stride.

'When he first started at United, he was a fair way behind the other lads, because he had only been going up in the school holidays,' Ted Beckham recalled. 'Most of the others came from the Manchester area, so they'd been nursed constantly by United. David had a fair bit to learn tactically, plus he had some growing to do, so it was no surprise he was a slightly late developer.'

Instead of being upset, Beckham resolved to work even harder at putting all the odds in his favour. That extended to his private life. He had remained very close friends with John O'Kane, who, by his own admission, did not share the same dedication to Manchester United or football. O'Kane was no less gifted than his team-mates, but his tendency to go on his own way resulted in turning up late for training once or twice and enjoying a night out.

This is not to say that any of this group were hardcore party animals, but, as Gary Neville has often gone on record to say, some players had to work harder to make an impression. He wouldn't have put Beckham in that category, but in the 1993/94 campaign, it appeared Beckham himself did, though this was perhaps encouraged somewhat by the club as well.

'Me and Becks drifted apart because we moved to different rooms in a house we stayed in,' O'Kane says. 'He gravitated to the first-teamers more and I stayed closest to my dig lads … it happens in football. One minute you're best buddies, the next you don't see them again. It's just the way it works – no hard feelings, we just move on.'

This extra year of development was spent with Eric Harrison, seeing what he could squeeze out of those players. It was a matter of discipline. In O'Kane's case, it was showing more application in training. In Beckham's, it was a matter of economy of possession. What might have initially come across as disobedience apparently seemed to be a case of a quest for perfection.

'Becks loved just pinging balls and playing Hollywood passes, to the anger of Eric Harrison, who used to rage at him for it,'

O'Kane remembers. 'He didn't listen … usually he'd ping a 50-yard pass to Colin McKee's foot. In my eyes, he was technically the best player I've played with. He had standards just like Keano's.'

Those standards meant ambitions much greater than the 'A' team, but that's where David Beckham found himself in the early weeks of the 1993/94 campaign. There was a crop of players coming through in the age bracket below: Phil Neville, but notably in competition with Beckham, Michael Appleton, a promising central midfielder, and Terry Cooke, a flying winger.

In the first team, United were also flying on all fronts, apart from in Europe. The squad was bursting with talent, and Ferguson's capability to rotate and rest players was comfortable and seamless. By Christmas, they had established an unassailable lead and were in the middle of a record unbeaten run. The best Beckham could do in the short term was make the most of his situation; this was made difficult by a winter in which only three 'A' team games were played. He did, however, score in two of them, against Morecambe and Tranmere, which resulted in a mini-promotion to the reserve side.

As the season reached its climax, and Ferguson made changes to freshen up his side as they reached the finals of both domestic competitions and dealt with a number of suspensions, Beckham found himself filling whichever spot was left behind in the reserve side. He equipped himself well, but the issue was the number of senior players still at the club who were blocking his pathway. That pressure was alleviated somewhat by the number of players who were allowed to leave in the summer of 1994. Clayton Blackmore, Mick Phelan and Bryan Robson all moved on, whilst Darren Ferguson and Robbie Savage also departed, freeing up plenty of opportunities for midfield places in the second string.

He still only made a token appearance in pre-season again, albeit in a fairly memorable encounter between Glasgow Rangers and Manchester United in a tournament at Ibrox. The game is best remembered for Eric Cantona getting sent off and earning a suspension which would rule him out of the start of the 1994/95 season. Funnily enough, Cantona – who had inherited Bryan Robson's number 7 shirt when squad numbers and names on shirts were introduced in 1993 – did not wear his regular number in this game, as this was pre-season and he was a substitute. Instead, the number 7 shirt was worn by Beckham.

He did make an appearance as a substitute in Clayton Blackmore's testimonial game on 16 August, which had been arranged as part of Blackmore's transfer to Middlesbrough. By then, Beckham had already started the 'season proper' in fine form, scoring twice for the reserves in the Lancashire Senior Cup against Rochdale. Even as the 1994/95 campaign got underway, it seemed a deliberate plan to continue to mould Beckham into a more resolute central midfielder.

Events throughout this controversial season changed the best-laid plans. But intentions were clear enough when Beckham made his full debut for the club on 21 September 1994. Here, he played in midfield alongside Nicky Butt, and Keith Gillespie played on the right-hand side, with Simon Davies on the left. Paul Scholes played up front and scored twice on his debut to earn his side a 2–1 win at Port Vale in the League Cup. A John O'Kane cameo from the bench late on made it a staggering seven members from the class of '92 in the first team. The game, of course, made headlines for other reasons.

'I smile when I think back to the days when I perhaps startled many people by ringing the changes,' Alex Ferguson said in 2011. 'In particular I remember the fuss my selection for the League Cup tie at Port Vale provoked. We had Roy Keane at centre-half and Brian McClair in midfield, but that was really the extent of our experienced players. Vale supporters, disappointed at the prospect of not being able to see some of our star names at their ground, took their complaints to the press and even to the House of Commons. John Rudge, who was manager of Port Vale at the time, told me that even his wife was one of the people who complained! What they didn't know of course was that they would be witnessing the launch of the David Beckham era, and we know how successful they went on to become.'

This particular chapter of the David Beckham era, as Ferguson dubbed it, continued with the youngster playing central midfield in the second leg – a 2–0 win at Old Trafford – and then again at Newcastle. The Magpies were tussling with United at the top of the table at the time, but Ferguson resisted the temptation to play a senior team. The 2–0 defeat at St James' Park was something of a learning curve; senior education was to come thick and fast for the Londoner.

First of all, United's untimely exit from the Champions League had been all but mathematically certified by a defeat in Gothenburg with one group game remaining. It expedited opportunities for players who otherwise wouldn't have got them. Gary Neville, Nicky Butt, Simon Davies and Beckham were all told on the morning of the game that they would start against Galatasaray at Old Trafford. In addition to that, O'Kane, Scholes, David Johnson and Kevin Pilkington were on the bench, making it a real youthful occasion, although Ferguson did opt for the experience of Cantona, Steve Bruce, Gary Pallister, Denis Irwin and McClair to complement the kids.

A footnote to this was the training exercises Ferguson ran the day before the game. His initial plan had been to play Gillespie on the right, but he realised he had made a 'boo-boo' because the Northern Irish winger was an assimilated player under the foreign player regulations, which placed a limit on the number of such players in a team. A reprieve for Beckham, and an opportunity in that vacant right-sided spot.

Within three minutes, the fledgling right side of Neville and Beckham had created its first goal – although the master provider of days to come was nowhere to be seen this time round. Neville punted a cross, which missed the middle of the pitch but fell kindly to Davies. The Welsh winger composed himself and fired across goal to put United ahead and set the tone for the evening.

Seven minutes before half-time came the moment Beckham and his family had been dreaming of – certainly, the moment Ted Beckham had been dreaming of for over 19 years, to see his son score at Old Trafford. The Turkish side couldn't clear their lines and the ball dropped invitingly to the approaching Beckham just outside the box. It wasn't exactly the cleanest strike in the world, but it was hit with assurance and precision, to take it across goal into the corner.

'The joy on the youngster's face there!' exclaimed ITV commentator Brian Moore. 'He struck it superbly!'

Two further goals followed as United recorded a 4–0 win: a pleasant way to end their campaign, even if it was somewhat bittersweet. 'I was proud of the young players,' Alex Ferguson said afterwards. 'I told them to go out and enjoy the match and they did. I knew they had the talent, but you always question whether they have the temperament to cope with a big match at Old Trafford. This game proved they have.'

Winning against Port Vale was one thing. But recording such an emphatic scoreline against a hardened European side – particularly one the United senior team had struggled against in three consecutive games – was enough to get some reporters sitting up and taking notice.

'Manchester United's European Cup season is a thing of the past, but the future looks full of glittering potential for the English champions,' wrote Steve Curry in the *Daily Express*. 'If there was consolation in their exit from Europe's most prestigious club competition it came from the teenage talent manager Alex Ferguson paraded at Old Trafford last night. If the Theatre of Dreams is the catwalk of football then there were four young models who strutted their stuff along it with a swagger and a sway that eased the pain of United's exit. Gary Neville, David Beckham, Nicky Butt and Simon Davies might not yet carry the same resonance as Eric Cantona, Ryan Giggs, Andrei Kanchelskis and Lee Sharpe. Yet out of the depression of another abortive European campaign there was a laser of light.'

The two years since his debut had been an education well taken. Beckham confessed to feeling 'a lot more at home' than he had done on his debut. 'For us boys, it felt like the European Cup Final, never mind that United were going out whatever the result,' he said.

Due to his involvement in the European game, Beckham missed the final reserve game of the year, which was played the day after. It would be another month until the next time the second string took to the pitch, by which time another significant event with potential ramifications for Beckham's future had taken place.

On 10 January, Manchester United broke the British transfer record when they agreed to sign Andy Cole from Newcastle United. The fee was £6m, but the deal was worth £7m because going the other way was the £1m-rated starlet Keith Gillespie. Gillespie's nationality had made him a reluctant bargaining chip; Ferguson was keen to lower the foreign quota in the squad, and indeed was signing Cole because he was English and would hopefully provide a sharper instinct than the Welshman Mark Hughes.

There was greater turmoil waiting for the United boss. On 25 January, Eric Cantona sought a personal vigilante kind of justice when he jumped into the Selhurst Park terraces feet first, and was punished with a suspension that would keep him out until October. Cantona was one of the form players of the season so far – the other was Andrei Kanchelskis. But the Russian winger was complaining of a mystery injury, and was sitting alongside Beckham on the bench for the visit of Wrexham in the FA Cup at the end of January. Both came on to the pitch as late substitutes once the game had been won and the intensity had been drawn out of the occasion.

Beckham played all four reserve games in February, scoring in a 2–1 home win against Tranmere on the 15th. His development was coming on, but when Third Division club Preston North End made an enquiry to take him on loan on 27 February, Ferguson considered the benefits. 'We've agreed, because we have everyone fit,' he wrote in his diary of the season. 'David's one of the later developers in our club, and it'll give him good experience. He's coming on well, he'll be a really good player, but we felt a month there would maybe help put him in the running when we bring him back at the end of it. A wee bit of experience of playing in that division, where it's quite tough and you've got to battle, will help him.'

What was not helpful to Manchester United or Ferguson was the news of the following day, when Andrei Kanchelskis requested a transfer. Though it was seemingly unrelated to the Beckham loan, it would contribute to that spell at Deepdale being cut short.

Preston manager Gary Peters had taken a trip with his player-coach, David Moyes, to Walsall's Bescot Stadium on 20 February. That was where Aston Villa's reserves played their games; on this evening, they were entertaining Manchester United, who had David Beckham in the number 4 shirt.

'I remember, Gary Peters was the manager and he said to me, "We're going to see Manchester United face Aston Villa,"' Moyes told Talksport in 2019. 'David was playing. There was this wide right player, skinny as anything. Pretty small-looking and I'm thinking there's no way he's going be good enough for the Second or First Division. But Gary said, "No, we're taking him on loan." I have to say, the minute he came in, he was unbelievable. He was brilliant, the minute he came he was out taking free kicks, he was only a boy at the time as well. He had nothing on him and I thought, he's going to get booted all over the place. But he was practising his free kicks, his corner-kicks; he scored one goal that was direct from a corner at Preston. Practice.'

United lost 2–0 on the night, but Peters was undeterred and made his move. It was a temporary spell with dual purpose. United wanted to get their prodigy hardened up a little. Preston needed a boost to revive their hopes of getting into the promotion play-off picture. The loan move, and the timing of it, was smart. Normally the veteran professionals at the lower end of the league structure can be reluctant for a wet-behind-the-ears kid to come in and upstage them. But livelihoods were on the line. It helped that the new Preston boss was a Londoner. As he introduced Beckham to his players, it came with the information that the new kid on the block would be taking every free kick and corner 'because he's much better at it than any of you lot'.

That did put Paul Raynor – the Preston midfielder who had previously taken them – in a difficult position. 'His face was an absolute picture,' team-mate Ryan Kidd told *Four Four Two* in 2015.

Raynor was again upset when he was brought off for Beckham to make his debut during the following Saturday's game with Doncaster Rovers. The United youngster had actually played in a midweek friendly for North End, scoring a fantastic goal as a substitute and raising expectations ahead of his league bow.

Soon after he had come on against Doncaster, he met those expectations, taking a corner in windy conditions; the ball evaded everyone and went straight into the goal. 'I was a bit perturbed because I was taken off for David to go on,' Raynor later confessed. 'So I was chuntering on the bench, then he went and scored directly from a corner. I had to shut up then.'

One person not shutting up was Kidd, who believed he had got the last touch. 'I still claim to this day that I got a head on that and put it in myself,' he said. 'In those days we got a goal bonus, and because I very rarely scored as a centre-half the extra £50 or

£100 was massive. Gary Peters asked, "Who got that goal?" and before I could say "Me, gaffer" he said, "Bugger that, it's David's." If there's any chance I could have that £100 back, I'd be more than obliged!'

The game ended 2–2; Gary Neville, Ben Thornley and Chris Casper had all made the journey to watch their mate play. Thornley, by now, had suffered a horrendous injury which was to have a catastrophic effect on his career. But Neville, Casper and Beckham might have felt their own paths would be that little bit tougher when they heard the result coming in from Old Trafford – United had registered a huge 9–0 win over Ipswich Town.

Still, Beckham was determined to make an impression, and a decent start to life a little further north was made even better in the next game. Raynor, the one player who had cause to be upset about Beckham's arrival, had been won over by the United kid's attitude. 'He'd stay every afternoon after training, out there for ages and ages, which got him a bit of stick from the boys,' Raynor recalled.

Beckham admitted that he had resolved to stay true to his own professional manner in order to survive in the lower division. 'I needed to know I had the ability to play and survive in a league where I was probably going to get lumps kicked out of me,' he said.

The midfielder started against Fulham, wearing the number 4 shirt. Would the home fans be treated to another set-piece spectacle? As it turned out, they would, and this one was certainly much less fortuitous, leaving nobody in any doubt about the intention or the identity of the scorer. Beckham stepped up for the free kick in what would become trademark fashion, striking the ball with magnificent precision in off the post. Preston won 3–2. Their on-loan star was the name on everyone's lips.

'It is astonishing to watch the ball, still rising, zip into the corner as Beckham bends one past another bewildered goalkeeper,' said Preston legend Sir Tom Finney.

Beckham later described it as 'one of my favourite goals, I know people will be a little surprised' to Sky Sports show *Soccer AM*. 'I remember Terry Hurlock playing. I stayed away from him all game! It was a different time in my career, a special time.'

It was, apparently, as painful as memorable. 'One of the Preston players grabbed my head and started pulling my hair so hard I thought he was going to pull a handful out,' Beckham recalled. 'Absolutely killed me.'

The culprit? None other than veteran defender, and former United manager, David Moyes.

Things continued to go well. A 5–0 win over Bury was followed up by a 1–0 victory at Exeter. On the long coach drive, Ryan Kidd remembered Beckham reading an article on the Galatasaray game in *Match* magazine, and some of the Preston lads embarrassing him by reading it out loud. His final game on loan was a 1–1 draw at Lincoln City.

After the Preston team returned home, all the players spoke to David and wished him well for the future. David Moyes personally said he wished Beckham would stay. And that was indeed the youngster's intention, after a conversation with Gary Peters, who expressed the same. 'We did our bit because we gave him responsibility and it helped breed the confidence in his game you see today,' Peters said ten years later. 'He came to Preston determined to get on with everyone and to develop his skills.'

If Beckham had found attitudes towards him had changed at Preston, that was nothing to what was awaiting him when he went to see Alex Ferguson the day after he returned to The Cliff. Ferguson asked him how it had gone. The player said he had really enjoyed it and would quite like to return there for the rest of the season. Ferguson laid into the player with expletives, telling him he 'wasn't fucking going anywhere'.

There were multiple reasons for his bad mood. Ferguson had just returned from Scotland, where he had attended the funeral of

Davie Cooper, the former Glasgow Rangers player who tragically passed away at the young age of 39 following a brain haemorrhage. Whilst he was north of the border, there were back-page stories of Andrei Kanchelskis wanting to move to Rangers. When he returned, Kanchelskis was complaining that he had to have eight injections – two in each arm, two in each buttock – to play for his country during the international break, and that he wasn't feeling well enough to play for United. 'I find it amazing that anyone would allow himself to be given those injections,' Ferguson fumed.

After training that day, Beckham was amazed to find that his name was included in the starting eleven for that weekend's game with Leeds, on the team sheet stuck up on the noticeboard inside The Cliff.

Winning Nothing, then Everything, with Kids

NOBODY WAS to know it at the time, but Andrei Kanchelskis had already played his last game for Manchester United. He signed off with the third goal in a 3–0 win against Arsenal on 22 March 1995. Lee Sharpe was also struggling with injury, which meant Ryan Giggs had to play through the pain barrier with a hamstring problem. Alex Ferguson, once so blessed with width, was already regretting his decision to let Keith Gillespie go in January.

This combination of events had facilitated an acceleration to first-team contention for David Beckham. His impressive spell at Preston had gone – just about – better than expected. Nobody was surprised by the quality of his contribution. More impressive had been his temperament and adaptation to the physicality of the lower league.

It wasn't only on the wings where United had issues. Eric Cantona, of course, was in the early throes of his suspension. Paul Parker had been suffering with an ankle problem at the back end of the previous season. He played through to win the league and FA Cup, but it had come at a cost. He missed most of the 1994/95 campaign. Ferguson had used David May – the former Blackburn man signed as a centre-half – and then even Roy Keane at right-back. Eventually, injury problems elsewhere in the team meant that the manager had to throw in Gary Neville ahead of schedule for a proper run as the first-team right-back. It was best for everyone in the long run, but came with the teething problems one expects of being forced to play inexperienced youngsters.

Neville and Beckham would line up for the first time on that right-hand side they would become synonymous with, against Leeds United on 2 April 1995. It was Beckham's league debut for United. Neville was making his 13th league appearance. They failed to make an impression against Howard Wilkinson's side, playing in direct competition with the experienced Tony Dorigo and Rod Wallace. This was not a slight on their part – the Yorkshire side had unapologetically come for a point, just as they had done the previous season. And, just as they had done then, they got a 0–0 draw.

'Two years in a row and I don't think they've had one strike at goal,' Ferguson moaned, and one could sense the escalation in his frustration which was to result in a much more direct blast a year later.

The goalless game left United five points behind Blackburn Rovers in the chase for the league title. Ferguson's men (and boys) were challenging, once more, for the FA Cup as well. Kanchelskis had initially asked for his fitness to be reviewed for the semi-final against Crystal Palace, but Ferguson, perhaps feeling aggrieved at recent events, decided instead to give that chance to Beckham. It was a tough outing again for Neville and Beckham on the right. Palace were combative, and Ferguson felt after half-time that he would be better served with Nicky Butt competing, so he brought him on in the 49th minute. The game went to a replay, and Butt started ahead of Beckham.

United won 2–0 to get to Wembley, but Roy Keane was sent off and would miss three games – the last three games of the season – with the threat of more if the FA decided that his stamp on Gareth Southgate deserved a harsher punishment. Keane, however, had also picked up an ankle injury earlier in the game, and would be missing for a couple of extra games anyway. Meanwhile, the gamble on Giggs had backfired, and he now looked likely to miss the rest of the campaign.

Against Leicester City the following weekend, it was clear that much responsibility rested on Lee Sharpe's penetration. He rose to that challenge, scoring one and creating another to give United a 2–0 lead, before he too fell victim to the injury curse. His crisis was David Beckham's opportunity; Beckham came on as a half-time substitute. Within seven minutes he had made an impact. His corner was brilliant and met with conviction by Steve Bruce. The captain's header was saved, but Cole scrambled in the rebound. David was also involved in the fourth goal, scored by Ince in the last minute.

Sharpe did not recover in time for the visit of Chelsea on Easter Monday. That meant a start again for Beckham, who found the going just as tough as it had been when Leeds went to Old Trafford. At half-time, he was brought off for Simon Davies, but greater embarrassment was to follow for the Welsh youngster. Ferguson accused him of failing to follow instructions and almost costing his team a goal. In the 75th minute, Davies was hauled off and replaced by Scholes. Davies requested a transfer the following day. His request was granted, although he was not sold for another couple of years.

A little bit of tough love and example-setting by the manager, then. Before, they had seen talented youngsters like Jules Maiorana or Adrian Doherty fail to establish themselves for different reasons. Maiorana in particular could be cited as collateral damage in that it didn't matter how talented you were, if you fell out with the manager, it was only going to end one way. Now, those examples were being set within the 'class of '92' to show them they weren't exempt. Gary Neville, around this time, had accumulated so many disciplinary points that he was fined £1,000. Ferguson claimed Neville was 'pleading poverty' and wanted assistance; the player complained he had been on reserve-team wages and couldn't afford the fine. 'I'm heartbroken for you,' Ferguson had told him in the dressing room. 'You'll need your cup final bonus now.'

Without knowing it, or without meaning to, the Davies episode had a fairly significant impact on Beckham's own contribution for the rest of the campaign. He came on as a late substitute in a 3–2 win at Coventry City on 1 May, but the following evening he was back in the second string, scoring in a 3–0 win at Rotherham, playing in the middle of the park. Playing the full 90 minutes in the last two reserve games at West Brom and at home to Notts County made it clear he wouldn't be involved in the crunch league fixtures.

Ferguson had privately conceded that he would not be able to count on the penetration from wide, and there was no point in trying to replicate what Kanchelskis and Giggs brought to the team through other players who possessed different qualities. At the same time, he felt Blackburn were struggling with the psychological pressure due to a number of poor performances and dropped points. Perhaps that is why the midfield and attack were flooded with combative players in the likes of Ince, Keane, Butt, Hughes and Scholes.

Ultimately, it wasn't enough. United drew at West Ham on the final day and lost the league by one point, despite having a superior goal difference to Blackburn. That invited many observations about what went wrong and where it did. Andy Cole shouldered a lot of the personal blame for a few misses against the Hammers. Cantona inevitably took a percentage. The inexperience of the youngsters in those goalless games against Leeds and Chelsea looked all the more pronounced now. Whilst that point was fair, it was also fair to say United – kids and all – had put together an impressive run-in and it was, in fact, arguably an autumn run of three defeats in five games which contributed to the anti-climax of spring.

In the FA Cup Final, against Everton at Wembley, Beckham was considered (and even had a shirt printed), but Nicky Butt's greater experience saw him picked on the right-hand side. The 1–0 defeat was indicative of United's underwhelming end to the season.

In his evaluation of the disappointment, Ferguson looked for silver linings. 'Perhaps most satisfying of all is the emergence of the kids,' he wrote in his diary of the season. 'Gary Neville has come on brilliant … Paul Scholes also came on [in the final] and made an impact, and Nicky Butt has now made himself a first-team player. Next season I shall be looking for others to follow their example.'

If you were reading between the lines, you might consider that David Beckham's name was deliberately omitted from that post-season missive from Alex Ferguson; that the intention was to lay down a challenge to be accepted, to be one of those names to break through and establish themselves.

That, however, would be ignoring the fact that Ferguson spent the summer trying to woo Darren Anderton from Tottenham Hotspur once it became obvious that Andrei Kanchelskis was on his way. It was a transfer saga that dragged all through the summer and past the exits of Mark Hughes to Chelsea, Paul Ince to Inter Milan and Gary Walsh to Middlesbrough. Anderton, though, remained loyal to Tottenham. In fact, by the time Kanchelskis signed for Everton on 25 August, there had already been two games of the league season played. And, by that time, David Beckham had already made quite an impression.

Pre-season had started with no suggestion of what was to come. Beckham travelled with the first-team squad on the tour to Malaysia, but a shortage of numbers meant the manager was trying out different formations. It was a 5–3–2 or 5–3–1–1; a seriously lopsided team, with only the width of Sharpe and no fit natural strikers other than veteran Brian McClair (now successfully retrained as a box-to-box midfielder), invited criticism for the manager back in England. How could he have allowed his team – which looked so strong a year ago – to get to the point where it seemed they were down to the bare bones, with little goal threat? A poll in the *Manchester Evening News* suggested many United fans would be happy with a change of manager.

He refused to bow to the pressure, though when he realised Anderton would not be coming, he must have felt some relief when towards the end of pre-season there was one shining light. First, Beckham scored in a 2–2 draw at Shelbourne; but he made much more of an impression two days later in a testimonial for Jimmy Bonthrone (a friend of Ferguson's) at East Fife. Beckham scored the last goal in a 4–0 win: a blockbuster from fully 30 yards which immediately ensured he would be in the plans for the opening day of the season.

Before that trip to Aston Villa, there was further woe when captain Steve Bruce was ruled out and joined Giggs and Cole on the injured list. It made for a very unfamiliar-looking side (in terms of shape rather than personnel) at Villa Park: Peter Schmeichel in goal; a back five of Gary Neville, Parker, Pallister, Phil Neville and Irwin; Butt, Keane and Sharpe in midfield; and McClair and Scholes up front.

Villa were no mugs: this was a good team with some great players and would, later that season, go on to win the League Cup inspired by the likes of Dwight Yorke. Yorke was in sensational form against United in this first-day fixture, scoring in a first-half romp which saw the hosts head in at the break with a 3–0 advantage.

Ferguson brought on Beckham for the younger Neville at half-time. The game was lost, but it didn't stop United from chasing it, and they certainly deserved more than the one goal they got in a second-half fightback. That said – what a goal to come away with. Around 15 minutes from the end, Beckham received a pass from Keane, set himself up for a shot and fired horribly wide, to the jeers of the home fans. The midfielder had been the best source of ammunition playing in an inside-right role, though; and when Keane found him in an identical position to before in the 84th minute, Beckham's arching effort this time was exceptionally accurate. The shot arrowed over the head of Mark Bosnich, who was just three yards off his line – one of the best goalkeepers in the land flummoxed by the audacity and confidence of his opponent.

'I for one will always have fond memories of that game, even though we lost,' John O'Kane recalls. 'We both came on as sub and played really well. Becks scored and we celebrated together. That evening, Alan Hansen made the quote which he's probably most infamous for.'

That quote, of course, was a prediction from the Liverpool legend that Manchester United wouldn't win 'anything' if they continued to play the kids. And, although the events of the season to come would prove him wrong in remarkable circumstances, nobody thought the remark was unreasonable at the time. Even Alex Ferguson, famed for using negative comments about his players as motivation, steered clear of this one. There was, instead, a quiet resolve amongst the class of '92.

'There was an element of "We'll show him",' remembers Kevin Pilkington. 'I'm sure plenty of the other lads were thinking it too, especially with him being an ex-Liverpool player.'

There was a strong response. United did enough to earn wins over West Ham and Wimbledon at Old Trafford before major tests followed, first at champions Blackburn and then at FA Cup holders Everton. The extent of the Old Trafford transition was laid bare in their trip to Ewood Park by the fact that four key players from their last visit there were missing: Kanchelskis, Cantona and Hughes, who had all scored in a 4–2 win in October 1994, along with Paul Ince. United were looking to the future – so too were Blackburn, hoping to build upon their platform as champions despite a sluggish start to their league season. Kenny Dalglish had resigned as manager and been replaced by Ray Harford. Broadcasters BSkyB were also serving as visionaries: they chose this game to launch their Replay 2000 initiative, on-screen technology which would show lines of offside. The thick red and white lines were informative enough. Despite the game's final scoreline, there were no narrow margins between the teams, as United put on an exceptional display. After Lee Sharpe and Alan Shearer exchanged goals, it was time for David Beckham to take centre stage again. There was a scrappy build-up as the ball pinged around the Blackburn box before it fell to Beckham; the cultured midfielder seemed to be in an ocean of calm, and he curled the ball with some finesse into the far corner. In terms of technique, this was every bit as brilliant as his opening-day effort, and a fitting match-winner as it turned out to be.

It was 'one of the greatest performances turned in by any Manchester United side since Alex Ferguson took charge', according to *The Sun*, and followed by an equally impressive showing and result at Everton – a 3–2 win where Beckham hit the bar from a free kick, and was also chief playmaker, setting up the opening goal for Lee Sharpe and the winner for Ryan Giggs.

The response from Villa Park had been emphatic, and, well, perfect. But United's run of victories was ended by a 0–0 draw with Rotor Volgograd in the UEFA Cup, and that trip to Russia came at a cost. Gary Neville, Roy Keane and Denis Irwin all picked up injuries. A very youthful team took to the field to take on Bolton Wanderers at Old Trafford the following weekend. The front six was entirely made up of 'fledglings' (if we are to include

Lee Sharpe, on the basis that he was a prominent member of the first group given that label by the press at the end of the previous decade). To top it off, David Beckham had the opportunity he'd always dreamed of – to play in the middle of the park for the team he had always supported.

If this was an audition, it was not only passed in convincing fashion – it also provided the United manager with a style of play he had probably hoped may one day materialise, though even someone with his ability to forecast the future would have felt this was much sooner than expected. The football played in the first half of this game was nothing short of spectacular, and in particular, the combination play between Beckham, Butt, Scholes and Giggs made you forget completely about the convention of football formations. It didn't matter that there wasn't a recognised striker in the side; this was merely about talented footballers who had grown up with each other and had an understanding of each other's movement that bordered on the telepathic. Scholes netted in the 17th minute, but it was Ryan Giggs's goal in the 33rd which really set pulses racing and tongues wagging: a move of pace, guile and penetration, and a rare one that Beckham was not involved in on the day. His own performance was accomplished, and it stuck in his memory as a 'great performance' in which the team 'could have scored ten'.

Following the general rule that nothing goes on forever, United had a bump right around the corner: a sobering evening for the kids who had taken everyone by surprise so far. That came in the unexpected form of York City, who came to Old Trafford and executed a 3–0 League Cup win that was as emphatic as it was shocking. It was true that there were young players in the team, but aside from Pat McGibbon, who was making his debut, and perhaps Kevin Pilkington in goal, there was plenty of first-team experience. Beckham was now included in the number of whom better was expected than this heavy and embarrassing reverse.

An improvement was expected when Eric Cantona returned from his suspension in early October, and though that provided a temporary morale boost, it also brought some inconsistency. Cole and Keane also came back, reducing the number of available positions in the team. When Beckham was called into the side, he was ensuring that his all-energy performances were noticed. He had a fine game against Southampton, creating the last goal in a 4–1 win with a corner that was headed in by Cole. In the following game, he scored the third in a 4–0 win at Coventry.

Against Chelsea – notoriously difficult visitors to Old Trafford, without a goal conceded in their previous three visits – Beckham proved to be the saviour, rescuing a point with a sublime chipped finish after Andy Cole's shot rolled back to him. David's form was holding up, but he, like the rest of the team, was to endure a difficult winter.

There were some heavy defeats. First at Liverpool, Beckham's maiden experience of Anfield at senior level, where Ferguson blasted his side for putting in 'the most lifeless performance in years' in a 2–0 defeat. Then at Leeds, where an equally vitriolic reception awaited. And, finally, a 4–1 capitulation at White Hart Lane.

Ferguson, who presumably thought he had already dealt with the major part of his squad overhaul, now realised that some more surgery was required in defence. Injuries over the winter period had decimated that area of the squad and exposed its limitations. William Prunier infamously came in for a short-term spell which did not go well. Longer-serving players were beginning to realise their own time was close to an end.

Paul Parker, whose ability and form had never been questioned, was finding it difficult to return from his injury issues. This had some consequential issues for Beckham, who would play in front of him. Over winter, Gary Neville had been required to play in the middle of defence. Parker is sympathetic to the struggles that Beckham endured in those days.

'It was different and a little difficult, probably for both of us,' he says. 'I was feeling my way back from an injury and he was only just breaking into the team. He was very different from this Russian flying winger I used to have in front of me. It was a different way of playing. He was a young lad and I had a lot of time for him, partly because of us both coming from the same part of the world. I tried as hard as I could to help him but I admit I was struggling … in a way I suppose the emergence of Gary Neville was the best thing that could have happened for him. They were close, they were used to playing alongside each other and had a good relationship on the pitch. I think they did each other a world of good.'

There is, of course, the generally accepted conventional wisdom that defeats can actually help a player's development. The Spurs defeat was the fifth in 19 games, which was quite a high tally for that United side. In this tough environment of senior players fighting for their future, it was commendable on their behalf and a testament to the healthy environment at the club that those elder statesmen did not shirk from their overall responsibility. Instead of seeking excuses – and plenty were there – they sought to put things right through leading by example.

'You do try and protect them as much as you can but some things are just impossible to manage,' Parker says. 'You can't control results and so you hope results like that can be character building. You can be beaten and you can be well beaten if you don't get the fundamentals right. York City got what they deserved, we got what we deserved. The same at Leeds. The same at Spurs. Those kind of games when you play for United, those are ones you really remember. Of course there are many great memories, they outweigh the bad ones, but sometimes you need to be reminded of them because there were so many. A bad defeat sticks in the memory. You don't want to talk about it but you definitely remember it.'

Ferguson also took responsibility, taking Beckham out of the firing line for a couple of weeks and putting him back in the reserves. There was an instant response, as the midfielder scored in a 2–0 win at Bolton at the end of January. An impressive performance against Blackburn reserves on the 31st of the month put him straight back in the manager's first-team plans.

Three days later, Beckham was on the bench at Selhurst Park for the trip to Wimbledon, but came on after just 15 minutes when Steve Bruce was injured. On the stroke of half-time, with United in a 1–0 lead, Beckham struck an impeccable free kick that hit the crossbar. Goal-line technology might have awarded the goal to the midfielder (that wouldn't be the last time the player's goal tally would be debated in such a way), but home defender Chris Perry inadvertently put the ball into his own net anyway. Beckham excelled in the second period, setting up a goal for Cantona to seal the win.

Beckham apparently had a list of Manchester United heroes which was as long as that of Robbie Keane's boyhood clubs, and would be considered to be just as improbable if only there wasn't the evidence to back it up. His Red Devils credentials were not in question by anyone. Bryan Robson was an obvious name from the 80s. Mark Hughes was so revered, Beckham even took his old digs room.

Eric Cantona was idolised by most outside and inside of Old Trafford, and Beckham was front of the line, almost literally. Cantona's approach to training is legendary. His extra training sessions transformed the attitude of the Old Trafford club and rubbed off on the impressionable youngsters, who would come back from their own sessions at Littleton Road and wait outside the changing rooms at The Cliff in the hope that the French star would select them to help him practise. Always there, without fail, would be David Beckham, though it is worth remembering that this was in tune with his own dedication to bettering his game.

Seeing that Cantona did the same – and observing the results on the pitch – strengthened his resolve to continue.

It is probably impossible to overstate the cumulative, consequential effects that this had at Old Trafford, and indeed on the game in general. Just as the class of '92 were influenced by watching Cantona, there was a group of young players watching the class of '92 make waves on the senior scene.

'My relationship with David, and the others from his group, probably goes back even before he broke into the first team properly,' remembers Danny Higginbotham, at the time an apprentice about to sign professional terms. 'He would have probably been an apprentice at the time. It's a long day as an apprentice. You have double sessions, jobs to do. But even after that, him and the likes of Gary Neville and Nicky Butt would come and train with us when we were under-12s and under-13s at the time. We were coached by Eric Harrison, Nobby Stiles, Brian Kidd and Tony Whelan. David would be training with us and working on his free kicks. People talk about it as if it was a God-given talent.

'Maybe a part of that is true but it was just as much a product of hard work. Two training sessions as an apprentice, one with us, and then he'd be putting up tyres in the goals to practise after all of that. When people saw the finished article they just assumed he was a natural ... they were obviously influenced by the senior players, and it left an impression on us about how hard we had to work. It didn't mean that working so hard guaranteed you would make it into the first team, but, that if we didn't work at least as hard we didn't stand a chance. That was the least that was expected. David Beckham was the best he could be because he made the most of everything that he had and he left no stone unturned in his quest for personal development. Their ability matched with their endeavour and work-rate got them to be the players they were for Manchester United. I didn't make it that far, but I have no doubt that witnessing that made me the best player I could be.'

Back to Beckham, and how he and his colleagues were being influenced by Eric Cantona. It was a developmental influence with evidence of its benefit in the future; but also a tangible influence, with evidence of its benefit in the present. Cantona had become familiar with the new system around him. He had Ryan Giggs to his left: still a flyer, but a little more responsible with his bursts of pace following the hamstring trouble of the previous year. He had the power of midfielder Roy Keane behind him. But to the right and in front of him, there were new options. Whether or not he ever fully got to grips with playing alongside Andy Cole is a matter for another examination, but he began to embrace the cultural style Beckham brought to the team from the other side of the pitch to Giggs. As Cantona settled, the form of the team improved. And as the form of the team improved, the confidence grew; and as the confidence grew, so did the form of the individuals.

Assisted by the experience of Peter Schmeichel, Steve Bruce, Gary Pallister and Denis Irwin at the back, who were all fit after the defensive injury crisis of the winter, United had a platform of composure on which their young pups could perform.

Beckham was back in action as a late substitute for Lee Sharpe in a 2–0 victory over Everton. United had played particularly well in this game, their seventh consecutive win in all competitions. Ferguson's team were going to need to be perfect to chase down leaders Newcastle, who had a six-point advantage and a game in hand. The two teams were due to meet at St James' Park, where victory for the home side would surely end the title race. Beckham and co would have to send out a message in their game before, at Bolton Wanderers. They did that, terrorising their relegation-threatened local rivals from first minute to last.

Five minutes into the game, Giggs almost scored with an extravagant effort; in fact, there would probably have been some commotion about whether the ball had crossed the line, if not for the presence of Beckham at the back post. The midfielder reacted quickest to head the ball into the net. That was the first of six goals in the afternoon, with United flexing their muscles to let Newcastle know goals could come from anywhere – a set piece, as Beckham delivered for Bruce to kill the game in the 15th minute, from midfield, attack or even the bench, with Scholes coming on to score twice. Scholes's emergence ensured a different selection poser was being played out on the back pages – should he be starting in front of Andy Cole?

Beckham's appearances were sporadic during the subsequent run, which is remembered for Cantona's mercurial intervention where he scored in five consecutive games, three of them 1–0 wins, including that game at Newcastle. The experience of Lee Sharpe was preferred on the right in the crunch games. But even that was an indication of where Sharpe now stood in the manager's thinking. Beforehand, he would have played Giggs from the right, and now Sharpe was having to accommodate. Ferguson had concerns over Sharpe's lifestyle and the influence it was having on the group of youngsters coming through. In March, he shaved his head, which infuriated the boss – only for Cantona to walk into training later with the same cropped hairstyle, and be the beneficiary of Ferguson's indulgence. It was clear that Sharpe's time was almost up, and that meant a position on the right would be available if Beckham demonstrated the requisite application.

Thus began another period of Beckham's United career which is usually overlooked but was significant. These infrequent first-team sojourns and returns to the reserve side indicated a key issue. If David wanted to become a permanent member of the senior set-up, well, he had already displayed his quality – now it was time to illustrate that he had the physicality and temperament to handle life at the business end of a Manchester United season where prizes were on offer. Think of Beckham and you think of the liner, bombing down the right and swinging that right foot. You think of him behind his halfway line, ready to strike a long diagonal ball to one of the attackers. But the David Beckham of the final weeks of the 1995/96 season was a different animal – almost a cross between the tenacity of Nicky Butt and the timing and instinct of Paul Scholes. After acquitting himself well as a substitute in the league game against Spurs, Beckham was rewarded with a starting berth on the right-hand side in the FA Cup semi-final against Chelsea – the biggest game of his career so far.

Ferguson described the game as the best semi-final in his time at Old Trafford to date – and David was one of the key figures of the day. He met a Giggs cross early on, but his powerful shot hit the post. One might argue that the first test of his physicality was failed when he was beaten in a tackle and Chelsea scored from the attack; but his opponent in the tackle was former team-mate and idol Mark Hughes, who had no room for sentiment as he bundled over his former protégé and crossed for Ruud Gullit to score the opener.

The fickle hand of fate then pointed the other way. Chelsea manager Glenn Hoddle had decided to keep Terry Phelan, his left-back, on despite suffering with a calf injury. United made no apologies in attacking that side of the pitch, profiting in the 55th minute when Phil Neville's cross was headed back across goal by Cantona and converted by Cole.

Four minutes later, Craig Burley must have had visions of Cantona's kung-fu kick – there can be no other explanation for why he embodied Daniel LaRusso and 'crane-kicked' the ball across the field aimlessly. It caught Phelan on the hop. The veteran was already having to turn around, but by that point Beckham had seized on to the ball and shaped his body cleverly in front of the defender. It wasn't the cleanest of strikes, but it was perfect as far as Beckham and his team were concerned. United were going back to Wembley.

'It was unbelievable and a dream come true,' the player said afterwards. 'I'm a central midfielder but I'll play anywhere to be in this team. It would be a dream to play in the final, but there are still senior players to come back so I will just wait and see.'

But David had now done enough to – at least temporarily – become a member of Ferguson's starting eleven, playing from the start in United's remaining fixtures. In the penultimate game of the season, United faced Nottingham Forest at Old Trafford. Three days earlier, they had been pushed to their limits by a stubborn Leeds side, and Forest – set to be major antagonists for one of the title challengers, as they faced both of them in the final week – were equally resolute as the game headed into half-time. United were irresistible, though, and would not be denied. In the 42nd minute, Giggs weaved his way through the defence and pulled the ball across for Scholes – now given that starring striker role ahead of Cole – to convert.

Right on the stroke of half-time, it was two. United were awarded an indirect free kick on the left-hand side of the box. Beckham, though, elected to shoot anyway. Forest goalkeeper Mark Crossley punched the ball away, and it fell to Cantona, who hit a speculative volley. Uncharacteristically for him, it wasn't perfect, but it did end perfectly. The shot was careering wide, probably for a throw-in, but Beckham, arriving from the left, met the ball with a clever header, using the power to give Crossley no chance. In the 55th minute, Beckham grabbed another, this time combining with Scholes and Irwin to slide the ball into the far corner.

United added two more – form players Ryan Giggs and Eric Cantona making the final score 5–0 – but there was no doubting who was the man of the match.

'When Beckham got the second goal it lifted the pressure off the players, and they were able to enjoy the rest of the match,' Ferguson said after. 'In the second half we saw the real United with fluent passing and movement. Beckham played brilliantly and he fully deserves his man-of-the-match award.'

The *Manchester Evening News* commended Beckham's end to the campaign: 'He's had to live with the constant demoralising argument that his Ukrainian predecessor's defection was the loss from last summer's exodus to really hurt United. But, having scored the goal that took United to Wembley in the FA Cup semi-final, he turned in a man-of-the-match display yesterday with two goals to boot.'

Beckham himself gave an equally professional performance in his post-match interview. 'I think that getting the points in the bag was what we wanted,' he said. 'The goals are a bonus. Now, we'll train every day as normal and wait on Newcastle's results.'

This was a statement performance: enough to guarantee his place in the cup final team, even if there was a temporary suggestion that it might be under threat due to Liverpool playing a 3–5–2 formation with wing-backs. First, there was the small matter of the final league fixture. United knew a win at Middlesbrough would bring them the title, and they achieved that result with some comfort, scoring early to take the tension out of the game.

Whilst not exactly diluting the joy that came from winning his first league title, Beckham later confessed to subscribing to the theory that kids dreamed of winning cup finals and not league titles. Particularly this one: he had spent the last 20 minutes of the semi-final not only naturally hoping that United got through to Wembley, but that it would be his goal which took them there.

Not for the last time, the conversation about style over substance was on the table as England's two biggest clubs prepared to face off in the showpiece occasion of the season. Beckham would be one of four home-grown players in the young United side. Liverpool had a few of their own and, with Jamie Redknapp, Steve McManaman and Robbie Fowler all in impressive form that season, were arguably more highly rated in the press. Perhaps that accounted for their nickname – the 'Spice Boys', a moniker attributed to them due to the success of the pop group the Spice Girls. The Liverpool youngsters attempted to live up to their reputation by arriving at Wembley in cream Armani suits.

'1–0,' Alex Ferguson told his assistant, Brian Kidd – the idea being that Liverpool's youngsters were distracted from the job at hand. That said, the 90 minutes of football that afternoon was a true test of concentration and commitment. After five minutes, Beckham found himself in a good position after being fed by Ryan Giggs, but his effort from the edge of the box was well saved by David James. That remained the best chance until five minutes from the end, when Beckham took a corner from the right-hand side. It was not his best, but resulted in a goal, when James could only punch it straight to Cantona. The Frenchman had his own date with destiny, and it was almost inevitable that this game should end 1–0, Cantona.

'The moment was up there with any I've ever experienced,' Beckham said in 2003. The boy who dreamed of playing in a cup final for Manchester United had now not only done so, but enjoyed the sweetest victory possible.

A Star is Born

EVEN MANCHESTER United's double victory wasn't enough to convince Terry Venables – now England manager – that some of their youngsters were good enough to make the squad for the European Championship, which was to be held that summer in England. Jamie Redknapp, Steve McManaman and Robbie Fowler all enjoyed call-ups to the squad, whilst David Beckham, Nicky Butt and Paul Scholes were omitted.

At the highest level of the game, tomorrow sometimes becomes more important than yesterday. That is to say, opinion and anticipation of what is to come can sometimes supersede what has been accomplished. Some might say that is necessary for the evolution of the game, but it does mean that sometimes, as in the case of international tournaments, reputation sometimes comes before form. As it transpired, the Liverpool trio did not make a major impact on England's Euro '96, and Venables's side lost in the semi-finals, on penalties again, to Germany, so it is difficult to make a conclusive case that the inclusion of United's youngsters would have made that much of a difference.

Unlike Butt and Scholes, Beckham had the consolation prize of a place in England's under-21 team for the Toulon Tournament in France. There, he was coached by former United manager Dave Sexton, and was about the only bright spot in a disastrous campaign for the Three Lions. A victory in the first game against Belgium was followed by defeats to Angola, Portugal and Brazil.

Sexton, however, reserved special praise for Beckham, saying he was 'convinced' he had seen a 'World Cup star of the future': 'David Beckham of Manchester United is a good mover and a natural athlete, who reminds me of Peter Osgood. Most important, he has a good temperament.'

It's probably fair to not point the finger at Venables too much. Even Beckham's club manager had started to have other thoughts about who should occupy the right-hand position in midfield. Karel Poborsky, the winger from the Czech Republic who had impressed as they reached the final, was signed for £3.5m. The restriction on foreign players in European competition had been lifted due to the implementation of the Bosman rule, which allowed players to leave their clubs for free at the end of their contract. United signed five foreign players that summer, including Ole Gunnar Solskjaer – who, ironically enough, would be a very real threat to Beckham's place in the team. That is for the distant future, though.

This was not new territory for David, who had spent 18 months proving himself worthy and capable of a place in the team. He was described as the 'best player in pre-season' by Ferguson after a couple of spectacular goals, and so he had earned his place in the starting line-up for the Charity Shield against Newcastle. It helped that Poborsky's transfer had become unnecessarily complicated and wasn't completed until a couple of days before that trip to Wembley.

The headlines of the day were not dictated by Beckham or Poborsky or even Eric Cantona; instead, Newcastle's new £15m signing, Alan Shearer, was the talk of the town as well as of the Toon Army. Shearer had decided to sign for Manchester United that summer, but Blackburn Rovers chairman Jack Walker refused to sanction the transfer and instead encouraged Newcastle to make their big-money move. With the Uniteds of Manchester and Newcastle coming head-to-head, clearly Shearer would be keen to show his one-time pursuers what they were missing.

Despite those five new arrivals, none started, but there was still a fresh look to the line-up, thanks to squad number changes. It was a case of many younger players 'graduating': Gary Neville took the number 2 shirt, Phil Neville the number 12, Nicky Butt was handed the number 8, and David Beckham was granted the shirt number of the player whose old room he had slept in when he was in digs – Mark Hughes.

Hughes was known as a scorer of great goals rather than a great goalscorer; perhaps the number 10 shirt possessed a special power which could be adopted by osmosis. That would be some explanation for the extravagant goal he scored against the Magpies: a 25-yard lob after an exquisite Cantona pass. The performance could not, however, be reduced to a simple goal – Beckham had created the first two in a 4–0 win where he and Cantona had been the master tormentors.

'Maybe for a half-second at least, Shearer might have been caught in two minds about his career ambitions,' reported the *Daily Telegraph*. 'He must have targeted the majestic Cantona with envious glances, (and) swooned about the creative touches of David Beckham.'

If it was some effort to share headline space with United's star man, it would be something extraordinary to upstage Cantona. And yet the word 'extraordinary' doesn't quite seem to do justice to what followed. In 2016, reflecting on the 20th anniversary of the event which is about to be described, Rob Smyth wrote in *The Guardian*, 'Innocence is finite; Beckham's would die within the week', referring to how the midfielder had celebrated his first Wembley goal with such delight.

Manchester United's memories at Selhurst Park since the inception of the Premier League had been almost as rich as at Old Trafford. A win against Crystal Palace in April 1993 put them on the verge of a first league title in 26 years. Their return to the same venue two weeks later to play Wimbledon was played in front of an audience of over 30,000, with approximately half of those United fans.

The most famous visit had, of course, been in January 1995, with Cantona's red card, kung-fu kick and subsequent ban. On the most recent visit, in February 1996, Beckham and Cantona had starred in a crucial win, but the midfielder was not yet really established as a starter. On 17 August 1996, that changed forever.

The best football stories – the best stories, period – have great subplots. Beckham had asked sportswear manufacturer Adidas to send him a pair of their new Predator boots. They obliged, but the only pair they had left in his size had been made for Glasgow Rangers midfielder Charlie Miller and had 'Charlie' stitched on the tongue. When David put them on before the game, his fellow players relished ribbing him about it.

United's performance was one of their most comfortable at the once-intimidating stadium. Cantona scored early on: a fine lashed drive which the Frenchman celebrated with an arms-up pose. Denis Irwin then got a goal early in the second half to secure the points. The visitors' comfort in the game was summed up by Jordi Cruyff, who, with five minutes remaining, had an effort on the Wimbledon goal from around 45 yards. He had seen Neil Sullivan coming off his line, but his left-foot shot had no power or direction. In one of his later books, Beckham generously described the effort as being closer than it was – saying that if it was on target, it would have gone in. The truth was that on its first bounce, the ball was closer to the edge of the box near the corner flag than it was the goal, and Sullivan was able to collect it with some comfort.

A couple of minutes later, Nicky Butt nicked the ball from Efan Ekoku, and Brian McClair nudged it to Beckham. The midfielder turned on to the rolling ball around five yards into his own half. The momentum was perfect.

'Not you now!' Brian Kidd moaned from the bench.

Perhaps Beckham's memory had been triggered by Cruyff's tame attempt to recall those days at Littleton Road where he would try this audacious move with some regularity.

'I hit it and I remember looking up at the ball, which seemed to be heading out towards somewhere between the goal and the corner flag,' Beckham recalled. 'The swerve I'd put on the shot, though, started to bring it back in and the thought flashed through my mind. *This has got a chance here.*'

Now, some historical context. In footballing parlance, Beckham had tried what was commonly known as the 'Pelé'; and it says everything about the difficulty of the task that the Brazilian, widely regarded as one of, if not, *the* greatest ever, was synonymous with this remarkable example of ambition despite his effort against Czechoslovakia in the 1970 World Cup not actually going in.

It *had* been done before, technically. John Bailey, the Everton defender, had scored from inside his own half against Luton Town in 1982. It had even occurred at Old Trafford – Tottenham Hotspur goalkeeper Pat Jennings scored from his own box after his long punt bounced over the head of Alex Stepney. But Jennings's kick was a clearance, and Bailey's was a pass that had been timed so poorly the player later admitted he 'turned away in disgust'. Of course, there was the case of José Luis Zalazar, though that had evaded the British media; in more recent times, Eric Cantona's 1993 effort at Stamford Bridge, an acrobatic shot which bounced over Dmitri Kharine and hit the crossbar, was still relatively fresh in the memory. And finally, in 1995, Nayim of Real Zaragoza scored the winning goal in the European Cup Winners' Cup Final against Arsenal, hitting the ball on the half-volley from fully 45 yards out wide on the right.

None of these examples compared with what Beckham was attempting. This was a clean shot, not with the benefit of being on the run, not with the wind assisting, not on the bounce or with any other advantages. This was a plain shot from halfway down the pitch. Immediately it was clear to see this effort had more conviction than Cruyff's. Sullivan was off his line again, but not so far off that he should have been caught out. The shot was struck perfectly; the descent of the ball was sharp and deceptive to the Wimbledon goalkeeper, who backtracked immediately but knew where it was ending up. Without a bounce, the ball struck the back of the net.

Nobody inside Selhurst Park could quite believe what they had witnessed. History. David Beckham had arrived. He had arrived as an established figure into the United team a little later than his peers, but he had provided a seminal moment which would forever be associated with him before any of them.

In a sense, this wasn't even Manchester United against Wimbledon. It was David Beckham against Neil Sullivan; but people were more prone to give the goalkeeper sympathy rather than ridicule, and he took it in good humour after the game. 'What can you say?' he told the press. 'He beat me fair and square. I didn't think I was too far out, and certainly didn't believe there was any danger. I couldn't believe it when I saw him shape to shoot. I thought he was taking the mickey. Even so, I had the ball covered for most of the way, but it suddenly swerved and dipped and I was beaten. The lads were good about it afterwards. They accepted it was a moment of magic. I suppose the only consolation I'll have is that at least I'll be seen on TV most weeks now!'

Beckham's instant response was to celebrate like Cantona had done earlier: his usual energetic runs replaced by this calm exterior, soaking in this life-changing moment. Afterwards, in the changing room, Cantona approached Beckham to congratulate him on his achievement. 'Believe me,' Beckham said, 'that felt even better than scoring it.'

New team-mate Ronny Johnsen had made his league debut in the game and described it as 'the best goal I've seen'. Gary Pallister had been around Beckham for much longer, but even he was surprised: 'My first thought was: "You cheeky sod!" Even as I watched the trajectory of the ball I was thinking: "Nah, nah, don't be daft." But then suddenly I saw the Wimbledon 'keeper, Neil Sullivan, back-pedalling, really starting to panic, and while the words "surely not" were still forming in my mind, the ball sailed over his head and hit the back of the net. To say I was stunned is an understatement. I could believe neither the audacity of the lad for trying such a thing, nor the incredible technique to pull it off. I think the initial reaction of the team was that it was quite funny. We understood the astonishing execution we had witnessed, but were dumbstruck that he'd had the nerve to try … he was catapulted from the status of richly promising rookie to superstar with one swing of his boot … in retrospect, that was the moment when David Beckham's life changed forever. Everybody talked about how Pelé had once tried it and failed … it was picture-perfect. It announced to the world a precocious talent and immense self-belief to go with it. What other kid would have tried that in a Premiership game?'

Alex Ferguson declared it the 'goal of the season', whilst others went even further than that. Take the conclusion of the *News of the World*: 'There's no argument David Beckham's unbelievable strike will be the goal of the season. The only debate is whether it is the greatest goal ever.'

According to his former best mate, this was the ultimate evidence of practice making perfect. 'It was no surprise he did it on the big stage,' John O'Kane says. 'If you practised like he did, chances are it would inevitably work. It did.'

Back in the days before online streaming and instant access to such things, it was a wait until *Match of the Day* aired that evening to see the goal that everyone was talking about on the news and on the radio.

Back in Manchester, news of Beckham's incredible moment was spreading like wildfire. 'If we weren't at the games we'd be listening to them on the radio,' Danny Higginbotham recalls. 'I was recovering from a broken leg and it was the first day of the season … I remember them saying David had scored from the halfway line. So Dad sent me out to get a copy of the *Pink* and they were raving about it in there. Like everyone else I tuned into *Match of the Day* to watch it that evening. It was everything and more when it came to people building it up and hyping about what an incredible goal it was. It was absolutely genius. You see players attempting it a lot more often now but at that time it was relatively unheard of. Neil Sullivan wasn't even that far off his line, which make the effort even more outrageous. It doesn't bounce. It goes in the top corner. It had to be precise. There are moments in time which stand out. That goal was probably the making of him. He hadn't been in the England squad for Euro '96 and now he had announced himself to the world. If you ask anyone about David Beckham as a footballer, especially Manchester United fans, that goal is one of the first things they talk about. It elevated his profile. He had arrived massively.'

A goal worthy of the hype. Beckham had scored classy goals before, but this was almost a transformation before our very eyes: as he takes the first touch, he still appears to be the energetic, scrappy and eager to please youngster who still has a lot to prove. By the time the ball has arched into the net, the world was different.

'They'd just won the title,' Higginbotham says. 'There was still a lot of talk about how good they could be. The '96 team had a good blend of experience with the likes of Bruce, Schmeichel,

Pallister. David did something that nobody had ever done, not even Pelé, and it suddenly changed the idea of what was possible for this group of players. The reaction from some was almost like "How dare you?!" They couldn't believe the arrogance. The confidence. But think of the pressure. When David gets the ball, he's thinking, "I've got to score with this." Can you imagine the backlash he would have got from the manager? From his team-mates? He wasn't Pelé. He was a 21-year-old kid. But this was the first moment where you understood how he could thrive under pressure in a way that few other players can.'

A counter argument to this is that Beckham's miracle had single-handedly raised expectation levels, not just for him but for the players around him. Ryan Giggs already had a handful of goals which had invited and even justified comparisons to George Best, but this was new – different. It was the first time someone had done something so outrageous that standards of what you thought you knew could essentially be ripped up because new ones were being set. There was no telling how Beckham himself might react to that change, but one could argue it did nobody any favours back at Old Trafford. What, for example, of those kids like Higginbotham, who were close to making the first team?

'It changed the expectation levels for all of us now the world had seen what David was capable of,' he admits. 'Manchester United were expected to win every game anyway and now there was an added expectation of doing something extraordinary. OK, you're not expected to score from the halfway line every week, but nonetheless there is a new standard. He set the standard for himself and for others. When you think about it, it makes the career he had all the more remarkable. He was asked questions time and time again in his career, and every single time he answered them. That is the sign of not only a great footballer, but an incredible mentality.'

Yet even that almost became its own problem. Beckham did consistently back up the hype, as we'll come to discuss. In doing so, this new standard of normality almost instantly diluted the power of that incredible moment of approximately 4.45pm on 17 August 1996. So much so, that by the end of the campaign, the goal did not even win the BBC's Goal of the Season award. Granted, that award was given to a wonderful Trevor Sinclair overhead kick, groundbreaking in its own way; yet even on revisiting the footage there is a certain amount of majesty that exists in watching Beckham's goal by comparison to Sinclair's, or indeed any other from that campaign. You are still minded to take a sharp intake of breath as you ponder and question the audacity of the shot; those who were alive and are lucid enough to recollect what it meant for David Beckham will fully agree with the simple assessment he acknowledged. It changed his life forever.

'David was quite shy in his immediate reaction to it,' Pallister recalled. 'Obviously he loved it and milked the applause … the lads were all buzzing about it and I think he was a little embarrassed by all the attention.'

Alex Ferguson went into default mode afterwards: just as he had done time and time before, he rejected the request from television channels for interviews after the game. Ferguson had infamously shielded Ryan Giggs from the media spotlight and had done so with a great degree of success. That Giggs had proved a triumph on the field, and a model professional, was a clear vindication of the manager's methods. But Giggs, for all of that admitted brilliance, had never done anything quite like this. To boot, the landscape of the game had changed dramatically between the time of Giggs's debut and now. The catalyst for that change had been at Old Trafford – Eric Cantona. Even when Cantona's antics at Selhurst in January 1995 transformed the sport in terms of intrigue and scandal, the Frenchman remained notoriously quiet with the press, much to Ferguson's delight. One could argue that, for different reasons, Beckham's contribution to Selhurst Park history was just as seminal as Cantona's, just as extraordinary, and so there was no reason for Ferguson to change tack as far as that was concerned.

Instead, Ferguson faced up to the press, made his 'goal of the season' remark and added: 'He's very young and he has a way to go. We will just take our time with him and he will develop into a very good player.'

That development came with mixed messages for the next game. Karel Poborsky played on the right against Everton, but Roy Keane was injured, so Beckham moved infield to play alongside Nicky Butt. The Toffees came away from Old Trafford with a 2–2 draw. So too did Blackburn the following weekend, with Beckham restored to the right side.

Glenn Hoddle had just become England manager, succeeding Venables after the summer. There was already speculation that Beckham would be among those to benefit from the wind of change, but even if the Wimbledon goal made a call-up inevitable, there was still a certain charm about the way he found out – by reading Teletext at his parents' house.

Ferguson, meanwhile, opined that it might be too much too soon – a lot of pressure for a young man to deal with.

'If you have talent, you should be playing with the best in the country – and the boy has talent,' Hoddle told the press. 'A lot of players have made their England debuts at 21. But I can understand Alex's worry. It is not just what you do on the pitch, it is how you handle things off it. Beckham can look at other players in the squad, such as Alan Shearer, and learn how they deal with situations. If he is not given the chance, he cannot learn. Beckham can become a great player at club and international level, but no one is saying he is the finished article. Alex knows that, I know it and the boy knows it. He was saying he wanted to protect him. I go along with that to a certain degree. We will not overdo it with the boy. He needs to be handled properly at that age. Alex knows him better than I do and I have to respect his feelings. You've got to be sensible. He did the same with Ryan Giggs and it worked out fine.'

Actions speak louder than words, though, and Ferguson was dismayed to say the least when Hoddle sat alongside Beckham for a press conference ahead of the World Cup qualifier with Moldova, in which it was expected the United star would make his international bow.

'He is a footballer,' Hoddle said, 'he'll get paid the rest of his life, and get acclaimed, for what he does on the football pitch, not off it. Those things spin off because you are playing well on the pitch for the next ten years, not the next ten months.'

Beckham made his debut in a convincing 3–0 win and applied himself well. Back in Manchester, Ferguson was keen to get feet back on the ground, but would have been concerned by a bipolar performance by both his team and Beckham at Derby's Baseball Ground. The Rams were physical and uncompromising, making for a tough test. Beckham was booked and also guilty of a couple of misses when he should have done better; but, then, he did score an absolute blockbuster of a goal from 30 yards to earn his team a point.

Roy Keane's injury problem was going to rule him out of the first Champions League game, which happened to be in Turin at Juventus, the winners from the previous season. The manager intended to play a three-man midfield, and Beckham would be a part of that, so he was tested in the role at Elland Road. It was another triumphant cameo: United won 4–0 with Beckham pulling the strings.

In Italy, though, Beckham, Butt and Giggs came up against Antonio Conte, Didier Deschamps and Zinedine Zidane, an experienced trio who absolutely controlled the pace of the game in a dour but professional 1–0 win for the holders. 'In Keane's absence, it was left to young Butt and David Beckham to scuffle for the bits, like little Jack Russells in among the Dalmatians,' Steve Curry wrote in the *Express*. 'It will have made them realise just how far they have to come to have their pedigree confirmed.'

Challenge accepted. The goal at Derby had already been sufficient to erase concerns of Beckham being a one-hit wonder (really, his goals from the previous season should have been enough, but Selhurst had presented a new hard, and harsh, reset), but more impressive than the goals was his on-pitch contribution. Like Butt, like Scholes, like Keane, Beckham worked relentlessly in both defence and attack. In the autumn of 1996, it is fair to say his influence was pivotal in helping United's season remain competitive.

He was the only scorer in a 1–0 win over Liverpool, and he answered Curry's call to improve in Europe, scoring against Rapid Vienna and at Fenerbahçe to help turn around that poor start. In the latter game, the *Mail* said he 'confirmed his spectacular rise to star status with club and country with the 55th-minute opener which silenced the frenzied fans inside the Fenerbahçe stadium'.

That trip to Turkey was followed by the worst run of form United had suffered in years – six out of nine games were lost, including the infamous 5–0 defeat at Newcastle and the club's first two home defeats ever in Europe. In the midst of this, though, was a win at home to Arsenal where *The Sun* insisted: 'The future for United, and indeed England, lies with the brilliance of David Beckham.'

Those last five words were repeated verbatim by the *Express* after Beckham scored a stunning goal at West Ham in December. There was another fine strike from the edge of the box at Forest on Boxing Day, in a performance which was described as 'outstanding' by the *Mirror*. There was a certain amount of class in this one: 'Beckham, full of confidence, simply leaned back and chipped in his seventh goal of the season,' said the *Express*.

It was nine goals now for the 21-year-old, and his six in the league were all worthy candidates in any goal of the season competition. Two more were to follow in quick succession. The first was a late winner in the FA Cup against Spurs at Old Trafford: a significant moment as it was his first free kick at the Stretford End (his second overall – his first had come in a 6–3 defeat at Southampton in that dreadful run).

A week later, however, against Spurs again at White Hart Lane, he scored an even greater goal. United were leading 1–0 with eight minutes left, and the hosts were pushing forward. The ball fell to Ronny Johnsen, who played it into Beckham, who was central and facing left. Suddenly realising the space around him, he turned and pushed the ball forward, adopting the increasingly familiar position of pulling his left arm back almost like a trigger to arch his body over the ball and generate power. And what power. The ball was struck with some ferocity, sailing over Ian Walker and into the top corner.

'Ferguson was leaping out of his dugout, a manager of 22 seasons enthused like a boy at the magician's ability of Beckham,' observed *The Times*.

Six weeks later, he was dishing out more capital punishment, smashing in a volley off the crossbar to earn United a point at Chelsea. More memorable for the player on that day, however, was the first meeting with Victoria Adams, a singer in the pop group the Spice Girls; Victoria, of course, was known as 'Posh Spice'. Beckham was too shy to ask for her phone number, and was ultimately grateful and indebted to Martin Edwards, the United chairman, who invited her to a game against Sheffield Wednesday at Old Trafford three weeks later.

There were no more goals for the youngster that season, but there was plenty of consolation. First, he was voted the PFA

Young Player of the Year: an inevitability, really, considering the number of spectacular strikes in the campaign. Despite the disappointment of a Champions League semi-final exit at the hands of Borussia Dortmund (the first leg saw Beckham have an effort cleared off the line), there was a breakthrough performance in Europe against Porto, where he played on the right of a midfield three in an emphatic 4–0 win.

Better luck greeted United in the Premier League. It was a competitive, if barely classic, season, but Ferguson's team ensured some positive memories by retaining the title. The crunch game came at Anfield, where United won 3–1 – Beckham's corners created two first-half goals for Gary Pallister.

In the last game of the season, United played West Ham, safe in the knowledge they were champions and had a trophy parade to look forward to. The weekend papers had been full of the news of the burgeoning relationship between the global pop icon and the Manchester United midfielder. Beckham went to take a corner in the 12th minute in front of the visiting fans, who made it their business to chant derogatory things about 'Posh Spice'; United scored, the best antidote, and whilst the rest of the team celebrated with Ole Gunnar Solskjaer, the scorer, Beckham 'ran to the West Ham supporters, slid on his knees and waved his fist in celebration' as described by the *Mirror*. He wasn't to know it at the time, but this relatively tame reaction to some fairly close-to-the-knuckle abuse was, apparently, incitement enough for a career of vitriol and abuse from the Upton Park faithful which was more personal than pantomime.

Thus ended a breakthrough season in the career, and life, of David Beckham. Though, again, 'breakthrough' hardly feels like a strong enough superlative. Every professional footballer has a spell that is considered their best; they all have moments they perceive as defining. Few have enjoyed – or 'experienced' might be a better term – such a trajectory as that David Beckham did from August 1996 to May 1997. And yet, one could argue that the period from May 1997 to July 1998 was even more turbulent.

Interest in British football had exploded. There was a certain public investment in Paul Gascoigne following Italia 1990, tears, a knee injury and a move to Italy. But when he did finally get to Lazio, there was a void, a space for that type of personality in British football. That void was filled by Eric Cantona – this divisive, difficult-to-understand foreign player who was a hero to United fans and a villain to all others. His influence had determined the direction of each of the five Premier League seasons so far. The regularity of football on television, and Cantona's various misdemeanours, had contributed to his elevation not only as the 'King' of Manchester United but the most dominant figure in English football.

Cantona was always one to shock an audience, but the announcement that he would retire in May 1997 was stunning even by his standards.

The King had abdicated his throne. There was a prince in waiting.

Seven

IF YOU were of a cynical predilection, you may be inclined to believe that David Beckham's acquisition of the coveted Manchester United number 7 shirt in the summer of 1997 was part of his masterplan. Of course, this *would* be highly cynical: Beckham was just 22; the idea of escalating celebrity wasn't something that anybody was envisaging, let alone planning; and, fundamentally, he was in fact attached to the number 10 shirt he had been wearing.

'That meant a great deal to me,' David explained. 'Denis Law and Mark Hughes had both worn it before me. Maybe the history that went with the number was why I scored so many goals wearing it.'

Perhaps that superstition sounds ludicrous, but it does bear some examination. Especially in the new age of squad numbers, to inherit one of the shirts numbered 1 to 11 was indicative of a genuine first-team promotion. Prior to 1993, club football in England had been played with just numbers 1 to 11 on the starting team. To be associated with a number in those days, you would have had to have worn it with some distinction. That was certainly true for Law and Hughes. The pair had a reputation for scoring spectacular goals, crucial goals, and sometimes spectacular crucial goals. Perhaps Hughes felt he had something to live up to. A certain personality. Beckham obviously did, and so one cannot discount the psychological influence the number had on his style of play. As Hughes was a personal hero, there were many reasons why David had such a connection with the shirt.

If he had read the signs, perhaps the changes which were to come wouldn't have been such a shock. First of all, United had been linked with the Brazilian playmaker Juninho, who was tipped to leave Middlesbrough following their relegation. He seemed a natural replacement for the recently retired Eric Cantona and, as Juninho was leaving the Riverside anyway, the fact they were managed by Bryan Robson would surely make the transfer convenient. Juninho wore the number 10 – adored by Brazilians for players who *weren't* Denis Law and Mark Hughes – but would probably have taken the 7.

The transfer never went through, as United were caught off guard by an offer to sign the experienced Teddy Sheringham from Tottenham Hotspur. Sheringham had been offered to United for £3.5m, a relative bargain, but had to complete the transfer quickly. Juninho was tempted by a move to Atlético Madrid, where he eventually went, and Alex Ferguson, wanting to secure a successor to Cantona without too much drama, felt that with the English player's experience, it would be a sensible move.

Sheringham had always worn the number 10, and it was he who initiated the change which led to one of the biggest brands in football history. 'There was a story about who'd wear the number 10 shirt for Manchester United – as it was between David Beckham and myself,' Sheringham recalled. 'I asked Sir Alex Ferguson: "Who's the young kid who's got the number 10 shirt?" He replied: "Oh, that's a lad called David Beckham." So I asked Sir Alex: "What's the chances of me getting his number 10 shirt?" He then asked Becks, who said "no problem". I'd never been a number 7 in my life, and not being a Manchester boy I'd never realised how much of an honour it was to wear the number 7 shirt for United.'

Ferguson actually called Beckham, who was on holiday in Malta with Gary Neville. David was distraught. 'No explanation, no alternative and no argument,' he said. 'I was devastated, trying to work out what I'd done wrong. Then, a month later when we turned up for pre-season training, he had a new shirt ready: the number 7. The boss handed me Eric Cantona's squad number. The surprise of that honour stopped me in my tracks.'

In his second autobiography, *The Second Half*, Roy Keane actually claimed that he had been offered the shirt (this was indeed corroborated by Ferguson). 'The manager pulled me into his office and said that he wanted me to wear the "7",' Keane said. 'I said, "No, I'm not bothered." And he said, "I know Becks will f**kin' want it and I don't want him to have it." The little power battles. I'd had 16 since I'd signed for the club. I was comfortable with 16. I think it might have kept me on my toes, being outside the 1 to 11. I didn't think I was a No. 7. I said, "Give it to Becks." Becks got it, and it suited him – and Cantona.'

So it wasn't Cantona, and it wasn't Keane, but it wasn't even Beckham who found his name emblazoned upon the number 7 shirt the next time it took to the field – a printing error meant that "BECKAM" was, embarrassingly, the name adorning the famous shirt. The marketing department were presumably hoping that allocating the number to England's bright new hope was a straightforward ticket to commercial success, but they weren't going to shift many copies with the misprint.

The aberration took place on a wet afternoon at Wembley for the Charity Shield. Beckham came on with the score 1–1 against Chelsea, but didn't take any of the penalties as his team won 4–2.

Ferguson had decided that his midfielder was going to start the season from the bench; the *Morning Star* reported that the manager was 'worried about the physical effects the past year' had had on the player, and in particular, his 'meteoric rise to England stardom'. Beckham had played a big part in England's Le Tournoi success in the summer – starting and starring as England defeated Italy and France in a pre-World Cup tournament.

'I think we're very, very fortunate,' Ferguson had said before the game. 'In Scholes, Butt and Keane we have a tremendous three in there. And if we want to use Giggs on the left-hand side or farther forward to give us more penetration, we can do that. I can then bring in Beckham when I feel it's right, perhaps in two or three weeks' time. You have got to take the long-term view with young players. I thought we did the right thing with David in December when we gave him a two-week rest. We saw the effects of a long season towards the end. He was starting to plod a bit, his willingness was there but the sharpness had gone a bit. He's still a maturing player physically, he's still a frame to fill out. I think he's still got a few pounds to put on.'

David was on the bench at White Hart Lane on United's opening day of the season. Teddy Sheringham missed a penalty on his return to his former club, and Ferguson brought on Beckham in the 65th minute with the scores level. Sheringham combined with Butt for Butt to open the scoring, and eight minutes from the end, Beckham, in his wide right area, hit a long diagonal pass to Giggs; the ball evaded the Welshman, but struck home defender Ramon Vega and went into the net. The champions went on to win 2–0.

This intervention wasn't enough to get him a starting place, so it was another rescue act he found himself brought into at Old Trafford against Southampton three days later, with no score on the board. In the 78th minute, Beckham latched on to a Giggs cross and scored the only goal of the game. 'It doesn't matter who got the goal, but I am very pleased,' Ferguson said afterwards.

Actions spoke louder than words, as that goal was enough to restore an eager Beckham to the starting line-up. Against Everton at Goodison Park, having suffered abuse from the home fans again, the midfielder scored another crucial goal – this time, an uncharacteristic angled header which set his side on the road to another 2–0 win. He celebrated by cupping his ear to the crowd.

A fairly melodramatic start to the season, then; and, punctuated as it often is by the early September international break, Ferguson would have been nonplussed by the England camp's more relaxed approach to players talking to the press. As it transpired, Beckham's comments were fairly innocuous:

'I'm still only 22 and learning the game. If you're in the limelight you're going to get people taking pictures and wanting to catch you doing things. It's part of the job, although I can't understand why people get a kick seeing me coming out of a restaurant.'

Innocuous, but nonetheless worth remembering for later on. Beckham was on a yellow card and therefore a risky selection for Hoddle – a caution and he would miss the crunch game against Italy in October. England, though, had to win against Moldova at Wembley to make that game against the Italians a crunch one. With his side 2–0 up, and Beckham trouble-free, Hoddle brought off the midfielder in the 68th minute. His contribution had been worthwhile: his cross had been headed in by Paul Scholes for the crucial opener.

The pair combined to score an almost identical goal in United's first game after the break – the winner against West Ham. The first scorer in that 2–1 win had been Roy Keane. The Irishman had been named club captain after Cantona's retirement, but his influence would be more notable by its absence this campaign, as later that month he would succumb to a knee injury at Elland Road.

In the past, this might well have meant Beckham would move infield. But Nicky Butt had now established himself as a key player in big games, whilst Paul Scholes had definitely been converted into a midfielder rather than a second striker. Ronny Johnsen had proven himself to be a fine defensive shield as an anchor man. Beckham was now considered such a strong fixture on the right-hand side that Ferguson was seeking suitors for Karel Poborsky; in December that year, the Czech was sold to Benfica for £2m.

There was no problem in the short term. It seemed as if Keane would not be missed. United overcame Juventus in a seminal 3–2 victory and scored 13 goals in two games – seven against Barnsley, followed by six against Sheffield Wednesday. Defeat at Arsenal before the November internationals didn't seem as if it would be too damaging.

England played Cameroon and won 2–0. It should have been straightforward, with support building in anticipation of the World Cup (Hoddle's side had drawn in Italy to secure their place in France), but instead Beckham found that he and his girlfriend were, bizarrely, the target of abuse from some England fans. Presumably indicating that this sort of attention was reflective of the unfavourable image of unintelligent, beer-bellied lager louts, Beckham puffed out his cheeks and pulled out his shirt as if to illustrate a pot belly. Provocative, perhaps, though before one questioned the maturity of a 22-year-old, it would have been better to question whether it reflected the real attitude of that section of the Wembley crowd; surely any reasonable-minded person would dismay at the sheer pointlessness and counter-productivity of it all.

Against Wimbledon at Selhurst the following weekend, Ferguson decided to give his under-the-weather star a breather and put him on the bench. He brought him on with his team winning 1–0 midway through the second half. 'It wasn't until David Beckham entered the fray and scored within seconds of a 65th-minute substitution, that United looked the likelier side to triumph,' wrote Ian Parkin of their 5–2 win in the *Morning Star*. 'Beckham, a surprising omission from the starting 11, seems to save the unique for Selhurst Park. Last season, he beat Neil Sullivan from fully 60 yards. This time, it was only from six, but it was the first time that he touched the ball. He made his mark again after Wimbledon's Neil Ardley (67) and [Michael] Hughes (69) had clawed the home side back into the game. His 35-yard deflected shot put United back in front and showed individualism that was typical of all his side's goals.'

In early December, Beckham scored the decisive goal in a 3–1 win at Anfield; his 20-yard free kick was struck with such power and precision that David James could only stand as the ball rebounded off the crossbar and just over the line.

At the turn of the year, it was time to face another baying crowd, this time at Stamford Bridge in the third round of the FA Cup. Beckham made himself even more unpopular, scoring the opening goal after 23 minutes and then cupping his ears to soak in the boos. Five minutes later, he scored a fine free kick to rub salt in the wounds; United went 5–0 up before the holders restored some dignity with three consolation goals on their way out. The swagger of the victory was only likely to offend.

Ferguson couldn't have been too impressed with the drama; there can be no doubt he enjoyed the sort of routine of the following week, with the understated yet magnificent Ryan Giggs scoring a double against Spurs (both goals created by Beckham). And maybe the United boss was unhappy with Glenn Hoddle for starting the ball rolling back in September 1996, but the trajectory of David Beckham's career was only going one way from the moment he stood behind the halfway line at Wimbledon and took aim at goal. Ferguson was wrestling with public property now, and couldn't ever quite come to terms with the fact that this was a factor he couldn't control.

This trajectory, this inevitable torpedo of fame, had all the right ingredients and facilitations. Eric Cantona's retirement had been one factor. Beckham, having understood the personality that was required to wear the number 10 shirt at United, almost shifted with the mood that came with the number 7. This was a shirt which carried the professionalism of Bryan Robson; it also possessed the history of swagger and arrogance of George Best and Eric Cantona. Whichever way you looked at it, when you considered the profile of those three individuals, the shirt often belonged to the headline name at Old Trafford. Cantona hadn't only vacated the shirt, but the spotlight. He was no longer in the English game. Beckham, with his front-page place guaranteed by virtue of his relationship, was a ready-made replacement.

Concurrently, the press itself was undergoing a transition of its own. The death of Princess Diana on 31 August 1997 ought to have had a transformative effect on the way the tabloid press reported; the thirst for salacious and sensational headlines was as strong as ever, though, and in January 1998, Roy Greenslade for *The Guardian* pondered, 'Who will be the next Diana?', with Beckham and his girlfriend listed alongside celebrities of the time who were often in the press due to controversy over their relationships, such as television host Anthea Turner. What Greenslade offered as a cautionary note was seen as an opportunity; less than two weeks later, David and Victoria held a press event at Rookery Hall Hotel in Nantwich where they 'announced' their engagement.

'Watching them flash their engagement rings for the press, I thought they looked rather sweet together,' wrote Laura Thompson of *The Guardian*. 'But, let's be honest, what the hell is going on, when the news of their engagement shares space on the covers of yesterday's newspapers with the story of the possible impeachment of the US president?'

Thompson's salient point was then somewhat undermined by a subsequent character assassination of the couple's personalities; clearly unfair, but the sort of invasion that the press generally feel is provoked when a couple deem it necessary to declare their personal news at an event to which they are invited. Certainly, Beckham's September comments seemed to contradict that ignorance of why people would, and indeed should, be interested.

A contradiction does not, however, make a hypocrite. Beckham was 22. He was a footballer who was still maturing as a professional and a young man. Clearly he was old enough to know and appreciate that dating a globally known pop star would generate a certain amount of interest, but it was fair to expect that he should be able to do his job without being abused; and, even if he expected that he would be abused by rival fans as part of the job, being targeted by his own fans in such a manner when representing his country was a hardship that no one had been subjected to.

Beckham was seen as fair game by everyone in the days and weeks that followed. United returned to Chelsea for a crucial league game on the last day of February. Home defender Frank Leboeuf had stoked the fire by saying: 'Beckham possesses great ability but is a spoilt little child.'

This did not stop the United star from putting in a good shift as his side claimed a 1–0 win. Stamford Bridge was just as welcoming as it had been before. 'The memory will endure of one Chelsea fan abusing Beckham for his choice of girlfriend while simultaneously singing homophobic insults his way,' sportswriter Paul Hayward penned. 'Not so easy to deal with when you're 22. There is something about him that sets off antagonistic responses in men: his good looks, talent, wealth and famous partner for starters. In the demonology of football terraces he has broken the code by embracing the alien worlds of the catwalk and recording studio. Beckham is the true crossover footy star of our age. George Best with knobs on.'

The attack from Leboeuf was the sort of thing Beckham could now expect. It was also precisely the kind of thing that Ferguson had been cautious of when adopting his protection approach with the younger players. People saw an asset and, perhaps naively, Beckham had entered tentatively into this new world feeling everyone would have good intentions. Yes, he was now becoming the figurehead in the British game the way that Gascoigne and Cantona had before him, but he was vastly different in terms of character. There was nothing particularly flashy about his play in the same way as Gazza; nothing as eccentric in the same way as Cantona. He was hard-working and largely uncontroversial; a role model, even at this tender age, but role models did not sell – and by not getting drunk and causing mayhem on trips abroad, or not reciting poetry or inventing strange quotes, Beckham was unfairly accused of having no personality, as in the words of Laura Thompson.

People wanted to know all about him, but were not truly satisfied with the truth that he was humble and shy. Beckham had compromised with the trust in those good intentions, and it has to be said that the trust was sometimes rewarded. Journalist Neil Harman was contracted to work with David on a 'first autobiography' which was set to be released at the end of the 1997/98 campaign. Harman's memories of that period are revelatory when it comes to understanding David's psyche.

'I was granted considerable access at the time – obviously long before he was world famous – and we discussed most things … he didn't shirk any questions, though he was so young back then,' Harman says. 'It was very early on in his relationship with Victoria but that was what made him most paranoid, discussing that. He always thought there was a snapper around every corner and for the most part, he was right. He lived in a secluded flat in Leigh at the time. I recall shutters across all the windows, which seemed to me to be taking security to its nth degree, but I suppose he was just being cautious. He asked me to go to collect the takeaway one evening so he wouldn't be followed. Amazing really.'

The best way for a footballer to silence any critics is by performing on the pitch. Sport – especially football, in the way that a dramatic narrative can be weaved in the form of a storyline – has a peculiar and arbitrary set of rules which can determine if and when redemption and justification is necessary and if and when it is accomplished. It is a process that makes a mockery of the idea that football is real life, whilst masquerading under the guise that it is. And, as far as that affects footballers, it might as well be, because the vitriol is real and not pantomime. The media world David Beckham had entered into was not the one he had grown up in. Ferguson was right to be protective – following an intuition about dangers he was not quite yet aware of.

Justification for David Beckham would have to come on the pitch. His own on-field contribution was fine, if people genuinely considered it: his late intervention as goalscorer (a rare left-footed effort) and provider again for Giggs turned a 0–0 draw at Villa Park into a vital 2–0 win a couple of weeks before that Chelsea victory. But when the Champions League quarter-final against Monaco came around, United suffered a destabilising injury crisis. They had coped admirably without Keane, but then the in-form Giggs picked up a hamstring problem and Gary Pallister struggled with his sciatica. Nicky Butt was absent for the game against Arsenal, so Ferguson was four key players short. The Gunners won at Old Trafford, a result made worse by Peter Schmeichel pulling up with an injury after he had raced upfield to try to get on the end of a late Beckham corner.

In the second leg against Monaco, United had only to win, the first game having ended scoreless. But David Trezeguet scored a stunning sixth-minute effort to turn the tie on its end, and then

Paul Scholes had to come off at half-time. Beckham was forced into the middle and played a good game, but without him on the right or Giggs on the left, the width and penetration was lacking. They got an early equaliser in the second half, but were eliminated on away goals. Paul Hayward of *The Guardian* mused that there was a bright spot amidst the disappointment: 'There is a resilience, an innate hunger about this United side that drove them forward again. After half-time they were transformed. Their leader was the hard-pressed David Beckham, who had to combine ball-winning duties with the job of being United's primary creative force.'

Valiance in defeat effectively summarises Beckham's influence on United's fortunes as the season drew to a close. He scored three goals in United's final seven games and was, remarkably, involved in 12 consecutive United goals as scorer or provider. His last goal of the campaign was the last goal scored at Old Trafford for the season: a smart volley from the edge of the box against Leeds United. David subsequently ran to the corner in front of the Leeds fans and raised his arms up like Cantona to goad them. He was given the week off for the final game of the season at Barnsley. Ferguson rotated his squad, as Arsenal had already won the league.

Selection for England's World Cup squad could be taken for granted for Beckham, but was coming with a couple of heavy caveats. The most important one was where he would play and indeed *if* he would. The other was almost a secondary issue. Glenn Hoddle had decided to invite Paul Durkin, one of the country's leading referees, who would also be officiating during the tournament in France, to be around the squad in their warm-up games to give advice about foreign referees and how easily yellow cards could be picked up. Beckham had two years' worth of Champions League experience, but it seemed that this process was as much for him as for anyone.

'I don't want to see yellow cards thrown about for things that could have been controlled,' Hoddle said. 'If the referee has made a mistake we'll live with it – but the silly situations, the stuff David has got involved in, the things that happen when the ball is dead, he has got to learn you can't do that. I've spoken to David and he knows he can't react the way he sometimes does at Manchester United. There are certain situations between him and the supporters which have got to stop. It's something he must be aware of in the World Cup.'

Beckham wasn't in Manchester any more. Back at United, he might have expected his manager to turn that responsibility back around on to the supporters; either way, he would not have been expected to respond to such comments personally. But here on England duty, he was. Understanding that his chances of featuring would be facilitated if he agreed with the national team boss, his professional side prevailed. 'You've got to keep your mouth shut,' David admitted to reporters. Famous last words; although, to be fair, it wasn't his mouth that would get him in trouble.

Evita

IN THE last warm-up game on English soil before the World Cup, on 23 May 1998, Glenn Hoddle used David Beckham as the right-sided central midfielder in a 3–5–2 formation which featured Tottenham Hotspur winger Darren Anderton as right wing-back. England drew 0–0 against Saudi Arabia: an unimpressive display which did nothing to hurt any of the players who started when it came to their selection for the final squad for France.

As far as Beckham was concerned, however, there was going to be a certain sense of embarrassment. It was rumoured that he would not be selected for England's World Cup opener against Tunisia.

On the morning of 12 June, three days before that game, the players had come out for an early training session before it got too hot. In front of the group, Hoddle berated him during a drill, reportedly saying, 'You're obviously not good enough to do that skill.' If that didn't seem personal enough, consider the reason Hoddle gave Beckham when he told him he wouldn't be playing: he wasn't focused enough.

These comments, and the personally directed remarks about retaliating to abuse from the stands, seemed overkill for a player who wouldn't even be starting. It seemed that Hoddle wanted to remind Beckham, and the press, who the boss was.

United coach Eric Harrison was out in France scouting for the club, and on the evening before the news of Beckham being axed was made public, journalists Bob Cass and Joe Melling tipped Harrison off. Harrison said he felt 'insulted' himself, and so called the England training HQ to speak to Neville and then Beckham, who was 'obviously upset'.

'I emphasised to David that in my opinion he was totally focused,' he said. 'Hoddle was wrong and would be proved wrong. I told David that he was a great player and he must remember that – today, tomorrow and at all times. Hoddle could not keep him out of the England team, I added, and when he brought David back into the team he would score his first goal for England.'

Beckham admitted he hadn't played very well in a training match, but said he hadn't thought it would result in him being dropped. 'When my name wasn't in the eleven,' he said, 'it felt like somebody had hit me in the stomach. I thought I was going to be sick.'

Beckham asked Hoddle for an explanation, at which point the lack of focus was suggested. The player rejected that immediately, saying that the tournament was all that had his attention, but it was to no avail.

The news was reported as if Anderton was the one who had taken his place, despite them both sharing the pitch in previous games. 'You try not to think about things like that,' the Spurs man told the press. 'It could turn out that I play there but the only person who knows is the gaffer. The irony is that, if I had gone to Manchester United when they wanted me in 1995, David might not even have had his chance there.'

England won 2–0 against Tunisia; but Anderton's performance was under the spotlight. This was perhaps unfair: he had different qualities to Beckham, and it could be argued that neither of them was a natural fit for a wing-back role. Martin Samuel in the *Express* said the Spurs player was 'lucky to get in ahead of Beckham and didn't really show anything to edge the Manchester United man out', giving him a match rating of 5/10. Elsewhere in the paper, there was a lot of praise for the man who had missed out: 'So meticulous is he [Beckham] in his crossing and passing that he only wears his boots once before discarding them, arguing that once the leather has stretched even a tad there can never be the same contact a boot tight to the foot can produce. For a man who enjoys the fine details of life, that will have impressed Hoddle. It might even have caused a flashback to his own playing days when a tapping of the toe of his boots allowed him to make a better contact with the ball. Perhaps, though, the overriding factor may be that Manchester United star Beckham is just too good a player to leave out, however strong Anderton's claims that he has done nothing much wrong since his return to an England shirt.'

It was, perhaps, not the wisest move from Hoddle to have Beckham face the press after this game; but that's what happened, and the United star was naturally defensive about his own position. 'Of course it has crossed my mind that the preferred starting line-up might have included Darren and not me all along,' Beckham said. 'He's a good player who has had his injuries, but he's come back and done well to get into the team and now could stay there. I haven't started, and if we keep doing well, why should the team change? It's seven games to the final, and suppose we get all the way without me? Not that I don't want us to win, but these things go through your mind. Hopefully, I'll get my chance. I feel if I could get on for 20 minutes, I could do the business. I've won trophies at Manchester United, I've worked hard at what I do. I've played in the middle or on the right for England – I genuinely feel I could do either job. I'm a determined person and this makes me try extra hard to get back – but I know it's going to be tough.'

He was again on the bench for the second group game against Romania. In the 33rd minute, Paul Ince had to come off with a knock, and David Beckham's World Cup adventure finally got underway. The argument for his inclusion wasn't exactly emphatic: England lost 2–1. It was now up in the air whether he would get into the team for the last group game against Colombia.

After the game, Hoddle attempted to downplay the fuss, saying: 'I love Beckham to bits. After all, I brought him in. But he's got to understand that football comes first. His focus was not there, but now he understands what I'm looking for.'

His club manager, Alex Ferguson, was quoted by the press defending his star. 'Beckham is entering a different type of world and the celebrity status means he does not get a lot of peace,' he sympathised. 'It is difficult for a young lad.'

Hoddle told the press he was going to start Beckham and Michael Owen against Colombia in Lens, and that it had been his plan all along. David was delighted to know he was playing, but disappointed with the explanation: Hoddle had confessed he had hoped England would have already qualified by then, and it would have given him the chance to rotate his squad.

The day before the game, Beckham took himself to one of the training pitches at England's La Baule camp, and practised free kicks for a couple of hours whilst listening to Tupac. As per usual, the training paid off. England took an early lead, coincidentally enough through Darren Anderton, who hit a rasping drive into the top corner. Ten minutes later, a free kick was awarded 30 yards from goal. Beckham stepped up and struck it perfectly; the ball bent over the wall and into the top corner. England won 2–0 and were through to the next round.

Hoddle was delighted, and relieved, about the identity of the scorers. 'David's goal was a wonderful strike and Darren Anderton proved a lot of people wrong,' he said.

Beckham was the one, however, who felt he had done the proving. 'I was always focused on the game,' the midfielder said, pointedly. 'Nothing ever comes in the way of my game. I just needed a chance to show what I could do. I knew when we got the free kick that it had my name on it. As soon as I struck it I knew it was in. The gap was there and I hit it. It was a great feeling and it was nice to get off the mark. But I was most pleased with my overall performance. I played in the middle, got a lot of the ball and I feel I used it well.'

On the front page of the *Express* the following day was the headline: 'BECKHAM KEEPS ENGLAND'S WORLD CUP DREAM ALIVE'.

There was no keeping him out of the next game – England had drawn Argentina in the second round, a repeat of their controversial 1986 tie. Hoddle, perhaps knowing that, spent time talking up the idea that Beckham's gentle integration had been part of a greater plan. 'I have waited 18 months to play Darren and David in the same team,' he said. 'They can both play inside, they go outside, they balance each other nicely and we can change the shape at any time, which is what I have been looking at all along. It is an added string to our bow. Had David been focused, he would have played that first game against Tunisia, no doubt, but credit where it's due – he has come in since and has done well. Leaving him out helped refocus him – but there was never any tension between us.'

Fair enough: it was a plausible theory, considering Anderton's injury problems. In the preceding three seasons he had played 39 league games. But in his absence, Beckham had most definitely established himself, and the idea that he would be vulnerable to Anderton's return would only have really convinced people if that return had been sensational. As it was, it had certainly been good enough to get him back into contention for national team selection, but most observers agreed that Beckham should be first choice. Consequently, Hoddle's handling of Beckham at the World Cup so far seemed to be a matter of working from erroneous preconceptions. Instead of accepting that, or at least saying nothing, Hoddle's insistence that the player was not focused only caused a fresh upset.

In training in Saint-Étienne before the Argentina game, Hoddle announced a new free-kick routine which involved someone flicking the ball up for Beckham to volley in. Beckham was complaining of a tight hamstring and was reluctant to whack the ball with full force so early in the morning, before he had properly warmed up, so he lobbed the ball gently into the net when the ball came to him. This irritated Hoddle, who blasted in front of everybody: 'Can't you do it? Well, if you can't do it, we'll forget it.' The episode – embarrassing for both parties – did not reflect well on Hoddle. The football – usually the antidote – was proving to be the negative part of this summer for Beckham, who had just found out that he was going to be a father for the first time as the national team arrived at their new training base.

World Cups carry their own micro-climate. The period around each match is only a matter of days but can feel like a month. Every decision in a match is analysed, every player's contribution is under the spotlight, and each potential bump in the road can be blown up into a catastrophe. Managers usually pay the price. Hoddle would not have been pleased by the events which were to unfold, but he may well have been relieved that his role as one of the key protagonists in the latest England saga was hugely diluted by what transpired in the game against Argentina on 30 June.

It was a true match of two halves. The first period set a pace which suggested a World Cup classic for the ages was on the cards. Gabriel Batistuta and Alan Shearer exchanged penalties in the first 11 minutes; in the 16th minute, Michael Owen scored a fine solo goal to give the Three Lions the lead, latching on to a Beckham pass to beat two defenders and finish with style.

Just before the break, Argentina equalised – ironically through a cleverly worked free kick, set up by Juan Verón, scored by Javier Zanetti.

Two minutes in to the second half, Diego Simeone clattered into Beckham with an unnecessarily aggressive body check in the middle of the park. The England man was flattened face-first down on the turf. Instinctively – but with just enough delay to convince the referee, Kim Milton Nielsen, that there was some malice intended – Beckham flicked out his right foot, which connected with Simeone's calf. Hook, line and sinker: Simeone was still on his way down from an exaggerated pratfall as he gestured to the official in his opponent's direction. After a pause for dramatic effect of his own, Nielsen booked Simeone and then brandished the red card in Beckham's direction.

With the game still much in the balance, Beckham's indiscretion would have to wait, and the severity of it would surely be assessed on the events to follow. Sol Campbell had the ball in the net with a late header, but the goal was disallowed as Alan Shearer was adjudged to have elbowed the goalkeeper. The game went to penalties, and England, as was traditionally the case, exited at this point, with Paul Ince and David Batty missing their kicks. There was, then, any number of culprits for England's defeat; but, conveniently for the others, only one was going to shoulder the blame.

On the front page of the *Mirror* the following day was the headline: '10 HEROIC LIONS, ONE STUPID BOY'; the *Mail* described it as a 'MOMENT OF LUNACY THAT COST CUP HOPES'.

With such inevitable outrage, Beckham would have been hoping that his manager would protect him, but that defence was not forthcoming. 'David Beckham's sending-off cost us dearly,' Hoddle said. 'I am not denying it cost us the game. It was unbelievable. We could not have asked more from the players.'

Later on he had calmed down and told reporters: 'David is very down at the moment. It was a silly mistake, a foolish thing to do, but it was not violent. It would be wrong to put the blame on David Beckham's shoulders or anybody's shoulders.'

Too little, too late: it had been an invitation for the England camp to turn on one of their own. 'Without being too harsh on David, it cost us the game,' Arsenal forward Ian Wright said.

Such heat-of-the-moment comments are almost understandable. Some players, however, never let it go. Take Michael Owen, who reflected in his 2019 autobiography: 'I'd be lying if I didn't say that what David did that day … let every single one of that England team down … I still hold some resentment about it today.'

There was a more reasonable reaction from those more familiar with Beckham. Gary Neville admitted it was 'daft', but insisted 'nobody seriously thought it was a red card offence'. Neville said, 'With so much abuse coming from outside the squad, Becks now needed people to rally round, but there wasn't a lot of support from anyone around the England hierarchy … All the frustration that England had failed to win a tournament – again – was dumped on him, which was ridiculous.'

Alex Ferguson was of a similar mind – conceding it was 'foolish', but following with 'the reaction to Beckham's folly, in the media and among some so-called football fans, made me wonder if attitudes to sport in our country had gone totally insane. He could hardly have been more vilified if he had committed murder or high treason.'

If that sounds like an over-reaction in itself, then just consider the events of the time. Beckham had immediately issued apologies both public and private, saying, 'This is without doubt the worst moment of my career … I will always regret my actions during last night's game. I have apologised to the England players and management and I want every England supporter to know how deeply sorry I am. I only hope I will have the opportunity in the future to be part of a successful England team in the European Championships and World Cup.'

It was a futile exercise in firefighting. On 3 July, the *Mirror* published an image that filled their page 13: a dartboard, with David Beckham's face on the bullseye, with the headline 'STILL BITTER? TAKE YOUR FURY OUT ON OUR DAVID BECKHAM DARTBOARD'.

Beckham had flown to New York immediately after returning to the UK; there were pressmen waiting for him as he disembarked from the plane in America. Back home, the furore continued.

Glenn Hoddle told *The Observer* that he still intended to select Beckham going forward. 'There is no doubt the boy's got talent and a massive England future,' he said. 'I don't want to knock that down and I hope the public don't either. We would have lost something then, and I don't think that should happen.'

David's club manager made a more private case, calling the player personally to tell him not to worry about coming back to Manchester because he was loved and supported. 'Knowing he was behind me really helped me get through that summer,' Beckham later admitted; though he was panicked nonetheless by information from his parents back home that reporters would be camped outside the house on a daily basis.

Intrusion and headlines were one thing. Nobody quite knew what would happen once David Beckham stepped on to a football pitch again. Or, indeed, when he would. It was expected that he would play in the first pre-season friendly at Birmingham City on 25 July, with Blues boss Trevor Francis going as far as to talk about the prospect in his column for the programme. 'Let's surprise everyone up and down the country by applauding David on to the field,' Francis sportingly wrote. Only one problem: Beckham didn't play, and was instead selected two days later to play in Norway at Vålerenga. It gave Ferguson the opportunity to lessen the spotlight, first of all taking it out of the country and also timing Beckham's return with that of Roy Keane. The tour of Scandinavia was the perfect low-key preparation for the new season. With United due to face Arsenal at Wembley in the Charity Shield, it was likely to be one of the more high-profile curtain-raisers, as English football awaited the return of its vilified son.

Effigy

ONE YEAR earlier, David Beckham had been the victim of an accidental misprint at the Charity Shield where his name was spelled incorrectly on his shirt. It was a similar case at the 1998 event against Arsenal, though this time it was more considered and definitely deliberate that some Gunners fans created a banner with the imaginative 'DAVID BECKSCUM' in bold letters. A more physical demonstration came in the form of 90 minutes of booing, although again, the United midfielder was depressingly familiar with that being the case at Wembley Stadium.

Beckham didn't particularly impress on the day, but the subdued performance was matched by all of his colleagues in a resounding 3–0 defeat to the previous season's double winners, even if Matt Lawton of the *Express* insisted the number 7 had a 'noticeably quiet game'. Quiet, but even in victory, Arsenal boss Arsene Wenger was pushed to comment about the abuse and how the United star might handle it. 'People are fragile,' the Frenchman said. 'You cannot tell. A lot depends on how David's team is performing. It is easy to cope when you are winning. But it is much harder when you are losing. The pressure will be worse for him at other grounds. If he gets used to it, he will cope. I hope he does.'

Alex Ferguson was looking forward to at least getting Beckham in front of his own fans on the opening day of the league season against Leicester City. Before that, United's competitive campaign had commenced with a Champions League qualifier against Polish side Łódź; a 2–0 win at Old Trafford with a visiting support who couldn't care less about Beckham's World Cup indiscretion was a straightforward return to life in M16. And, all things considered, Leicester hardly boasted a notorious visiting support. Like fellow Midlanders Birmingham before them, they were probably as accommodating as they could be.

Beckham's career could almost be divided into three parts with clear distinction. The first is the formative era, which encapsulates everything before World Cup 1998. This was a time when, as a youngster, he was still trying to define his own style, so much so that he was fairly open about the traits he would adopt from previous wearers of the sacred numbers he carried on his back. It is ironic and endearing in equal measure to remember this age of innocence, where Beckham – who was destined to be such a trendsetter in his own right – displayed so openly his own impressionable side.

The second part is what we are about to dive into: a period from 1998 until 2003 where Beckham – born in London, built by Manchester – underwent a rehabilitation almost entirely through his own volition. Almost – but before we go down that path, let's first acknowledge the classic closed-ranks protection offered to the player by his club, exampled of course in that return to senior action on the continent to a more welcoming crowd. Back home, United were cautious.

'There was an extra presence of security around The Cliff in the first few weeks,' Danny Higginbotham remembers. 'The club was a family. You could be having lunch with Eric Cantona or Brian McClair or one of your mates from the youth team. Everyone treated each other the same, and we all looked out for each other, so I'm sure David knew we all had his back. That was the environment that Sir Alex Ferguson created. Having said that, I can't even begin to imagine what he must have been going through. It wasn't as if the controversy had all come from the red card. Remember that he started the World Cup not even in the team. All the papers were demanding that he played. Then he did, and made an impact. Then the World Cup was all about David Beckham. Then bang. The red card. Effigies outside pubs.'

The effigies are for a slightly later part of this story. It's fair to say that the press were taking each and every opportunity to sensationalise Beckham in the worst way, and the golden opportunity came in the days before the season began. Glenn Hoddle had agreed to release a diary of the World Cup which was due to be published and was given serialisation; of course, the in-demand subject was that of how he perceived his relationship with Beckham and how the events transpired in his direct opinion.

'I believe that with everything that has happened since, he needs help more than ever,' Hoddle wrote, whilst suggesting Beckham would benefit from sessions with Eileen Drewery, a faith healer known to the England manager. For some, the comments were so outrageous as to be unpalatable. Martin Samuel of the *Express* was one reporter who bucked the trend, saying that, far from the player being exiled by his country, he would in fact be forgiven if he had decided he'd had enough of the scrutiny and wanted to retire from international football. The difference between how his club and international managers treated him was profound.

In Manchester, Beckham was given all of the conditions to come through it. It's one thing to say lesser players or lesser men would not have come through this ordeal – and it was an ordeal – but such a statement cheapens the perception of how traumatic it must have been. One key word that must dominate any description of how Beckham recovered from the summer of 1998 is *strength*.

That is to say, ordinary men, even exceptional men, men and footballers capable of handling any pressure on a football field, anyone could well have seen their destiny take a different turn if they had been subject to the same level of persecution as David Beckham had been, and was imminently due to go through. Destiny, though, implies that fortunes are dictated by chance. From the very first game of the league season – right through to the last kicks of the entire campaign – Beckham was to prove master of his own fate, seizing responsibility and standing up to be counted.

United started sluggishly against Leicester. Emile Heskey scored after seven minutes. Ferguson had gone for a 4–4–1–1 formation with Paul Scholes behind Andy Cole; he was desperate to add another striker and was close to a deal for Dwight Yorke of Aston Villa. It was clear his team needed some extra firepower. When veteran Tony Cottee struck with 14 minutes left, defeat seemed inevitable. Teddy Sheringham was brought on and almost immediately made an impact; Beckham collected the ball from a cleared corner and hit a shot which didn't seem to possess much power. That is until it was met by Sheringham, who diverted the ball with a header into the net.

In injury time, United were awarded a free kick 30 yards out. Prime territory for Beckham to strike. 'If United had a free kick 30 yards from goal, there was a level of expectancy,' Danny Higginbotham says. 'It was as if they had a penalty. You knew something would come from it.'

The Old Trafford crowd were not disappointed. It was classic Beckham rather than a Beckham classic; the ball dipped over the wall, and the scrambling Pegguy Arphexad in the Foxes goal couldn't get there. United's number 7 did what he needed to do – hit the target. He had rescued a point for his team.

This reminder of Beckham's contribution as a footballer rather than front-page fodder was welcome, but not enough of a distraction for West Ham fans, who were preparing to give the midfielder his first official 'welcome' at an away ground in England.

Geoff Hurst – the Hammers legend who had made a rather more positive contribution to the country's history of World Cup achievements – played down fears of an atmosphere that might become too hostile: 'They'll get a hot reception, always have done and always will do. And Beckham will get as hot a reception as anyone. That's part and parcel of the game of football, the normal critical response from an opposing crowd. I'm sure Beckham has got the ability to overcome any of the stick he may get … he's got to ram the voices of the opposing fans back down their throats, and that can start at Upton Park. David has done a silly little thing, which a lot of players do. But to isolate David's actions on the day would be unfair. To say we would have won against Argentina if he'd still been on is silly, and we've over-reacted. He must expect a certain amount of criticism at various clubs. To become a great player, you've got to overcome it.'

That conciliatory tone fell on deaf ears to home fans who hung an effigy of Beckham – in an England shirt, complete with sarong, as the player had been spotted in the Indonesian fashion garment – from one of the local pubs. The game itself was a non-affair. Beckham played the full 90 minutes alongside debutant Yorke, but the pair were unable to inspire anything above a goalless draw. Much ado about nothing, then; though the images of the effigy would remain as a dark memory of the British game. James Lawton, the *Express* columnist, watched the game at Upton Park and wondered if Beckham was partly responsible for the scale of the ferocity because of his willingness to play up to the camera and engage in celebrity.

'Beckham isn't as brilliant or as beautiful as the young Best, or as wilfully destructive as Gascoigne, but he is required by his situation to carry the burden that broke both those players at a time when they should have been expressing gifts unique in their generations,' Lawton wrote. 'Part of the burden is resentment. Of youth, of talent – of sheer, blazing good fortune. If Beckham could not play football so conspicuously well, he would carry no more pressure than the toast of the local disco, but his rewards would not include £20,000 a week and the favours of one of the most visible young women of the time.'

David was at his best against Charlton, excelling as creator in a 4–1 win at Old Trafford. The first task for United in the Champions League group stage was Barcelona, where Beckham showed there was something about the traditional winger in him by beating Spanish defender Sergi to set up Ryan Giggs. His *pièce de résistance* came in the 64th minute. Barça had recovered from a 2–0 deficit to level things, but then surrendered a free kick in a similar position to the one Leicester had given up. And this one yielded the same result, albeit somewhat more spectacularly. The ball was struck with such wicked power that the netting almost seemed to get in the way of it. It was not enough to win the game – Barcelona equalised again to make it a 3–3 classic.

Beckham had been the best performer for the hosts, which made Bixente Lizarazu's comments ahead of the second group game – against the French defender's club side, Bayern Munich – a little harsh. Lizarazu was referring to Ryan Giggs's absence when he told reporters, 'He is the player we regarded as most dangerous. David Beckham is a good player, too, but he can be stopped. If you put a good man on Beckham you shut off the supply. Giggs offered more than that.'

Perhaps the Bayern man was indulging in self-deprecation: he was nowhere to be found when Beckham fashioned space to create one of United's goals in a 2–2 draw. On form, there could be no question that the player deserved an international recall after his suspension had expired, and events since then had panned out in such a way that the merit of bringing back a controversial player was not such a hot topic. Paul Ince – once of United, now of Liverpool – was dismissed in a game in Sweden in an incident described by fellow former United midfielder-turned-critic Johnny Giles as 'idiocy'.

'Already on a yellow card, his tackle was utterly reckless, and clearly delivered by a man out of control,' Giles said. 'It is interesting to compare the public reaction to Ince's irresponsibility with that of David Beckham in the World Cup game in France. Beckham's behaviour was, obviously, quite wretched, but at least there was some element of doubt about whether he would be sent off. In Ince's case there wasn't even a flicker of debate.'

Beckham would still have to sit out the first game of the October schedule. That was against Bulgaria at Wembley, where England plodded to a 0–0 draw.

'From the most reviled man in England three months ago to potential saviour,' wrote *Guardian* journalist Paul McCarthy, 'it's the kind of perilous journey to which Beckham has grown accustomed throughout his short career. Yet never has his country needed him more … To be brutally frank, Beckham on one leg and blindfolded could do no worse than the putrid imposters who tried to pass themselves off as an England team at Wembley.'

His recall would come in Luxembourg. Glenn Hoddle felt that would be of some benefit. 'In a strange way, this might be the best place for him to come back instead of at Wembley in front of his own crowd,' the England boss said. 'It will be nice and easy for him. He's looked very sharp and very keen. I don't think people have been against him as much as was expected. The boy started the season in great fashion by sticking in a fantastic free kick in the last minute, and that's where his season has come from. His performances have been very good and I've been pleased with him. The stick hasn't been as major a problem as some people thought it might be, and although he's put up with a bit, it's been pretty balanced. Nobody has gone way overboard as we thought. Now, when he puts the England shirt on again, he will be determined to play well and start well.'

A routine 3–0 win followed. Beckham – who had not been a tremendous fan of Hoddle speaking about him to the press – was decidedly nonplussed about the faith healer remarks, but, again, with his fate in Hoddle's hands, simply turned up and behaved in a professional manner. As far as that translated into squad morale – well, most players just felt the problems were in the past. Emile Heskey was called into the squad around this time and insists that he was not aware of any fractured relationship. He was, however, aware of the treatment Beckham was getting from the crowd. On his return to Wembley, in a friendly against the Czech Republic, Beckham was horribly jeered by the England fans. Heskey, a non-playing member of the squad, was alarmed. 'I remember it being really loud,' he says. 'I can remember admiring how David was able to block it out. He could do that better than most. I don't know many people who could get booed like that by their own fans and go out there and want to perform, and perform to a high standard like David did. People would always ask me if I heard the crowd when I was playing, and the truth was not really, though I think it would have been different if they were all booing me like they were David.'

Beckham's relationship with the national team following would continue; his relationship as an England player under Glenn Hoddle would not. Hoddle was dismissed after giving a controversial interview to *The Times* in January 1999 in which he said people were reincarnated 'to learn and face some of the things you have done – good and bad'. He said, 'You and I have been physically given two hands and two legs and half-decent brains. Some people have not been born like that for a reason. The karma is working from another lifetime. I have nothing to hide about that. It is not only people with disabilities. What you sow, you have to reap.'

It was not all plain sailing for Beckham. Certainly, in the period before Christmas 1998, it seemed as if his and United's season was careering out of control. In a draw at Derby, Beckham lashed out at Darryl Powell, mirroring the World Cup incident. Powell was not Diego Simeone, however, and referee Paul Durkin was not Kim Milton Nielsen; the Derby player was booked for the original foul, and had no complaints.

'I patted him on the head to say sorry, really,' he said. 'I just wanted to get on with the game. What he did after that was nothing really. It wasn't vicious. I think he gets singled out unfairly because he's got so much skill and ability. We've seen it before in England with players like him, but he seems to be handling the attention OK.'

Durkin agreed. 'I think David is responding brilliantly,' said the official. 'To be quite honest, he doesn't deserve the barracking he is getting at times. He knows he has to be very careful and try not to be provoked and I think he is coping admirably.'

The tone had changed just a few short weeks later. December was a poor month: four draws and two defeats before Christmas undermined trophy hopes. Middlesbrough won at Old Trafford in a game where United were led by Jim Ryan, the temporary assistant manager (Alex Ferguson missed the game, and Brian Kidd had just joined Blackburn as manager). James Lawton of the *Express* was particularly displeased by what he saw from United's number 7. 'The really low ground was occupied by David Beckham; but for a stupidly peevish foul on Ricard, which could have as easily earned a red as a yellow card, Beckham had displayed all the passion of a pacifist at a war rally,' Lawton wrote. 'He carried the demeanour of a recalcitrant puppy. Old Trafford caretaker Jimmy Ryan explained that he pulled Beckham off in the 63rd minute because his replacement Scholes was a more likely scorer. There were more popular theories. One was that Beckham was an even-money shot to turn the yellow in to red. The other, my favourite, was that any prolonging of Beckham's presence was a serious affront to the eyes of any watching professional. The truth is that Beckham has been underperforming quite desperately for some time now. Here, the simplest challenges of control and commitment seem beyond him. Some speak of him as England's player of destiny and talk about his frustration that neither Ferguson nor Glenn Hoddle seem prepared to trust him with responsibilities in the centre of midfield. Any more performances like this and he will have to be grateful to be squeezed into the team, let alone any team seriously intent on winning.'

United were suffering from a serious case of double vision in December and January. They played Spurs twice – in the league and the League Cup – and would face Middlesbrough again in the FA Cup third round. Before then, there was still time to play Chelsea twice. The first game ended in a 1–1 draw at Old Trafford, and the second, on 29 December, was another stalemate which had been preceded by the reopening of the old row between Frank Leboeuf and Beckham. Press reports carried comments made by the Frenchman at the Oxford Union two months earlier. He said Beckham was 'arrogant' and continued: 'He had a very sad summer. Mine was very nice. But I don't think about him. I am not as young as him. He has his life and I have my life. He said something silly about me. He said my ears were like a clown's. You might win, but you know you can lose the next day and so you shouldn't be too arrogant. He is too arrogant and has a lot of things to learn about football. But I am sure he will become one of the best players very soon.'

In a dull game, Leboeuf was actually fortunate to stay on the pitch: he was already booked when he made the cynical decision to drag Beckham to the ground. He was given a reprieve, and Beckham, to his credit, did not retaliate. After the game, Ferguson said he would give his midfielder a rest, as he was suspended for the cup game against 'Boro anyway.

Beckham was back for the visit to Leicester, but took a back seat for the majority of the game (save for setting up the final goal of six, which was Jaap Stam's only goal for the club). Ryan Giggs was in fine form, but Dwight Yorke and Andy Cole's partnership instead stole the headlines; the pair had hit it off as a fine tandem and were creating and scoring goals by the bucketload.

Ferguson's team were multi-dimensional, with threats all over the pitch. There was a genuine purple patch of form – late winners against Liverpool in the cup and Charlton in the league were followed by another huge away win, this time by eight goals to one Nottingham Forest. Beckham set up just one of the goals, one of Ole Gunnar Solskjaer's four, but new Forest boss Ron Atkinson reserved special praise for his performance.

'I thought David Beckham had a smashing game … he's almost good enough to get in our team,' he joked. 'Then they've got three strikers who all go up and score goals. They might just make it into our side as well.'

Yorke, Cole, Giggs, Solskjaer, Paul Scholes – players were stepping up with crucial interventions when necessary. Once he was back into the groove, Beckham was no different. It was from his quality delivery that Ryan Giggs scored the only goal at Coventry, and that Dwight Yorke got the winner against Southampton the following week.

'The best United could offer was the wide and dreamy craftmanship of David Beckham,' reported the *Express* on the latter game. 'He reminded us and Inter Milan that no-one strikes the ball more sweetly.'

No reminders were necessary of the Inter Milan game, though. In their midfield was chief antagonist Diego Simeone, and he was not only keen to play up the history between him and Beckham, but also not shy to confess that he was the villain of the piece.

'Obviously I was being clever, so let's just say the referee fell into the trap,' he told newspapers. 'By letting myself fall I got the referee to pull out a red card immediately. It wasn't a violent blow. It was just a little kick back with no force behind it, and was probably instinctive. The referee was right there, just two steps away, and probably punished that intention to retaliate … you could see my falling transformed a yellow card into a red.'

Kim Milton Nielsen amusingly waded into the debate, blasting: 'This proves Simeone is a sissy. He is a man without honour just trying to score cheap points before he has to stand face-to-face with Beckham and 55,000 angry people. He knows they will be on his back, so it is easy for him to blame me.'

Beckham, meanwhile, had mostly kept as low a profile as possible, although he had been the focus of a spread in James O'Brien's XY section of the *Express* in mid-February, where he explained some of what he'd been going through and how it had affected him.

'It's generally safer to have nothing to do with journalists,' he said. 'They put unnecessary pressure on players, managers and now even referees and I find it hard to understand how people who claim to love the game try so hard to damage it. But I'm beginning to think that it's good to do things like this because it gives you the chance to put the record straight … There is no way I could have survived the World Cup aftermath without Victoria. That's why I went straight to New York to be with her. She didn't say a word when I saw her, just gave me a big cuddle. She was about a month pregnant – no one knew except us – and was as pleased to see me as I was to see her. No way did I expect things to turn as nasty as they did but, once I was with her, I knew I'd get through it.'

David used the opportunity to voice his opposing opinion to Hoddle now he was part of England's past – 'Personally, I didn't agree with the comment about me not being focused … I've been brought up to believe that whether you're playing on Hackney Marshes or in the World Cup, you give it everything you've got'

– before insisting he wanted to stay at United 'for the rest of my career and continue to repay the debt I owe to the boss, the club and the best fans in the world'.

Only 23, he was quizzed on what the future held. 'I have no great desire to play abroad but you can never say never; United might get sick of me and sell me abroad or to London,' he said, before adding, 'Management holds no appeal for me. What I would really like to do is open a school of excellence for kids – boys and girls. It's not a normal ambition for a footballer, but it's something I've always wanted to do. A lot of people helped me get to where I am and I want to put something tangible back into the game. It's something I feel strongly about. I think it's important to remove the idea that football is an exclusively male domain. When I was at school some of the girls were as good as the boys and getting them involved more might help to remove some of the macho nonsense that mars the game.'

Inevitably, though, some of that nonsense was involved in the build-up to the clash between United and Inter in the Champions League quarter-final. These were the days before the formal Premier League pre-game rituals of line-ups and handshakes, but such formalities were customary before European matches. So, observers were keen to see what would happen when Simeone and Beckham crossed paths, but they were left underwhelmed by a straightforward firm handshake. Pleasantries did not extend to the field: this was an era where Italian sides were infamous in their physical approach, particularly against susceptible and weaker sides, which the English were deemed to be. Beckham was already getting a taste of close attention in the first couple of minutes, but demonstrated his concentration with a free kick which clipped the top of the crossbar soon after. It was an eventful start and came with an exclamation point in the sixth minute, when Beckham's whipped centre was met by Yorke in the middle. In first-half injury time, the trick was repeated; thanks to second-half heroics from Peter Schmeichel and Henning Berg, United held on for a deserved two-goal advantage to take to Italy. It was enough to see them qualify for the semi-final against Juventus.[1]

There was semi-final football waiting for United in the FA Cup, too. Their form since Christmas had been nothing short of remarkable: 15 wins and five draws from 20 games, with Beckham proving an increasingly influential force, had provoked talk of an unlikely treble of league, FA Cup and European Cup glory for United. In their way in the FA Cup were Arsenal. They contested a goalless draw at Villa Park and went to a replay at the same venue three days later. For the second game, Ferguson rotated his team, but Beckham – who had played the entire 120 minutes in the first encounter – would have to play from the start again. This, too, would go for the maximum duration, but nobody at Old Trafford was complaining; in fact, they were just proud to be included in one of the greatest football matches in English football history.

It was Beckham who got the show started. In the 17th minute, Teddy Sheringham laid off a short pass. The momentum of the roll of the ball was perfectly in sync with that of the midfielder's run, but plenty was left to do. From 30 yards out, the United star blasted a stunning curling effort past the considerable frame of David Seaman. Of course, Beckham's repertoire of goals from open play was already so outstanding that it might not top his list of greats. But it could, for some. It was a wonderful strike, made all the more remarkable by the fact that Seaman just wasn't beaten *like this* from that kind of distance. United went on to win, but Beckham's classic goal was overshadowed even before the night was out thanks to Ryan Giggs, who had his moment of a career when he slalomed through the Gunners' defence to smash the ball home and take United to Wembley. Even Beckham later

---

1 Twenty-four hours after David had created that brace of goals for Yorke, Victoria gave birth to a son, Brooklyn – a bizarre bookend, considering David had discovered he would become a father after his first altercation with Diego Simeone.

admitted, 'It's only me who thinks about it now,' although the passage of time has meant a new appreciation for the goal has developed primarily *because* of its forgotten nature.

His contribution was not overlooked by the PFA, who included him in the nominations for the Player of the Year alongside fellow United players Roy Keane and Dwight Yorke. Keane, like Giggs, was imminently to experience his career-defining moment, whilst Yorke was most definitely at his career peak, aided by that partnership with Cole and also the supply line of Beckham.

One week after the second game against Arsenal at Villa Park came the second against Juventus in Turin. Giggs had scored a last-minute equaliser to take a 1–1 scoreline to Italy, but he was out of the second leg. After 12 minutes, it seemed as if his team-mates would be out too. Two Pippo Inzaghi goals put Juve 3–1 up on aggregate. In the 17th minute, Beckham stood over a free kick, and remembered telling his friend and colleague Gary Neville that he felt their opponents were there to be beaten.

Seven minutes later, it was Beckham's corner which was met by Roy Keane at the near post; the skipper's header looped over Angelo Peruzzi into the far corner. Game on. Ten minutes later, though, Keane was booked for a late foul on Zinedine Zidane. It was a huge blow – the Irishman would not only miss the final should United get there, but, reasonably speaking, his capacity to be the same dominating force for the remaining two-thirds of the game should have been significantly reduced. It wasn't, and history has recorded the entirety of this game as the definitive Roy Keane masterclass – a lesson in influence and selflessness. On captaincy. Leadership.

And rightly so. But it is worth remembering the almost-as-masterful display of Beckham, who, within 60 seconds of Keane's booking, had played his part in another goal – this time cleverly laying the ball off for Cole, who crossed for Yorke to head in the equaliser and the pivotal goal of the tie. United now had the lead on away goals, with the advantage of more than half a game remaining to add more. Despite both teams threatening to do so, it wasn't until the last few minutes that another goal came, this time an insurance effort by Cole after great work by Yorke. Beckham – who had feared early on that this would be 'another Dortmund' – was heading to the Nou Camp and the Champions League Final with Manchester United, emulating his father's heroes.

Martin Samuel heaped praise in the *Express*, explaining how 'the dead ball expertise of David Beckham shocked Turin to its foundations. His 24th-minute corner from the left was struck with perfect specifications to meet Keane.'

So there were now two finals to look forward to, but a league title to compete for; and David Beckham was as influential as any player, if not more so. On 1 May, just after half-time in the game against Aston Villa, Beckham struck a magnificent free kick to give United a crucial 2–1 win.

'It was a superb free kick,' Dwight Yorke said afterwards. 'I know one day I will probably get my chance to take one – when he's not on the pitch because the gaffer has decided to give him a rest. The guy's superb, and it's all down to hard work. You've got to practise to improve yourself and that is exactly what Becks does. Like everything else in life, practice makes perfect. Sometimes after training he will spend an hour just taking free kicks.'

Beckham wasn't the only one preparing. His skill had become so feared that opponents dedicated time especially to dealing with it – for what good it did.

'We spent all week looking at the Beckham free-kick business,' Villa defender Gareth Southgate lamented. 'We decided if he was in a certain position I would drop back on to the line, and that worked the first time. In the second half he was a bit further out, and we thought we would be able to defend without me back there. To be honest, I don't think eight men on the line would have stopped that one, because sometimes you just have to hold your hands up and put it down to a fantastic piece of skill. From a goalkeeper's point of view, and admittedly I'm no expert, it must be difficult to know where he's going to put it. It is impossible to tell until it's five yards off his boot. That's why it's no disgrace to lose to a goal like that. At the moment, Becks is the best in the world at it. He seems to get an awful lot of stick because people are jealous of him, but he is magnificent. There are very few players in our country we can consider to be world class and he stands among them. You have to admire the talent he has.'

The Beckham–Yorke connection yielded another goal at Anfield in a 2–2 draw. United had the chance to win the title at Blackburn, but a 0–0 draw did neither side any good; it in fact relegated Rovers, making it a very unhappy spell for Brian Kidd. It took the title race to the last day of the season. United were masters of their own destiny. If they won against Spurs, it wouldn't matter what Arsenal did at home to Villa.

Beckham was inevitably featured as one of the key players in the build-up, and gave a rare interview about how this season had turned around for him. 'At the start of the season I think a lot of people were wondering how it would go for me,' he said. 'They wondered whether I would crack up, or whether I would go abroad. All I actually wanted to do was come back to Manchester United and start playing again. That was important to me. And the manager said that as long as I got back here and rejoined my team-mates I would be fine. Looking back now, I'm pleased with the way it's gone for me. At times it was hard when the rival fans got on my back. The lads here have been brilliant and at no time did I ever have any doubt about wanting to stay at United. I knew I was going to get a bit of stick at away grounds, but when you're playing for the biggest club in the world you expect that anyway.'

It was fair to say that away from London and some of the usual suspects (the England crowd being among them!), the treatment dished out to Beckham hadn't been as bad as those early weeks had threatened it could be. Perhaps it helped that visits to Leeds and Liverpool were so late in the season. This ought not to deflect from the remarkable journey Beckham had been on. There were boos at every away ground; the only thing that changed from week to week was the scale and anger.

There were boos too from the visiting Spurs fans, who were caught in that classic quandary of not really wanting their team to win as it would give their huge local rivals a distinct advantage. That was the dilemma they were faced with when Les Ferdinand scored a freak goal to give their side a 26th-minute lead. Perhaps, then, Beckham's 43rd-minute intervention was not the most unwelcome; his whipped effort carried the sort of power you would see on a cross, but this was an intentional shot (described by the *Mirror*'s Harry Harris as 'vicious'), which smashed against the inside of the post and into the net. The equaliser relieved the tension; Andy Cole's early second-half strike settled the title.

Part one of the treble was in the bag. Ahead of the FA Cup Final against Newcastle United, Ferguson had teased Beckham, telling him he was considering resting him because he would be required to play in the centre of midfield against Bayern Munich in the Champions League Final. It was serious enough to make Beckham wonder; he was, however, picked from the start at Wembley. And, after six minutes, it was clear he would have some practice playing in the middle when Roy Keane's game – and season – was prematurely ended by injury. Keane's replacement, Teddy Sheringham, scored within five minutes of being on the pitch, and try as they might, Newcastle were never able to wrestle this game out of the control of Ferguson's side. A second goal early in the second half from Scholes – who would also miss the following game due to suspension – settled a game that was as routine as the United contingent could have hoped for. This was Beckham's second FA Cup, and an audition well and truly passed.

'Everyone has been saying facing Munich without Roy because of his ban would be a major hurdle for us,' Ferguson said after the game. 'But I think we proved today that isn't the case. David took over Roy's role and was outstanding.'

United's success was indeed a genuine collective effort. This was reflected in the awards for Player of the Year: David Ginola picked up both, from players and writers. Ginola had an exceptional season for Tottenham, but his victory was always seen as a consequence of split voting, even in contemporary times. The Monday after the cup final, reporter Martin Samuel explained how it had all transpired in his eyes: 'In March, when many of the votes were cast, I would have gone for Dwight Yorke. By the closing date, in April, I had switched to Roy Keane. Patience has its own reward, however. Because while this particular award carries scant kudos, no prize and is not recorded anywhere except on this page today, David Beckham is my Footballer of the Year. I can decide this without bitter regrets in a month's time and without discovering some genius has given it to David Ginola by mistake. That's the beauty of joining an association of one. Your guy always wins. Beckham is ending the season as Footballer of the Year by a distance. It might have taken some time to shrug off the club-mates on his shoulder but as Manchester United charge up the final straight there is only one runner in sight, checking behind to see if he can afford to slow down. Yet he never does.

'By which discipline do you judge him? Stamina, ability, professionalism, behaviour on field, behaviour off field. He's streets ahead in them all. If you want a game of football he's the best player on the park ... Beckham has endured taunts and abuse that would have driven others demented and has turned them, incredibly, to his advantage. He has enough money to be lazy, yet never is, and enough celebrity to be flash and egotistical, yet does not appear to be. He is a player who crosses on the run and invariably drops it on a two-bob bit. Can you imagine how many times he must have practised that skill as a youngster, a teenager and now as a professional to perform with such consistency? No one is born with that much natural ability. It comes only from pure graft – and ask anyone around Old Trafford and they will confirm Beckham is the hardest worker of all.'

Samuel dubbed Beckham 'the King without a crown', but even if he was already considered part of footballing royalty, there were no airs and graces about the United midfielder. The team had been handed the FA Cup by Prince Charles; David had been so preoccupied with finding Victoria to wave to with the trophy, that he had to be reminded by the Prince of Wales to pick up his winners' medal. Later that evening, he and his partner found much amusement from a split lip he had picked up in a clash with combative Magpies midfielder Gary Speed; water was leaking through a hole that went straight through it, making for the most unique party trick of the night.

Any proper celebrations had to be put on hold. United had won a third double in six years – business as usual, almost – but were pursuing an even more glorious place in history. Against Munich midfielders Stefan Effenberg and Jens Jeremies, they were going to need Nicky Butt (rested completely at Wembley) and Beckham at their best. Possibly acknowledging that Beckham would benefit from a charm offensive to get himself ready for the big day, some at Old Trafford were keen to build up his confidence.

'The booing and constant jeering from rival fans whenever he's on the ball is something you would not wish on anybody,' said team-mate Ryan Giggs, 'yet David has handled it brilliantly because it's actually been the best season he's ever had. He's been magnificent for us and, gradually, he has silenced the boo-boys with his football.'

Club legend Denis Law agreed. 'He's not collapsed under the abuse,' said the Scot. 'Far from it. He's blossomed beyond belief and is a better player because of it. He's one of the best crossers of all time and his very best is yet to come.'

Watching on with interest would be new England manager Kevin Keegan; Beckham's enforced switch into the middle may well prove to be a watershed moment for club and country if all went well. In a newspaper interview, Keegan waxed lyrical about the player's ability and suggested the reason why he couldn't play infield is because no one is as good as him at crossing. 'If they start cloning footballers Beckham would be the first one you sent to the lab,' he said.

It was most definitely a compliment, though a little ironic, considering that Beckham was in fact an example of the improvement which comes from hard work on a training ground. And, in fact, Keegan was probably more accurate with his other assessment: the suspensions to Keane and Scholes claimed a third and fourth victim, as without Beckham on the right, United were robbed of inarguably the most prolific assist supply in open play in Europe. Ryan Giggs would be asked to play from the right.

At United's training camp in Spain, Beckham was interviewed by the press on these topics. 'I practise all the time,' he said. 'Throughout the week we do different drills, dead-ball stuff, set pieces and I train a lot on my own when everyone has finished. I stay out for an hour hitting balls – if the manager lets me. Sometimes he sends me in, he says "Get your rest, stop training." I've tried to sneak out, but he's got a view of everything from his office at The Cliff. It's nice to be talked of as the best crosser in the game, but if you think about it too much you start worrying, wanting to get it right all the time, and then you suffer. I have people asking who is the best free-kick taker between me and Roberto Carlos. But I don't think of things in those terms. It doesn't matter, does it? Anyway, after his one at Le Tournoi, I won't flatter myself.'

In truth, although Beckham had endured the ritual of comparison in the very early days of his career – could he be the next Kanchelskis? – those comments had been answered in the most emphatic and convincing fashion. Not by being the next Kanchelskis, but the first Beckham. In doing so, he had almost completely reinvented the idea of what it means to be a right-winger. For 90 minutes at the Nou Camp, though, he would have to do his best Paul Scholes impression alongside Nicky Butt in Roy Keane's clothes. And they did a largely capable job, though it was evident that Beckham's absence from the right was having an impact. Ryan Giggs played well in that position – he now had enough European experience to unsettle any continental defence wherever he was – but didn't have the same lacerating penetration he naturally possessed from the left.

An already difficult task was made near-impossible once Mario Basler scored a free kick in the sixth minute. The goal enabled the German side to sit back and protect their lead on the big Barcelona pitch. United were never found wanting for effort, but found their opponents near-impenetrable, particularly with the English side shorn of their two most devastating forces of attack in their natural areas. In the 66th minute, Teddy Sheringham came on for Jesper Blomqvist: it was a significant move, often overlooked as a turning point of the game besides the obvious point. Ferguson had gone for broke. His half-time team talk had been spent reminding the players of how close they would get to the European Cup without being allowed to touch it. It had not been enough to generate a response to break through; so on came the veteran England forward, playing in what could be explained as the Cantona role against Porto back in 1997: a withdrawn role in front of three midfielders and behind two attackers. It was a subtle move, but it enabled Giggs and Beckham to reposition – not entirely back to their usual places, but close enough for them to influence the game a little more. This tactic had worked with devastating effect against the Portuguese team. It was the only positional change Ferguson could reasonably deploy.

Bayern responded immediately, withdrawing a forward for a creator – Zickler for Scholl – and with the game open, the leaders had opportunities to add to their advantage. With ten minutes remaining, Solskjaer came on for Cole, whilst Bayern brought on Thorsten Fink for the legendary Lothar Matthäus in a symbolic move; an end-to-end frantic battle ensued. Solskjaer forced a save from Oliver Kahn immediately; Jancker hit the crossbar with an overhead kick, after Scholl had hit the post some minutes earlier. Three minutes of added time were allocated following the number of substitutions. In the first of those, United were awarded a corner. Peter Schmeichel – the legendary goalkeeper, who had announced earlier in the season that he would be leaving the club at the end of it – came up for it, hoping to score just as he had done almost four years earlier against Rotor Volgograd. He didn't, but his presence caused enough panic to send the normally composed Munich side into disarray. Beckham's corner was half-cleared to Giggs, who shot but couldn't get a full connection on it with his right foot. On the spinning ball, neither could Sheringham, but it was nonetheless a sufficient scuff to divert it into the near corner and send the United fans behind the goal into some sort of delirium.

Quite why they were so excited must have been because of the occasion: surely United supporters had been here enough this season for last-minute goals to feel part of the usual routine? There had been four in 1999 alone, three of them in the heightened hysteria of cup competition, two of them indeed in European competition. And, if you had a long enough memory, you might have recalled that United's quest for success this season had started by depending on the reliability of David Beckham's set pieces in the last minute of the first home game against Leicester.

Within 90 seconds of Sheringham's leveller, Solskjaer was out on the left, winning another corner, requiring Beckham to make one more sprint over to that side. As he did, the normally endlessly energetic midfielder wondered if he would have the stamina to endure 30 minutes of extra time. It wouldn't be necessary if they got this right.

Beckham's corner was good. It was automatic quality; the default setting for the number 7. In another world, Darren Anderton might have been playing this game instead; Sheringham, so infamously part of Anderton's routine where he would flick on his colleague's corners across the box, did so almost on auto-pilot. And then Ole Gunnar Solskjaer did what he did best on instinct too – sticking out a leg and prodding the ball into the net. Thirty-one years before, United's first European Cup had been won by one brilliant shimmy of genius in the body swerve of George Best. Here, it was decided with the ruthless and perfect execution of a training-ground drill. Practice – as it so often did for David Beckham – made perfect.

Manchester United had won the Champions League. Beckham earned praise for his performance, which grew in confidence as the game wore on, though it was perhaps a greater matter of concession that his presence on the right was more deeply missed than anticipated. It was an emotional night – all the more for taking place on what would have been Sir Matt Busby's 90th birthday – but Manchester United, under Alex Ferguson (Sir Alex, as he was soon to be known), were in the business of viewing things clinically. The victory would be celebrated, but, unlike Busby, Ferguson was not content with one such triumph. He would want a repeat, and need it, in order to cement a legacy as Britain's greatest boss.

Such an outlook – undoubtedly a positive thing – requires something of a harder perspective, colder and perhaps more harsh than the romance sometimes allows. This had been a particularly big week in the career of David Beckham, and in the life of the Beckham family. The Nou Camp had not only provided this remarkable memory for them. The success also meant Beckham had actually surpassed Bobby Charlton – his father's hero, and the man after whom he was given a middle name – when it came to Old Trafford trophy hauls. Charlton had won three league title medals, one FA Cup and a European Cup. Beckham now had all that and an extra FA Cup. This is not an invitation for comparison about ability or era, purely a statement of notable fact.

On a broader scale, it meant that the class of '92 had earned their place in history as worthy of mention alongside the Busby Babes. The Beckham/Charlton comparison is one of a number, most of them now favouring the modern group of stars. Munich undoubtedly affected the older generation. In order for the new crop to continue to justify their place in the conversation, they would now need to accumulate trophies at a rate that fate decreed many of the Babes could not. Of course, nobody was thinking in such a way at the time: this is an analytical viewpoint taken over 20 years after the event, with the benefit of hindsight at the end of entire careers.

In May 1999, David Beckham was most certainly living in the moment, even though there was plenty for him to look forward to.

Naughty Boy

THE JOURNEY from hero to zero and back to hero was one rarely accomplished in British sport. Once a competitor was down, they usually stayed down; they didn't resolve to reach even greater heights than ever before. In English football, David Beckham had the close-at-hand example of Eric Cantona, but the Frenchman had not, even at his most polarising, been the recipient of such hate and vitriol as Beckham. Perhaps Cantona was more inaccessible whereas Beckham seemed vulnerable. Cantona was reactive, explosive, but usually by his own rules and according to his own time. Beckham was responsive and engaged. He almost at times appeared to thrive on the attention.

Even though the sheer passage of time dictates that no story is ever truly complete, conclusions often need to be provided in order to satisfy the consumer. In the summer of 1999, the stage of Beckham's journey was very much seen as the end of a blockbuster movie: he wins the biggest prizes he can, gets married to the love of his life and lives happily ever after. His redemption arc was as complete for country as it was for club, at least so far as the press was concerned – rival supporters would need a little more convincing.

England had two European Championship qualifiers in early June and, in a huge contrast to the previous year, the Manchester United midfielder found his national team boss not only welcoming but a captivated, fanatical audience of one.

'It has been an education just sitting and listening to David,' Keegan said, before England faced Sweden. 'I can see how he is a very special young man as well as being a very special talent. David got hurt but answered all his critics – people who went too far – in the perfect way, on the football pitch. What he's done this year with Manchester United and England means he will achieve his ambition of having people look up to him and respect him. He can play that central role and it is clear that is the way he wants to go, but at the moment on the right he is the best in the country. We want the best of both worlds from him, everything he can give us – he can play narrow and go inside but we also want those fantastic crosses. It is up to us and him to find a way of doing that.'

Beckham appeared to exude a new maturity and contentment. 'If you've been through an experience like I have, you can either crack or come out stronger,' he told the press. 'It is difficult to take in what has happened to me because it all seems to have come at once. I am only 24 and I've done so many things, more than some people have done in their whole careers. After the World Cup I knew I just had to get on with things. It was hard at first with the attention I was getting but it affected my family more than me. My mum and dad were upset by a lot of the things that were said. It hurt me because it was upsetting a lot of other people close to me, but I do not hate people who came out with all that stuff, I just feel sorry for them. We're champions of Europe and champions of England so that takes away the pain. I made a few people eat their words, but I didn't feel as if I needed to vindicate myself, it was just a case of getting back to playing football and trying to enjoy it. I'm happier now than I've ever been.'

It was not, however, an enjoyable afternoon for Beckham and co against the Swedes. Prior to the game, defender Pontus Kaamark had remarked, 'David Beckham is one of the best players in the world right now and getting better and better. But we are making no special provision for him. That's not our way.' Yet Sweden – in this era, defensively very efficient – were rarely troubled, and instead irritated the home team at Wembley. Paul Scholes was dismissed early in the second half after getting two bookings, and Beckham himself was forced to come off in the 75th minute with a hamstring strain.

Visiting player Kennet Andersson had a tangible tone of relief in his words when he said, 'I thought everything was just too predictable. We were really worried that David Beckham and Phil Neville could hurt us down the right, because they have an understanding and Beckham is so good with his crosses that no team can expect to be untroubled all game. But they didn't ever get in the positions where we could be exposed.'

So far, if one were to evaluate the journey of Beckham's career, one would note the triumph and the turbulence and feel that it was one of the quintessential success stories: the 'boy done good' type of thing. It is on tracking the lines of what is to come that you have cause to question how much of it was chance and how much of it was design. The easy answer is the psychological jargon often trotted out: that some players have a self-destruct button, that sometimes when things are going too well, they have a subconscious need to instigate some form of controversy. Beckham, ostensibly in the happiest time of his life, did not seem to be troubled to the extent that would explain the outbursts of the coming months.

The hamstring injury kept him out of United's pre-season tour to Australia and the Far East, but Beckham was back for the Charity Shield against Arsenal. There were a couple of matters of significance with his appearance here. The first is that his magnificent free kick – which struck the underside of the crossbar and went in – was actually, eventually, a goal credited to Dwight Yorke, who followed up to make sure. If that ought not to really matter too much, aside from the principle of Beckham surely preferring that the records show that he scored 86 rather than 85 times for United, then it resonates a little more when acknowledging the fact that this would be the club's final registered goal at the old Wembley Stadium before it was demolished and rebuilt. It should have been fitting that the club who had enjoyed the most glorious recent past with it should have this superb goal to say goodbye to it. Not that Yorke was complaining; though he might have been dissatisfied with the final result of 2–1 to Arsenal.

It was a fairly quiet start to the season for Beckham, whose first notable contribution to the league campaign was to set up the second goal for Yorke in a 2–0 win over Leeds United at Old Trafford. By that stage of the match, he had already secured his place in the headlines by reacting to taunts from the visiting end and giving them a 'V' sign.

FA chief David Davies insisted that the player would not face charges for the incident. 'Nobody can pretend David Beckham has been treated by fans like every other player,' he said. 'Every time he takes a corner at an away ground everybody knows the reaction he has had.'

Before long, though, that tone had changed. Not soon enough to impact on Beckham's international call-up in early September – poor performances against Luxembourg and Poland were attributed to the slow recovery from that hamstring issue – but by the time he was back with England, the August matter had apparently escalated in seriousness. No doubt that was down to Beckham's behaviour in the meantime more than the first incident. First, he was criticised for allegedly kicking out at Steven Gerrard and stamping on Jamie Redknapp in a fiery 3–2 win at Anfield; and in a Champions League game against Sturm Graz, he was accused of lashing out at Tomica Kocijan off the ball. 'Beckham definitely made contact with me and was lucky to escape punishment because he kicked out at me,' Kocijan said. 'The referee didn't even give a foul and yet we weren't anywhere near the ball.'

Beckham was cautioned in the 72nd minute after clashing with Roman Mahlich; yet after the game, he received support from the unlikeliest source.

'Is Beckham more important than the whole game? The booking he received wasn't fair and the other incident, well that's just part of the game, isn't it?' said rival boss Ivica Osim. 'It helps to stimulate both my team and the spectators. But is Beckham better than the other United players? I think not. He did not have a very good game.'

The United boss gave his take on the events that had transpired. 'The lad tried to get Beckham booked,' Sir Alex said. 'I thought it was a harsh decision.'

This was the public face; privately, the United boss was furious that Beckham had attended a party in London hours before he was due to travel to Austria. The charade had given weight to the speculation that the midfielder would welcome a move to the capital – which he quickly rebuffed, saying, 'We're living as a family up in Manchester and we couldn't be any happier.' He would have been happier still if he hadn't been fined £50,000 for the episode. A controversial week was made worse by the news that the FA had requested an informal meeting with FA compliance officer Graham Bean, where Beckham could expect to be told that a repeat of the 'V' sign or similar could result in a five-match ban.

On 2 October, England boss Kevin Keegan took a diplomatic stance: 'It's not me personally who wants to speak to David, it's not my department and I definitely wouldn't let the FA speak to him while he was with me. When a player comes with England, he comes to play – it's another department that is involved here and they would have to come through me.' The meeting took place on 12 October with less fanfare; Beckham was accompanied by Ferguson, and afterwards, a spokesman simply said the 'matter is closed'.

It was finally time for Beckham's season to have some positive events. His goal against Croatia Zagreb inspired a 2–1 win which sealed qualification to the second group phase of the Champions League. The reminder of his talent hit home on the continent, particularly with reigning Ballon d'Or holder Zinedine Zidane, who tipped the England star to be his successor. 'I don't deserve it again,' said the Juventus playmaker. 'There are other players who have produced much more than me and who have also won more. I am thinking of Christian Vieri, Luís Figo and Rivaldo, but above all of Beckham.'

Beckham was also at the forefront for the waiting public in Tokyo, as Manchester United travelled to Japan to take on Brazilian side Palmeiras in the Intercontinental Cup. Television networks in the country were dedicating half-hour shows in prime-time slots on their top channels to United's number 7. The entire team were treated like the Beatles, but Beckham was seen as both Lennon and McCartney in this analogy. Before the showpiece occasion, Ferguson was quizzed on Zidane's comments, and replied: 'If it's David we'll be delighted. It would be fantastic for a Manchester United player to win it, but if it is taken over performances last season, I'd say four or five could have been nominated. It's a tribute to all our players, not just one individual.'

As if to emphasise the point, United won thanks to a true team effort; Ryan Giggs won the man-of-the-match award after tormenting his opponents throughout. Roy Keane – fittingly, considering he'd missed the European Cup Final – was the scorer of the only goal, courtesy of a fine Giggs cross. And there was also room for a goalkeeping masterclass from Mark Bosnich, who had been signed as a successor for Peter Schmeichel, but would, in fairness, never quite kick on from this highlight of his time at the club.

United returned to England to play a few games before travelling to Brazil to play in the World Club Cup; if it sounds like an unusually cramped calendar, then it certainly was that. The arrangement of this extra intercontinental tournament, coinciding with the ill-judged second group stage of the Champions League, meant United had to assess their options; the World Club Cup clashed with the third round of the FA Cup, and rather than move the tie, or have a reserve side play in it, the decision was taken to not participate in English football's most famous domestic cup competition.

Predictably – and understandably – this was a hugely controversial decision, made by United under political pressure from the FA, who were campaigning to host the 2006 World Cup. It was felt that United's presence at this new FIFA tournament would help immeasurably, and the club felt that they would receive sympathetic press following conversations. As soon as the decision was made, however, there was a media backlash, accusing the club of devaluing the FA Cup. Still, United were now in it to win it, and pledged to take a strong squad to South America.

Where possible, before Christmas, Ferguson rested Beckham, to try to help him finally get that hamstring issue sorted. He was on the bench for the home game against Everton; with his side 3–1 up at half-time, and no real need for his supply line, he returned to the bench with a cup of tea after the break.

On 21 December, it was announced that Barcelona player Rivaldo had been named as Ballon d'Or winner, with Beckham coming second. Convincing wins against Everton, West Ham and Bradford City were followed by a morale-boosting late equaliser at Sunderland to close out the century.

United's first game of the 21st century would come in Brazil, against Mexican outfit Rayos Del Necaxa. It was worth pausing to collect our thoughts at the convenient timing of the turn of the century to consider Beckham's contemporaneous standing in the world of football. The words of Zidane ought to be enough to articulate what the first 40,000 words of this book have been building to: there was a tremendous appreciation for Beckham's contribution on the pitch. In British football, more at this time than at any time in the future, it was almost necessary, or easier, to concentrate on one protagonist, one central figure. Beckham couldn't have been a more convenient figure in this respect.

If Eric Cantona had taken the domestic limelight when sports reporters had been looking for a character to replace Paul Gascoigne, then Beckham's acquisition of the number 7 shirt and his subsequent World Cup episode had made him not only a natural and obvious successor to Cantona as this public figure, but a willing and eager one.

Cantona had effectively transformed the way footballers were perceived. His various misdemeanours, played out in front of an exponentially growing television audience, made football front-page news, increasing public interest at a time when money was pouring into the game.

In 1985, Football League clubs had been locked in a dispute with broadcasters and eventually agreed a deal where nine games would be shown in a deal worth £1.73m. When Sky won the rights to show live Premier League football on the rebranding of the top flight, they secured the deal with an offer of £304m for five years. Those rights were renewed in 1996 for £670m, and it was accurately predicted that the next deal, to be announced in mid-2000, would top £1bn (Sky eventually paid £1.1bn for a package of 66 live Premier League matches for each of the following three seasons). The impact on player wages was just as significant. Cantona had renegotiated his contract when he had his lengthy suspension in 1995. United were reluctant to commit to a huge deal for such a risky player, so they ostensibly just extended his £10,000-a-week deal, though with bonuses it effectively worked out at £20,000. Of course, Cantona was gone; United's top earner was now Roy Keane – who, in the closing weeks of the century, had agreed a new contract worth £50,000 a week. The likes of David Beckham, on £25,000, could expect to double their pay when it came to signing their next contract. Keane was fully worth his place as the top earner due to his importance in the team, but Beckham had a fair claim to be Cantona's natural successor when it came to the lucrative aspect of marketing. He had filled that void to become the most famous player in the country, and, due to the popularity and exposure of the Premier League, and his relationship with one of the members of the most famous pop group in the country, probably the world now, too. It was probably fair to say at the time that their international profile was comparable, and if it is true that David's would eventually usurp that of Victoria, there was certainly a time on foreign shores when the United star was known as 'Mr Posh Spice'.

There is an amusing anecdote told by legendary football journalist Paddy Barclay, who had travelled to Brazil to cover the World Club Cup. In an exchange with a local store owner on the Copacabana, the proprietor noticed Barclay was British. 'David Beckham!' the businessman said to Barclay's delight – he was excited to discuss the beautiful game with a resident of a country that had arguably the most glorious interpretation of it. And, of course, the country which was home to the only player just voted better than Beckham in the world. Barclay nodded. 'Is it true,' the man said, 'that he wears the underwear of his wife?'

The growing celebrity – and financial power – had the potential, and indeed likelihood, to change anyone. But, possibly owing something to the latter experience being a shared one within the soccer community, and of course still being a part of the group of players he had grown up with, to those at Old Trafford, Beckham remained the same lad they had known for years. Of course, one might expect his closest friends to be defensive of him anyway, so it is worth taking the thoughts of Danny Higginbotham, a local lad who wasn't on the inside of that close-knit 'class of '92' group.

'I can only speak from my experiences with him, but I would say he did not change a single bit in my opinion,' he says. 'Obviously he had this lifestyle, and partly because of his wife it was more public than others, but everyone had different lifestyles, everyone does in life … so long as they were doing the business in training or on the pitch when it mattered, that was the important thing. Who cares? It shouldn't matter. From the outside, jealousy started to prevail. He never changed as a player. His style remained the same.'

One might attribute what was to follow to that consistency of style. Beckham was selected from the start against Necaxa, but United struggled to come to terms with unfamiliar opposition, conceding early and finding them embroiled in a scrap the BBC generously described as 'an epic'. Three minutes before half-time, Beckham went for a bouncing ball, but his right foot was high off the ground. As he tried to plant his feet on the ground in that spread-legged way he had always done since being a youngster, his studs became planted in the hip of José Milian, who went to the ground in agony, if somewhat theatrically. The referee, Argentinian Horacio Elizondo (though we can surely discount any premeditated desire to dismiss Beckham, if not the seizing of an opportunity to), did not have to think for too long before pulling out a red card.

'Obviously the pressure was on, it wasn't a great trip in terms of our reputation because of the controversy around the FA Cup exit,' Higginbotham recalls. 'You look at the incident and wonder if it was petulant like the one at the World Cup. But I think that would be very harsh. I do think that everything was magnified because of the situation.'

Despite initial suggestions about Beckham not being able to control his temper, the furore quickly fizzled out. Sir Alex Ferguson, at the time, had been furious with the officials, but both manager and player relented after watching replays after the game, and accepted the decision for what it was. Beckham was suspended for the game against Vasco da Gama, which United lost comprehensively to suffer elimination from the tournament (they had drawn the first game).

Back in the UK, United were to win the Premier League at a canter, but not without some cost. Ferguson had backed Beckham when publicly required to do so, but remained upset with his player over the incident with the party in London, and so was less inclined to be sympathetic when the next problem arose in mid-February.

David was an anxious first-time father to Brooklyn, and with good reason on top of the usual ones which face every parent. In October, whilst he was on international duty, Victoria had been told by the police that she and Brooklyn were the target of a kidnap plot for the following day. Kevin Keegan allowed David to get his family and take them to the team hotel. In order to try to live a normal life, extra security measures were taken. It was somewhat understandable, then, that in order to be closer to family, Victoria stayed in their London house whenever possible and especially when David had a couple of days off, as he did following a rare defeat up at Newcastle. He had planned to return to Manchester on the Wednesday evening before the weekend game with Leeds – a crucial top-of-the-table clash – but decided to stay home when Brooklyn fell ill. On Friday, Beckham reported for training, but in the morning papers, Victoria was pictured attending a charity function the previous night, and Ferguson was furious. In front of the other players, he ordered Beckham to train with the reserves.

He did as he was told, and asked Roy Keane after training what he should do. Keane told him to go and speak to the manager. 'I went to the gaffer's office, knocked on the door and walked into the biggest dressing-down I've ever had in my career,' Beckham recalled.

'You were babysitting while your wife was out gallivanting,' Ferguson blasted, provoking a response from David, who told him not to speak like that about his wife, and that he wouldn't like it if it were the other way around. Beckham was told not to report for the Leeds game.

Ferguson insisted his decision was the right one for the morale of the squad (that United won 1–0 at Leeds, with Beckham conspicuously sitting in the stands, was almost inconsequential) and wrote in his first autobiography that living in London was 'not fair to me, the club, his team-mates or the fans'. For his part, Beckham – whilst defensive of the principle – confessed that coming from London had exacerbated the issue.

'I picked the team and that's it,' Ferguson told the press after the game. 'I have the privilege of picking the team. What happened is just one of those things. What we do in response is inside the club and all things will be dealt with by the club.' When asked if Beckham would return to the team to face Wimbledon at Selhurst Park on Saturday, he added, 'I've got Roy Keane and Paul Scholes suspended, so there's every chance he will play.'

He did; but Beckham's bumpy season was not quite ready to go under the radar. In early March, there were reports that he had been transfer-listed by the club after the recent issues. These were unfounded stories, but Peter Kenyon, deputy chief executive, was nonetheless compelled to speak to BBC Radio Five Live, where he described the stories as nonsense and pure speculation.

Later in the month, United faced Leicester City at Filbert Street. The day before the game, Beckham had taken the decision to shave his hair off – news of the haircut had been leaked to the morning papers, and the player arrived at the ground with a baseball cap on.

'Arriving at the training ground at 3pm before a trip to Leicester City, I noticed the press lined up on the road into Carrington,' Ferguson recalled. 'There must have been 20 photographers. "What's going on?" I demanded. I was told, "Apparently Beckham is revealing his new haircut tomorrow." David turned up with a beanie hat on. At dinner that night he was still wearing it. "David, take your beanie hat off, you're in a restaurant," I said. He refused. "Don't be so stupid," I persisted. "Take it off." But he wouldn't, so I was raging. The next day, the players were going out for the pre-match warm-up and David had his beanie hat on. "David," I said, "you're not going out with that beanie hat on, you'll not be playing. I'll take you out of the team right now." He went berserk. Took it off. Bald head, completely shaved. The plan was that he would keep the beanie hat on and take it off just before kick-off. At the time I was starting to despair of him. I could see him being swallowed up by the media or publicity agents.'

Waiting for him at the ground were dozens of youngsters who were wearing flesh-coloured swimming caps as a tribute. Beckham wasn't dropped – Ferguson probably knew it would have been a ridiculous decision this close to the game, not least because of the extra attention it would have created – and indeed, somewhat inevitably, he scored with a trademark free kick. Ryan Giggs was first on the scene to celebrate with his colleague, rubbing the top of his shorn head. It was only his second league goal of the season, yet, perhaps inspired by the bracing fresh air on his neck, Beckham was inspired into a run of great scoring form to close out the season. The best was probably a fine solo effort against Real Madrid, albeit in losing circumstances as holders United were eliminated from the Champions League.

The following weekend, they received the consolation prize of the league title again – Beckham netting another free kick at Southampton in a 3–1 win which decided the destiny of the Premier League. 'Over the years, we've made it hard for ourselves and left it until the last game, so we wanted to win it today,' he said on the pitch at The Dell – traditionally a difficult place for United. 'We also needed to show a good performance after Wednesday. We've played some great football in the last few months and we've deserved this one.'

Trophy celebrations followed another 3–1 win, this time against Spurs at Old Trafford, which included another Beckham blockbuster. After the game, David took Brooklyn on the now-traditional lap of honour around the pitch to thank the supporters for their dedication over the season.

* * *

England had three warm-up games before the European Championship that summer: Brazil and Ukraine would visit Wembley, and the final friendly would be in Malta. Roberto Carlos – one of those Real Madrid players Beckham had skipped around to score in United's elimination – paid his opponent the highest compliment after a 1–1 draw.

'Beckham is England's main player,' said the full-back. 'Every time they have the ball they look to get it to him. If he gets the time and space to cross, he will cause any team in the world problems, but after a while it becomes so predictable. Teams will discover that if you can keep Beckham quiet, England will struggle to create. We changed things at half-time, and England couldn't cause us any problems because Beckham had to go very deep to get the ball. The idea was to let him have the ball in his own half and then close him down quickly. It meant he was usually facing his own goal and then had to go backwards or take a risk. England have some good strikers, but it's Beckham who controls the way the team plays on the attack. Stop him and the strikers are not so dangerous.'

Barcelona star Rivaldo concurred. 'He is the only English player who would get into Brazil's squad,' claimed the forward. 'When he crosses the ball it's like half a goal. If England are to do well, then they need Beckham to be playing at his best.'

To prove the point, it was from Beckham's corners that England grabbed their goals against Ukraine. First, Alan Shearer's header was blocked, but Robbie Fowler converted the rebound in the 44th minute. Midway through the second half, Tony Adams finished from another. It was a successful trial of a role that saw Beckham play at wing-back, though best mate Gary Neville didn't think it should be one for the long term. 'I don't think playing in a back five works for David Beckham,' he said. 'He hasn't played it often enough, whereas we know he has played well on the right side of a midfield four.'

In warm climes before the Maltese FA Centenary Celebration Match, Beckham was in relaxed mood as he was inevitably targeted for interviews. 'I don't think I have ever felt better than I do going into this tournament,' he said. 'I feel confident because I've come off a good season at United, where I've been playing well and scoring goals, and I can take that with me. There is a definite improvement in team spirit on 1998 before the World Cup. The manager and the staff have greater togetherness, and that shows around the camp and in games. Last summer ... I felt tired, coming off the back of United's last three games where we won the treble. It took a lot out of me. This year I'm here having had a break, and that did me good. The managers talked and it worked out best. I feel very fresh. I was happy with how I played against Ukraine. I saw a lot of the ball and, when I did, got good crosses in. The wing-back role is hard work, and you can spend a lot of time going back as well as forward, but it wasn't like that on Wednesday because when I pushed up, Steven Gerrard sat and fed me a lot of the ball, too. The more ball I see, the more I'll get into games, it's very simple. I probably could dominate more than

I have done for England, and I would still like to play centre, get in the middle and spray it about, because you are more involved straight away. But it's about working for the team.'

Once again, England's number 7 was the key creative force, setting up the first goal in a 2–1 win, prompting some special praise from the manager. 'Our set plays have been fantastic,' Keegan said, having decided to start the tournament with a 4–4–2 shape. 'If anything, it's been that good that it made us look as [though] if we can get set plays then we can win games. With David Beckham in your side and with some good movement and a bit of height, you should cause people some problems.'

If it seemed as if all was rosy, then it's worth backtracking slightly to the Ukraine game, where a pocket of the home support still, bewilderingly, heckled the man whose supply line had decided the game. 'There are people in the crowd who actually hate me,' Beckham said. 'That was proved when I took a throw-in against Ukraine at Wembley. There were a few fans who stood up and absolutely ripped me to shreds. I want to show people David Beckham the footballer. I want to show them I have changed in certain ways, matured and grown up. I have won medals with Manchester United, now I want to start winning some with England. We can go all the way at Euro 2000.'

Within 18 minutes of the opening game against Portugal, it was Beckham's right foot that provided the ammunition from which England plundered two goals. By the hour mark, the Portuguese had turned the game on its head to take a 3–2 lead, which they held on to for a crucial win. That did not disturb Keegan as much as the abuse hurled in Beckham's direction, again by a contingent claiming to be England support. The player was the target, but the chants regarded his wife and child.

'It was the worst thing I've seen in football,' Keegan said the morning after the game. 'I've taken plenty of abuse in my time but this was way beyond anything I've heard. It was very personal. If you'd heard that abuse, if your sons and daughters had to listen to that, you'd have reacted the same way. It was aimed at a lot of my players and I take my hat off to them that they didn't react more strongly. It was a lovely atmosphere and a shame it should end that way. There is a point where every human being has a limit to what they can take. It got way beyond that limit in Eindhoven. If I could have got back down the tunnel I'd have probably thumped them last night. I don't understand that kind of person and I don't think I want to.'

Keegan, normally an emotionally impulsive character, had shown some restraint – his considered comments made with a night's sleep behind them gave weight to how seriously he judged the treatment of his player – but his remarks showed he empathised with Beckham's reaction, which had been to direct a one-fingered salute at the travelling fans.

But the player – who had found himself the subject of a talking-to by the association for an identical situation early in the domestic season – now had the weight of the support of the manager and the FA. 'As the team left the pitch, some of the players were subjected to disgusting, foul-mouthed abuse from a small group who we would hesitate to describe as England fans,' FA spokesman Steve Double said, after hearing that UEFA would take no action. 'We would have liked to have seen them arrested for their behaviour. Although they were clearly English, they were not from a sector reserved for the England Members Club and we would like to disassociate ourselves from the sort of behaviour that they displayed. It is fair to say that everybody who heard what was being said was deeply shocked that their own people could have behaved in such a way. We believe they were drunk. We will be making observations about the security arrangements when the players leave the pitch for future games in the tournament.'

The defiant and defensive response had an impact. The press responded kindly – those journalists who had been annoyed by

Beckham's response clearly outnumbered by those who saw the behaviour of the fans as reprehensible.

England's next game was against Germany in Charleroi. As Beckham came out for the warm-up with the rest of the team, he was once again the focus of attention of the England fans. The tone was significantly different: 'One David Beckham ... There's only one David Beckham ...'

One thing you could not say about Beckham's journey to redemption – or however you want to describe the path he had taken since the 1998 World Cup – was that it had come overnight. Yet that could be a fair summary of how England fans suddenly changed their attitude towards him. If he was never *completely* flavour of the month for those disgruntled voices, the overwhelming noise of support was clear for all to hear. Did it have an impact? Well, it may have done, but considering recent form, it was business as usual for Beckham, who created the game's only goal. His free kick from near the touchline bounced and evaded two players, but not Shearer, whose header was clinical. For the first time since 1966, England had defeated Germany in a competitive game.

Hopes that the result would prove to be a good omen were extinguished by a crushing defeat against Romania in the final group game, which eliminated England from the tournament. Keegan's men had led at half-time, but threw it away in the second period. In the last minute, Phil Neville gave away a penalty that was converted. England lost 3–2. The supporters had a new Manchester United player to vilify. Gary Neville was thrown in too, presumably by association.

England were making their way back home. The immediate memo from Old Trafford was a reassuring rallying cry from the boss. 'The agenda with Phil and Gary is not an honest agenda,' Alex Ferguson said. 'It is an anti-Manchester United agenda. Any United player who plays for England is going to get unfair criticism. Sadly, it is part of the national disease. Unfortunately for Phil and Gary they are copping it this time. Last time, at the World Cup, it was David Beckham. However, both Phil and Gary have proved themselves time and time again. They have got more league title medals than any other player in the country and they will get more medals with this club.'

The world transfer record was broken that summer when Luís Figo made a hugely controversial move from Barcelona to Real Madrid for £37m. That fee would have been surpassed if Adriano Galliani, Milan's vice president, had had his way. Twice, the Italians made an offer of £40m – one before, and one after, a report which said Beckham was unhappy about the updated publication of Sir Alex Ferguson's autobiography which featured information about their fall-out in February – but those offers were dismissed out of hand.

'We realise that we do not have a chance of getting David Beckham, so we have made moves for two other players who we are confident of signing,' Galliani said in defeat.

Ferguson's book did indeed contain passages relating to the incident before the Leeds game, which concluded with the manager reasserting the idea that he was the one who called the shots. Perhaps that might explain the act of pushing the boundaries a little before the Charity Shield against Chelsea.

Beckham had let his hair grow out enough for it to be shaved into a mohawk, but was so tremendously fearful of the manager seeing it, you can't help but liken the player's recollection to that of a child trying it on with their parent.

'I walked in the changing room and he hadn't seen it because I was too scared to even show him,' he recalled in 2019. 'I'd gone into training the day before with a beanie on, trained in a beanie, gone back, walked in the hotel, had a beanie on, had dinner, beanie on, breakfast, beanie on, bus on way to stadium – beanie. Then as I got ready for the game I took it off, he said, "Go and shave it off" … I giggled and he was like, "No, I'm serious. Go and shave it off." So I had to find a pair of clippers and I shaved it off in Wembley Stadium. Manager always rules.'

If he can see the funny side now in hindsight, it appeared to influence his mood somewhat differently at the time. He was involved in the incident which saw Roy Keane sent off in a bad-tempered 2–0 defeat to Chelsea (though he ultimately ended as peacemaker, attempting to restrain Keane and pushing him off the pitch) and was also in an altercation with Manchester City's Danny Tiatto in Denis Irwin's testimonial. Tiatto fouled the United man, and got a wild swing back at him for his crime.

Australian Tiatto – with a reputation for being a 'hard man' – had been ordered to see a stress counsellor over the past year and gave some advice to his opponent: 'I was exactly like that a couple of years ago. Every time I got kicked I would immediately retaliate. I got sent off a couple of times, but then I saw that was no way to go on and it didn't help anyone – not me, not the football club. I decided from then that I had to turn my game around. Without a doubt it has helped me so much, I have become a much better player. It's not for me to tell David Beckham what to do but maybe he should do the same. It's up to him to sort himself out. I think sometimes that if he kept his head he would be an even better player. It's a testimonial match so I think the referee didn't want to make a big deal and nor did I. I just got up and carried on.'

That was the same attitude the United manager was taking, although you could most certainly count on Ferguson – who had previously commented on his 'despair' of such incidents as the haircuts – not forgetting. Call it defiance, call it testing the waters: Beckham knew what he was doing. That much is evident in his embarrassed approach to keeping the hat on again – Ferguson, having been through this before, was able to smell a rat with some ease. David was now 25, so something like this should not have even been a matter of concern. It was, though. His haircuts *were* a matter of national interest, regardless of whether you or I or Sir Alex Ferguson felt that might be a case of stretching the definition of 'journalism'. In this strange arena, despite David being quite entitled to do whatever he liked with his own body, in hindsight it could be considered not only a pointless battle to instigate, but one which would only count against him in the long run.

The United boss did, though, keep the disagreement behind closed doors for the time being, and Beckham's early-season form spoke for itself. His corner created the crucial opening goal on the first day of the season, and he then scored free kicks in consecutive away games against Ipswich and West Ham before, in the latter, making the winning goal with a penetrating pass which split the defence. Giggs could not convert; Cole could.

Beckham had been booed by those around the pitch at Upton Park, but had admirers on it. Prodigious Hammers talent Joe Cole had pleaded with Beckham to swap shirts. Beckham told him that they weren't allowed to do that; an hour later, though, as Cole reflected on his performance, he received a message from a steward that Beckham wanted to see him at the end of the tunnel; there, he gave him the jersey.

'I hope I haven't got him into trouble,' Cole told a reporter. 'He told me the club don't allow swapping shirts, but he did it anyway. For me he's the ultimate, a fantastic player, and I'm going to hang it on my wall.'

Ferguson certainly wasn't cross, and spoke in an admiring tone of his player. 'David is the best free-kick taker I've ever worked with, and we could see a few more goals from him this season,' he said. The United manager had been linked with a move for Dutch right-sided star Ronald de Boer. The player had signed for Rangers instead; Ferguson insisted it wouldn't have been as a replacement for the number 7.

'David's always been an option to play in central midfield if I could find a player who can play in the wide right role as well as he does,' he said. 'He's a fantastic crosser of the ball and he's got the work-rate to get up and down the pitch. He's simply too valuable for us in that area at the moment. De Boer would have given us an option on the right, but I understand his reasons for joining Rangers because he was concerned about the number of games he would have played for us. I don't have a problem with that. He's 30 and wants to be a regular. But the good thing is we have got one or two younger players, like Luke Chadwick and Jonathan Greening, who are developing well, so maybe in a year's time I will have other options on the right.'

Putting two and two together, one could deduce that the recent behind-closed-doors nuisance had influenced the United boss into considering his options, at least to the extent that Beckham couldn't dictate his own place in the team because of the monopoly he had on that position. However, talk of David playing in the middle had been reignited, and that was the plan for Kevin Keegan in an international friendly against France, with Darren Anderton back available following his most recent injury issues.

'I'd like to think I'll do well in the middle and stay there,' Beckham said before the game, whilst taking the opportunity to speak up in defence of the manager, who had predictably faced calls to be sacked after the poor summer. 'We have to accept some of the criticism made of our performances in the summer, but I think it's unfair that Kevin Keegan should have got so much stick. And now having to hear talk of the sack. It's the responsibility of the players to get England going again, to show that we really can be a side which can go on and win things.' The words of a leader – but even though the captaincy of the side was vacated by Alan Shearer following his retirement from international duty, and even though Keegan had spoken so glowingly about Beckham in the past, Arsenal legend Tony Adams was given the armband on account of his seniority.

England drew 1–1; not every performance has to be a spectacular victory to demonstrate it is worth keeping patience, as observed by Rob Shepherd, who wrote for the *Express*: 'Offered the chance to show he can perform as a catalyst at the heart of midfield, Beckham responded with a convincing, if not spectacular, display. It is too early to assess whether he really can blossom into a world-class playmaker, but those who would demean his contribution in that role surely missed the point of Beckham's influence. Most vitally he gave the England team a point of reference. Beckham acted as glue to mend the parts which had been shattered in Euro 2000. If his passing and touch were not quite as sublime as that of Zinedine Zidane – some yardstick that – they were composed. He demanded the ball – Beckham doesn't hide – and when he got it, for the most part, he made good use of it. Fundamentally, he imposed a passing philosophy on those around him which had been so lacking when England sunk to rock bottom.'

By the time England were playing again – this time in the last-ever game at Wembley, against Germany in a repeat of their recent clash – Beckham had been promoted to 'vice-captain'.

'It's a big boost for the lad,' Alex Ferguson said. 'He sets a great example in terms of work-rate and ability and, when you look at the England squad, I think there is a shortage of players who can lead by example the way David can. They have got some experienced players there, but he sets an incredible standard for them all to follow. I think it's a possibility that he will take the next step when Tony Adams retires. I think that that is what Kevin Keegan sees for him. Tony is obviously in the twilight of his career.'

The honour had been bestowed upon Beckham despite another controversial month at Old Trafford. He had scored in a 3–3 draw at home to Chelsea but suffered a head wound which needed stitches. It was said he would be rested for the game against PSV in the Champions League – he was on the bench, and was called off it with his team in trouble. United eventually lost 3–1, and Beckham was accused of spitting at German referee Markus Merk; the midfielder strongly denied the allegation, and footage backed him up.

'When we saw Beckham and Giggs were not on the team sheet, we couldn't believe it,' PSV forward Arnold Bruggink said. 'We were amazed. You can't take Beckham and Giggs out of the team and expect it to play the same way. Our coach was obviously pleased because the two players who make things happen and create openings for United had been left out. But it made us more motivated to win the game because we thought, "Why should United believe they can beat us with that side?" Maybe there was a touch of arrogance about United's decision not to send out their strongest team.'

Arrogance could be the right word; or over-confidence, perhaps. Beckham's benching was clearly precautionary, but Ferguson was having to juggle his squad in a way few, if any, managers before him had had to. There were two group stages in the Champions League, with eight games played before Christmas, and that in addition to the League Cup. United were dab hands at qualifying from the group stages these days, so could usually afford to accommodate one or two bumps along the way.

England, however, could not – not if they were to qualify for the World Cup. So Kevin Keegan resisted the temptation to play Beckham in the middle and went for the tried and tested right-hand placement. The player himself had seemingly accepted this, but was looking forward to this last occasion at the famous old stadium, which for once would hopefully be on his side.

'I've had two games in the central position and I feel I did well there against France,' he said. 'If I can get a run at playing in that position then, hopefully, I will stay there. Of course it's up to the manager, but I'd rather stay in the middle. I would be a bit disappointed not to. It has got to be my favourite position.

But staying in the team, whether in the centre or on the right, is all that matters … I think the fans will be behind me. In France they were unbelievable. It's important to go over and clap the fans after every game, but I made a special effort to go to them in the Stade de France because they had been singing the whole game … After the Portugal game maybe people sat back and thought about the kinds of things that were being said to me. After two years I sort of got used to it, but it's never easy. It has made me a stronger person.'

Clearly, though, Kevin Keegan was not able to handle the pressure which came with managing England. They lost 1–0 and gave a flat performance in the last game on the old Wembley pitch. 'I have had all the help I have needed to do my job properly,' he said, as he announced his resignation after the match. 'I've not been quite good enough.'

Probably the only player representing the Three Lions with any credit at all was Beckham. Martin Samuel of the *Express* wrote, 'In a time of managerial turbulence the one constant has been that Beckham is an outstanding international. It is time he was given a manager who recognised this and, more importantly, allowed him to live up to the billing.'

Beckham had picked up a knee injury against Germany; it was rumoured that he might have to go under the knife to put right a medial ligament injury. He was out of the first game after the international break at Leicester, and was the only United player with discomfort in a routine win over PSV. He was on the bench for the visit of Leeds – reports said he was suffering from a cold, too – but he was required to take the pitch when Roy Keane was injured after 30 minutes. His arrival coincided with his team taking a lead; five minutes after the interval, Beckham made it two with a deflected free kick. Close to the end, his cross created a third goal when an unfortunate Leeds defender bundled it into the net.

Whilst the national talk was whether or not the 34-year-old Tony Adams would retire in the wake of Keegan's resignation – making the England captaincy available again – Beckham seemed keen to audition, taking the armband at club level for the first time. Keane had given it to Phil Neville when he left the pitch; Beckham, on impulse, had taken it when he saw it on the floor of the dressing room at half-time, performing with trademark distinction. 'Roy Keane may be the captain of United for years, so I thought that may be my only chance to be captain,' Beckham said afterwards. Nobody else wanted it, so I just grabbed it ... All my goals came in the second half of last season. I've got five now and I'm pleased with that. I've just got to keep it going.'

Ferguson confirmed that he didn't know about that situation, but praised Beckham for taking control: 'I didn't realise at first that he'd done that. But if players want to take responsibility, that's good. Beckham is incomparable. I've not seen anyone with that range of passing before. Maybe Johnny Giles comes close. But you just can't beat David for range and quality from the right side of the field. It is absolutely phenomenal. He can play it short, he can play it through, over the top and switch play. He's got that great range. He ran the second half today. Maybe it was a reaction to being on the bench, because he doesn't like that. But he's been carrying a cold and I wanted him fresh for our game in Anderlecht on Tuesday.'

Ferguson did confirm, however, that he would name Ryan Giggs as captain for that European game. 'I'll give the job to Giggs because he has been captain before and he's one of the most experienced players out there,' he said. 'It is appropriate. Gary Neville doesn't want it. Obviously, Keane is a big influence, not only because of his presence but also because of what he does for the rest of the team.'

It didn't detract from the performance levels. Beckham was in exceptional form, despite the injuries and illness; arguably better than the previous calendar year, in which he had been voted second in the Ballon d'Or. Against Coventry in early November, he was the most influential player on the pitch, creating a goal for Andy Cole and scoring another free kick himself in a 2–1 win.

Coventry manager Gordon Strachan – a predecessor on the Old Trafford right wing, who, of course, had sometimes served as inspiration for the young Beckham's haircuts – spoke glowingly of the United number 7, whilst also insisting his current platform was a match made in heaven.

'Beckham has all the riches in the world but it hasn't changed him,' said Strachan. 'Riches don't change good players. You have to say that it is all down to the manager. It's not just at United. He did it before with Aberdeen, brought on a bunch there when I was one of them, and before that at St Mirren. He is huge in this.'

What do you give the boy who has *almost* everything?

The one thing he doesn't have.

Interim England manager Peter Taylor announced that David Beckham would be captain for the friendly against Italy.

Sir Alex Ferguson was first to respond, saying, 'It doesn't matter whether it is for one match or long-term under the new manager, it is a great honour for the club and David. David will relish it. He always accepts a challenge.'

Beckham remembered that he was staying over at Gary Neville's house when he received the phone call from Taylor; he said it was like a dream and that he had to sit down for five minutes.

'I'm surprised to be in this position because two years ago I wasn't liked by a lot of people,' he told newspapers, once he had composed himself. 'Now I'm leading out an England team, which is the most special thing that could happen to me. I don't know if Glenn Hoddle would ever have given me the job. He certainly wouldn't have done at the time. A lot has happened and been said, but I have kept my head down, enjoyed my football and won trophies. I still get a bit of stick, but it is wearing off. It is something I have had to overcome because, if I hadn't, my football would have suffered. The most important thing is to do well on the pitch, and if I listened to what was being said off it, it would certainly affect my game. Leading England out against Italy will be the greatest honour I can have in the game. After that red card, Tony was great to me, and it is astonishing to think that I am now captain of England. I have learnt from the way Tony acted towards me, and I am fully aware that one day I may need to give similar comfort to a player in trouble. Maybe this may change the way the fans treat me. Things have been getting better, but I still get some abuse. It is a case of getting my head down and ignoring that type of thing.'

In 2018, though, Taylor reflected that he may have got a little carried away at the time. 'It turned out to be a decent choice in the end,' he said. 'But the funny thing is, I look back now and it probably was a mistake. It really should have been Gareth Southgate or Gary Neville. It was maybe a little bit too early for David, but I just saw something in him. And he turned out to be a very well-respected captain, so it wasn't just me.'

Taylor had taken another gamble: this was a much younger squad than usual, with Gareth Barry, Rio Ferdinand, Kieron Dyer, Jamie Carragher, Seth Johnson and Emile Heskey all 22 and under and getting some time on the pitch in a 1–0 defeat to the Italians at the Stadio delle Alpi – an arena which already held fond memories for Beckham, memories which would not diminish because of the result.

'I'm very proud,' said the United star. 'It's the proudest I've been in my career. I want to be captain again. I don't want it to end. There have been some great moments for me with club and country, but captaining England has topped it all for me. It was something I've always wanted to do and now I've done it. If I could have picked anybody to walk out alongside when I was captaining

England for the first time then it would have been Paolo Maldini. That's simply added to the pride.'

That pride meant keeping hold of his shirt; even with Maldini on the pitch, referee Sandor Puhl, officiating in his last big game, asked for Beckham's jersey as a souvenir. 'I didn't swap my shirt because, of all the ones I have in my possession, this is the one I'll cherish the most,' David admitted. 'I've got quite a few in my collection and no doubt my dad will be putting in a bid for this one. He's got a lot of my shirts and medals, so I might frame it and give it to him for Christmas.'

Beckham had scarcely unvelcroed his armband before he was faced with political questions. Surely a Manchester United player, from a large United contingent in the national team squad, would find it difficult to blend with the growing Liverpool number on England duty these days? As well as Carragher, Steven Gerrard was becoming a staple of the squad, following in the footsteps of Michael Owen. Emile Heskey, too, was part of that Anfield group, having moved there from Leicester early in the year. Beckham's diplomatic skills were put to the test. 'Liverpool in particular have a group of emerging young players who are in some ways very reminiscent of how I and the lads at United came through the ranks,' he said successfully. 'Obviously we have proved ourselves now at United, but at Liverpool they're beginning to emerge like we did a few years ago, and I think England have a lot of reasons to be optimistic.'

On the rift, it's worth getting the opinion from the so-called enemy camp.

'As far as I was concerned, I never saw it,' Heskey, in an interview for this book, insists. 'There was a natural divide. You would sit with the Liverpool lads, the United lads would sit together. Then there was a mixed group. You wouldn't segregate; you'd sit and have chats with any of the lads. I'm not saying that others didn't feel that way – maybe they did feel there was such a rivalry between the clubs that they held on to it. But me personally, I never noticed it. I never thought someone wasn't passing me the ball because I played for Liverpool. It didn't seem any different than from when I played for Leicester, other than sitting with the Liverpool lads. When I got back into the England squad after I left Liverpool, I sat with the group made up of lads from other clubs.'

Perhaps it helped as far as Heskey was concerned that he had been in the England squad prior to moving to Liverpool – or, that he was a forward, and had a greater appreciation for what Beckham brought to the side – but certainly, the former Foxes star is not reserved in his praise for the quality of the then-United midfielder.

'You would be able to just make a run and you knew David would have the quality to find you,' Heskey says. 'His delivery would be inch-perfect. He would find you every single time. It would be up to you to finish it. His consistency was as great in a game as on the training pitch.'

And, whilst Taylor may feel in hindsight that Beckham at 25 was too young, it seemed a perfect age to serve as leader of this inexperienced team.

'At the time it was the best option, the right option for me,' Emile says. 'He was the stand-out performer, the talisman, the leader and yes, the global brand, so it made sense to the FA and eventually to Sven [-Göran Eriksson, the future England coach]. I know Sol wanted it and was disappointed, but David was the right choice and he grasped the opportunity with both hands. He was a wonderful captain. He wasn't a bawler and wouldn't scream, he'd lead by example with his performances. He didn't change as a person, but he did grow with the responsibility. He was happy to take it all on board. He was a great person to have to communicate messages from us as individual players or as a squad to the manager.'

Heskey could not be more effusive in his praise for Beckham. One of the longer-lasting criticisms of the United star was that he was undeserving of being mentioned in the same breath as the likes of Rivaldo and Zidane. Emile, though, believes David most certainly did belong in that category.

'Every footballer is different,' he says. 'You would not believe the amount of work David put in on the training pitch. People criticised him because he wasn't as skilful as Ronaldo, for example. Ask Coley about playing with him. Ask Dwight. Ask Alan Shearer. Myself. David was one of the best crossers of the ball, if not the best. He was able to control a game from out wide. He matured into a player who would command games. I think that's how he managed to turn everything around. Basically by being himself. He was a wonderful player, a wonderful individual, but obviously you need to show that on the pitch. It's easier said than done because of what he went through, but he did do that, and he won people over. He came into his own, commanding and controlling games. You always have one leader in a team and he was definitely like that for us with England. He matured into that type of player at the same time I was in the team. It was beginning to feel like he was the main man in the dressing room even when we had Alan Shearer and Tony Adams, players of that seniority, but obviously when they didn't play for England any more, Becks was the main man in his own right.'

In his own right: an interesting turn of phrase considering those earlier comparisons Beckham had made of himself to Mark Hughes, and those this writer made for him to Eric Cantona. There was no question of imitation any longer. Beckham had established himself in his own way – he had taken the weight of expectation in the number 7 shirt at Old Trafford, and had done what Cantona had in succeeding Robson. He had imposed his own personality on it, created his own legacy. At the same time, he had almost transformed the perception of what it took to be a winger. He wasn't as rapid as Ryan Giggs on the other side, nor as gifted at dribbling. That is not to say that he wasn't quick, or that he couldn't dribble. With around a decade of dedicated training and exposure to some of the best players around, Beckham's development had accelerated to the point where he was unequalled when it came to delivery. If he had control of the ball in any position on the right-hand side of the attacking half, you could almost guarantee that he would create a goalscoring opportunity if he had space. He was clever enough to generate that space on his own most times. If he was up against a particularly troublesome opponent, Gary Neville's overlapping runs would usually serve as a strong enough complement to create an opening. The quality and dependability of his crossing was metronomic.

So too, so far this season, was the quality of his free kicks, as Manchester City found to their cost just 90 seconds into the first game after the international break. Beckham struck a beauty of an arching shot from fully 30 yards into the top corner – it was the only goal of the game, and most certainly a strike worthy of the occasion.

Angry home fans threw coins at Beckham; one £1 coin struck his head. 'A coin hit me on the top of the head,' he said after the match. 'But you expect that. I've had this sort of things at a few places. You just have to get on with it and concentrate on your game. I didn't rise to it. The best thing was that all of them were £1 coins and I saved them up in a corner … On Wednesday, I had a bit of responsibility, being captain of England. There are always people watching everything I do wherever I play. Obviously, in a derby game, there were going to be sparks flying, so I was even more aware of the need to keep my head. You have to keep your temper, keep calm. Every one of the lads did that. There were a few incidents on the pitch, but the lads kept their heads.'

The game at Maine Road was the first derby since 1996. It was the fifth of seven consecutive wins, and of 18 victories in 24 games which would prove to earn United an unassailable advantage in their quest for a third successive league title.

A year on from Roy Keane's new contract, talk now turned to a new one for Beckham, whose current deal expired in June 2003. He could expect to at least match Keane's, or, considering his performances, probably even better it. One thing not on the table was a move elsewhere, though Beckham did send some red heartbeats fluttering when he said in early December, 'If I'm happy and my family are happy then I will stay where I am – if things go well with the club and the contract. But you don't know. You can never say about that. So I will have to wait and see over the next few months if the club talks to me.'

His position was done no harm when Germany legend Franz Beckenbauer heralded him as the best player in the world. 'David Beckham is the most exciting, talented footballer in the world,' he said. 'Beckham this year has been fantastic. If I had a vote, it would have gone to Beckham. If I had to name a player who has dominated football, then it would have to be Beckham. All the great stars this year have had periods when they have had a break or haven't been at their best. Zinedine Zidane and Rivaldo, for example, have not been at their peak for the whole season. But Beckham has not faltered. He is the man who all year has been consistent and who can continue to get better. I really like him. I like the way he passes the ball and the way he shoots. It's fantastic. There is nobody in the world like him.'

His club manager agreed, although he also took a share of the praise, attributing the excellent form to a professional response to being dropped against Leeds early in the year. 'The media monster was running out of control … I think the way David has responded has been magnificent,' said Ferguson. 'Basically, it's been a case of him becoming more mature. But he has also been conscious of not getting involved in too many things outside of the game. His form and attitude have been outstanding. One of the greatest tributes to him is that he no longer gets the same level of stick at away grounds as he did.'

United legend George Best was also a paid-up member of the Beckham fan club, despite a fairly negative quote which would later be attributed to the Northern Irish legend. 'He's been unbelievable considering the amount of publicity he gets,' Best said. 'I went through it all, and the only way to answer the critics is to walk off at the end of a match having stuck a 30–40-yarder away and to have won the game. And that's what he does better than anyone. Obviously he's under the microscope – he's playing for the biggest club in the world, the most successful in the Premiership since it started, he's been captain of England at a young age, and married to a very famous lady as well. The one thing he does do to his credit is handle it. He does what he's paid to do better than anyone, and he does do it on the pitch so they can all have a go at him. And you can't question his commitment and ability.'

Despite this backing, Beckham only finished joint tenth in the Ballon d'Or list, which was topped by Luís Figo. He was rated as the Premier League's best midfielder, though, and the stats backed it up. 'Imperious' barely comes close to describing the masterful display he gave against West Ham on 3 January: he made 111 passes, in the days before such metrics were analysed to such an extent that they influenced players' decisions on the pitch. It was revealed after the game that Beckham had made a staggering 677 passes in the attacking half of the pitch so far that season, and had scored or assisted over half of the club's 51 league goals.

'West Ham sat off us a lot more than we expected,' he said after the game. 'But we made it easy for ourselves by the way we played. It was nice getting the space we needed to pass the ball about, although sometimes that can actually make it harder for you because you can have too much time. Getting the early goal set us up. It was important because we had had a hard game at Newcastle and it helped relax us. We passed the ball around well and we had good movement with midfield players running through.'

Ferguson singled out Beckham for special praise when he said: 'He had a marvellous game. His passing and work-rate were phenomenal. He just never stopped. We had a lot of good performances, but you can't deny David the man-of-the-match award.'

If there was any lingering disappointment about missing out on the international player of the year awards, there was renewed discussion about the international captaincy when Tony Adams announced his retirement from England duty in January.

'If I was being really honest I wouldn't expect to be captain if Tony Adams was playing,' said Beckham at the launch of a new £750,000-a-year Police sunglasses deal. 'He is going to be missed. I really enjoyed being captain and hopefully I can be captain again. It would be a pleasure to be captain in every game.'

New England manager Sven-Göran Eriksson did indeed announce that he had no intention of changing the captain from the last game; by that time, there had been a significant dip in form for the midfielder. One of Eriksson's first acts as boss was to watch United's FA Cup tie with West Ham, but on this occasion the performance was nowhere near as controlling as it had been just a few weeks earlier. Ferguson tried to blame the below-par showing on his player suffering the flu, but against Valencia in the Champions League a few weeks later, his performance was poor enough to be described by *The Guardian* as 'peripheral'.

The discussion was prominent enough to elicit a response from the club. First of all, from assistant manager Steve McClaren, who said, 'David will be the first to admit he is not playing to his usual standards. He is one of the greatest players in the world. Playing to that level every Saturday and Wednesday is extremely difficult, and he has been through a dip in form. He knows it and he knows what he has to do about it.'

And Beckham himself even responded. 'There's a lot been said needlessly about the way I've been playing,' he insisted. 'About a month ago I had flu and should have sat it out and missed three games. But, being the person I am, I played through it and it was catching up with me.'

He needn't have worried about his place in Eriksson's eyes: he was indeed named captain for the friendly against Spain at Villa Park. 'It was great to have the armband still and walk out there in front of so many fans,' the skipper said after featuring in the first half of a 3–0 win. 'The manager told me last night that I was captain.'

Back at United, he found a manager unafraid to swing the axe to an underperforming star. What the media reported as 'dropping', though, the club were keen to insist was something else. 'I felt he needed a rest,' Ferguson said after leaving Beckham out of the squads to face Sturm Graz and Leicester City. 'There's been a lot of pressure on him and I decided to leave him out so he could regroup and regain his game.'

Beckham insisted there was no rift this time, describing Ferguson as 'a father figure', and in truth, he was not the only player given some time out as the manager exercised his big squad in games he was comfortable in navigating.

It meant the player was in peak condition to go back on England duty: due to the demolition of Wembley, the Three Lions were going on a tour of the country in their World Cup qualifiers. This first one after Keegan's resignation was at Anfield; it was a surreal occasion for all to witness the Kop signing 'There's only one David Beckham', but the United man repaid that support by scoring the winner.

'The manager [Ferguson] probably didn't realise it, but he was doing me a favour,' Beckham said. 'I've relaxed for several days and am now feeling in better physical shape than I've done for a couple of months. I probably needed the break.'

Eriksson concurred, quipping, 'I hope Alex Ferguson will rest him before every game we play in the future.'

United were back at Anfield on the last day of March, but lost 2–0. They followed that with an underwhelming last-minute defeat in the first leg of their quarter-final in the Champions League against Bayern Munich. Beckham was booked – he would miss the next game – making a mockery of comments made a week or so earlier by Gary Neville about Beckham's new-found maturity. 'He's more assured, and it's a necessity when you're made the England captain,' he had said. 'All of a sudden you've got to take on more responsibility, and it's not a problem for him. There's not a lot he's not seen. Sometimes at 25 or 26 you need that extra challenge, that extra motivation. Giving him the England captaincy will certainly have given him that, and he can be captain for years to come.'

There was a strong criticism of Beckham's performance against the Germans. *Bild* carried the following: 'David Beckham banked his third yellow card. Is that why he seems to have lost the desire to play? Mr Spice Girl really wasn't that outstanding.'

Paul Wilson of *The Guardian* wrote, 'United will not even have Beckham for the next leg either, although to be brutally frank the England captain did not put in the kind of first leg performance to make this a crying shame.'

Beckham was absent against Charlton and on the bench against Coventry as United recorded victories to put them on the verge of winning the league – Ferguson was keen to try to field a team that he could play in the return game in Germany. Another European success had taken on extra significance to the manager, who had announced that he intended to retire at the end of the following season; this despite repeated pleas in the press from various players – Beckham included – for him to reconsider.

In the afternoon after the Coventry game, Arsenal lost at home to Middlesbrough to gift United a very early championship. 'We want to keep winning and improving until we are regarded as one of the greatest teams of all time,' Beckham said after the game.

It echoed comments made by the manager around Christmas time. 'This is the best side this club have ever had,' Ferguson had remarked. 'I have spoken to Bobby about this a couple of times and he probably shares that opinion. It is difficult to compare eras. But with today's media profile, these players handle it very well. The statistics point to that also. They have surpassed the 1968 team. The '58 team? No one knows, but they probably would have been the greatest team ever.'

But when United were eliminated by Bayern Munich, and convincingly so, there was a new conversation being held: whether this group of players were even good enough to survive the final summer under the current manager. Defeat to Real Madrid the year before had provoked Ferguson into action: he had an agreement to sign Dutch striker Ruud van Nistelrooy, before the move collapsed due to justified concerns over a knee injury. That cancellation resulted in a stay of execution for Teddy Sheringham, who had enjoyed an extra year at Old Trafford, ending as top scorer and PFA Player of the Year. But Van Nistelrooy was now back, fit, and destined to move to United.

After losing in Germany, captain Roy Keane had blasted the team as being 'average', and some newspapers speculated that David Beckham may be a player allowed to leave so that Ferguson could build one last, great side.

Eric Harrison, Beckham's former youth coach, hoped it would be some time yet before his class of '92 lads were split up: 'I've always said that it would be a sad day if one of them split, or if they left for one reason or another, a very sad day for the club.'

And Beckham himself seemed to take umbrage with Keane's comments, telling Greater Manchester Radio at the end of April, 'This is a great team. So many people have said there should be changes and there should be this and there should be that, but we've won seven championships in nine years as well as FA Cups and a European Cup. I don't think that is really the sign of an average team. You should always stick together as a team. We have never been a side who have come out in the papers ands said things about each other, or other players. The manager makes the decisions. If he thinks the team needs strengthening then he will. Next season is going to be special for the manager, the team and the fans. I want to be a part of that. I love the club and, if contract talks go well, then I'll be staying.'

Those comments were broadcast on the morning of United's win at Middlesbrough, a game in which Beckham scored but put in an odd shift. 'Beckham had a bizarre game,' reported John Wilford for *The Guardian*. 'At times he strolled around the pitch as if indulging Brooklyn and his pals in the park. Then, suddenly, he would spring to life orchestrating intricate moves involving up to 20 passes. Boro's defence gave him the freedom to run at will. He was lucky to stay on the pitch, though, after an off-the-ball challenge on Cooper that escaped referee [Steven] Lodge's notice.'

Ferguson claimed not to have heard Beckham's radio interview; chief executive Peter Kenyon did, however, respond, saying, 'There are limits as to where we can go. There is no evidence that David is bored at Old Trafford; he is a key player for us and we'd like to retain him. We feel pretty confident we can reach an agreement with David, but if the demands fall outside of our limit then we won't be able to do it – that's just how it is.'

United had made a strong case for consistency by awarding the in-form Ryan Giggs a new five-year deal that matched Roy Keane's £50,000.

Ferguson was in no particular rush to part with Beckham, but was not especially enamoured with his behaviour after the end of the season. United's underwhelming end to the campaign saw them lose their last three games. The manager saw this as a sliding scale of standards and wanted to address that by adding the combative force of Patrick Vieira to play alongside Roy Keane. Vieira was willing; Arsenal, understandably, were not. Ferguson directed his attention instead to the player who was widely acknowledged to be the playmaker destined to shortly overtake Zinedine Zidane's reputation as the world's best (away from what the awards told us to believe) – Juan Sebastián Verón of Lazio.

That transfer saga would last for most of the summer; in the May post-season internationals, Ferguson was likely to have been frustrated to see pictures of Beckham reporting for England duty with the mohawk hairstyle he had attempted to have at the start of the season. It was a little hard to take the player at face value when reading his comments to the press: 'There's publicity about anything I do, so I've got used to it. There was no thinking behind it. It's not so much about the way you look as how you conduct yourself. It's just me. I'm not doing it to attract attention.'

As usual with Beckham – though not so usual in recent months – his football was good enough to get the attention on its own. England swept aside Mexico in a friendly at Pride Park, with David grabbing the third of four unanswered goals with a typically tremendous free kick. For the first time, perhaps the player himself saw the damaging aspect of such publicity. The morning papers were full of references to the extravagance of the new hairstyle more than they were the goal. On 3 June, a 'friend' told the *Express*, 'David has been sickened by all the fuss and comments over his hairstyle. He's had enough and wanted to shave it off almost immediately. Instead he will wait until a quiet moment away from the glare of the media.'

It was still present in Greece a few days later. This was a tricky tie against a Greek team emerging as one of their best ever, but a Paul Scholes goal midway through the second half settled the nerves, before a very late Beckham free kick settled the points. It would not be the last time this year that the new England skipper would break Greek hearts.

Practice Makes Perfect

MANCHESTER UNITED were aggressive with their player recruitment and retention policy in the summer of 2001. Ruud van Nistelrooy arrived for a fee of just under £20m to break the club's transfer record. A few weeks later, Juan Sebastián Verón's protracted move was also completed, breaking the record again, this time at a cost of £28m. In the meantime, Sir Alex Ferguson and Peter Kenyon had moved to reassure those midfielders who may well have felt under threat from Verón's arrival – giving Paul Scholes a new six-year deal and Nicky Butt a five-year renewal. The reports of these new contracts carried suggestions that an agreement was close with David Beckham on a five-year contract which would give him parity with Roy Keane.

On the first session of pre-season, Verón was pictured by the press wearing the number 7 on his training kit. Tongues wagged and keyboards furiously clicked as some reporters put two and two together; Milan needed little encouragement to test the waters with speculation of a £50m offer and a weekly wage of £150,000. Kenyon was quick to dismiss the idea that Beckham was now dispensable.

'Any enquiry would get short shrift,' the chief executive said. 'We are hopeful an agreement will be reached with David before the start of the season. That is our priority. We set ourselves a target of buying quality footballers and re-signing existing players. The only one left is David. I'm happy with the stage we have reached in negotiations, and we'll talk again after the trip to the Far East. I'd hope the arrival of Van Nistelrooy and Verón would show David we aim to be a competitive club in Europe. Why would he want to go anywhere else as a footballer right now?'

Kenyon's spin seemed deliberate, but Beckham's position in the United squad was underlined when they arrived in Kuala Lumpur for their friendlies. It was he, and not either of the new signings, who was the star attraction. Organisers of the three-match tour described interest as 'like Michael Jackson and Madonna rolled into one'. John Merritt, spokesman for the tour organisers ProEvents Management, said: 'Beckham is quite simply a superstar over here. United just grow bigger every year and so do the number of fans they have in this part of the world.'

Speaking to MUTV at the end of the tour, Beckham spoke glowingly about the new arrivals. 'I think the manager has made two great buys, and all the players have said that,' he said. 'I definitely wouldn't swap those two for anyone in the world. I think that says it all. They're two world-class players and Ruud has proved it in his first two games, scoring three goals, and Juan is a great footballer. The manager can always do it. He always picks players who can fit straight into the team, because we're a tight team with a great team spirit. At the end of last season, people were saying "What's going to happen to Manchester United?" We won the league with five games to go and people were talking about a crisis. But there is no crisis and there never will be. People can say what they want, but we've got two great new players, a new coach, a manager who is world class and world-class players.'

Van Nistelrooy scored on his debut in the Charity Shield against Liverpool, but United lost 2–1 (their fourth consecutive defeat in the curtain-raiser!); when the real business kicked off the following week against Fulham, the champions were a little sluggish and had to come from behind twice to win. The first of those equalisers came from the magic boots of Beckham, whose free kick smashed in off the near side of the crossbar, before a Van Nistelrooy brace secured the win.

Before the game, Beckham had given the clearest indication yet that he was ready to sign a new contract. 'I want to stay at Manchester United, and if everything is right I will stay,' he said. 'I have always been a fan of the club and I am happy there. I have grown up at the club, most of my friends are there and my family are comfortable coming up to watch me play. The next round of talks are in September and we'll have to see what happens there, but I would say the three previous talks have gone quite well. I have said in the past I would like to know who the new manager is – and I would – but it's good to know that Sir Alex Ferguson will be staying on at the club in some capacity. I know virtually everyone else has signed new long-term deals and I am seen as the odd one out at the moment. That is bound to cause speculation, but I love Manchester United and I want to stay.'

For the moment, though, it was United's defence that was dominating the headlines, and more accurately, Jaap Stam. Ferguson was concerned about how his back line was leaking goals, but Stam was giving the manager an even greater headache: he had a book that was due to be published, in which he suggested that Ferguson had tapped him up before his transfer from PSV. In more recent years, both player and manager have rejected the idea that the book was to blame, but there can be no doubt that Italian side Lazio had picked up on the speculation, and decided to spend some of their Verón money on the Dutch defender. A bid of £16.5m was made. Ferguson had cause to consider this seriously, and, in a self-confessed rare error of judgement, saw the money and convinced himself that Stam was the cause of the defensive problem at the club.

'He'd been out for months and, when he came back, Steve McClaren and I thought he had lost a yard of pace,' Ferguson recalled. 'We played Fulham and he didn't have a good game, and at that moment Lazio come in and offered £16.5m. So then Jaap goes to Lazio and he played fantastic. So it was a bad decision. I should maybe have waited a bit longer.'

Stam – who had been named in the PFA Team of the Year every season he had been in England – was on his way. Some still do not buy the idea that the player's injury was to blame. At the time, the message carried in the press was very much: cross Ferguson and you're out of the door. And Stam – the best defender in the league, if not the world – was such a high-profile example that it meant nobody was safe. Stam was absent from the trip to Ewood Park as negotiations intensified.

United's number 7 was the talk of the after-match following an eventful 2–2 draw, as described by Richard Tanner of the *Express*: 'David Beckham was both villain and hero as Manchester United's defensive problems continued on a thrilling night at Ewood Park. The England captain headed into his own net to bring Graeme Souness's newly-promoted side back into the game after Ryan Giggs had given United a first-half lead. But after Old Trafford old boy Keith Gillespie had put Rovers in sight of victory, Beckham came to United's rescue with a quickly taken free kick that caught Blackburn goalkeeper Brad Friedel off his line and still organising his wall.'

With their defensive and midfield reshaping, United stumbled to another draw, this time at Villa Park. Beckham had to come off after 70 minutes, suffering a groin strain; he was now a major doubt for England's crucial World Cup qualifier in Germany. Coach Rudi Völler had shared his compatriot Beckenbauer's view of the England skipper and acknowledged it would be a boost for his team if he was missing. 'You have many outstanding players, but Beckham is different,' Völler said, after admitting his eight-year-old son pretended to be the United star when he played football in the back garden. 'He has rare qualities.'

But Beckham did make the plane, and was going to be given every chance to prove his fitness. This provoked a little fighting talk from Uli Stielike, one of Völler's assistants, who was less diplomatic than his boss. 'Sebastian Deisler is faster than David Beckham … in terms of ability he is the better of the two,' Stielike claimed. 'He has everything needed to become a great player. He is perfect from a skills point of view, and can hit inch-precise crosses. He is also dangerous in front of goal and possesses great vision. He, Michael Ballack and Sebastian Kehl have no reason to hide away when faced with Beckham and company. Beckham's one advantage is that he has more experience. Being England's captain has helped him mature as a person – he is no longer the young hothead he used to be.'

The skipper was named in the team, but it seemed to be a gamble that backfired for Eriksson when his side fell behind in the sixth minute. Michael Owen equalised in the 13th minute, before the much-lauded Deisler thrashed at a golden opportunity with little composure.

Just before half-time, a Beckham cross was blocked and headed out to Steven Gerrard, who hit a fantastic shot from 25 yards to give England the lead. It was another Beckham delivery which sent the travelling supporters in Munich into dreamland; the cross from the right was headed down by Heskey, into the path of Owen, who grabbed a second. Owen then scored a remarkable third, before Heskey made it five. The Germans were stunned, but so too were the England players themselves, who were well aware of the history they'd made.

'Everyone can now see why I was so desperate to play,' Beckham said after the game. 'You work hard throughout your whole career to be part of nights like that. But the injury wasn't a smokescreen. I simply wouldn't do anything like that. It was nice for me to get through 90 minutes. I felt the groin towards the end, but I'll be fit for the Albania game. The manager was going to bring me off, but I didn't want to come off before the end on a night like that. We've proved that we can go to places like Munich and show what we can do. They had a great record before, but records are there to be broken, and that's exactly what we did. When the world sees that scoreline, they'll be amazed as we are. We all sat in the dressing room saying: "What has gone on?" We might go down as legends. We have got to keep our feet on the ground for the game on Wednesday, even though nights like this don't come along very often. Tonight will mean nothing if we mess it up against Albania.'

England won in comfortable – if less spectacular – fashion against Albania to round off a hugely successful international break. Beckham was keen, however, to point out that success was not a relative thing. Winning meant winning, just the same for country as it was for club, and anything less than a trophy would be a disappointment.

'I would definitely see it as a failure as an England captain if I didn't hold up a trophy during my England career,' he said. 'I have won quite a few trophies with Manchester United, and the feeling you get from winning trophies is immense. But I think success with the national team is a must. It's about time we did something in a major competition.'

Overall, Beckham's tangible contribution hadn't been as obvious as, for example, Owen's in the previous two games, but the influence and confidence that came with the captain declaring himself fit and available gave the squad a tangible boost. Asked if the midfielder was a symbolic figure for his team, Eriksson replied: 'Yes, I think so. We are doing well and he is playing excellently. He's an outstanding player and, of course, I'm proud of him. He's hard-working. When people think about Beckham, it's his right foot, but it's not just about that. He's a complete footballer. Every time we come together, he's becoming a more complete player. Every time, he takes more responsibility.'

Back at United, Ferguson gave Beckham a rest on the bench against Everton. It was a masterclass from Juan Sebastián Verón that had given United a comfortable win, but Beckham came on as a late substitute and scored another stunning free kick to ensure, according to reporter John Richardson, that 'a certain Argentinian shouldn't hog all the headlines'. The reality was that Verón and Beckham would share them throughout a stuttering few weeks in which they were the better performers in an erratic United side.

Against Lille, Beckham struggled with the personal attention of Edvin Murati, the left-back who had played against him for Albania the week before. Murati said he would try to wind Beckham up, and that 'I'm sure he'll remember me.' As usual, it was the United star who made the lasting impression, scoring a last-minute winner.

On Thursday, 27 September, former Manchester City star and now outspoken pundit Rodney Marsh launched one of his controversial broadsides in Beckham's direction, saying he 'lacks the edge to be a great' like himself, Pelé, Best, Gerrard and Owen; it's hard to know which parts were meant to be tongue-in-cheek. Regardless, two days later, David did his talking on the pitch. Without Keane and Giggs, Beckham was captain in a league game at White Hart Lane, and it threatened to be a calamity in the first half. Spurs led 3–0 at the break – Beckham remembered Ferguson coming into the dressing room and, with the players expecting a hairdryer, the manager simply said, 'Let's try and keep the score down now.'

The pride of the players was suitably stung – even their own manager didn't believe in their power of recovery. What followed was 'one of the most amazing 45 minutes of football in which I've ever been involved', according to Beckham, though such a comment suggests he was a passenger rather than one of the inspiring forces. It was fitting that he and Verón scored the last two goals in an epic 5–3 turnaround, and it was in these jovial spirits that he went away on international duty with England.

This would be a special occasion – not only because the game with Greece would decide whether England would qualify for the World Cup, but because it would be played at Old Trafford. Beckham found it impossible to contain his excitement: 'It's still hard to take in that I am captain of England. I always dreamed it would happen, but to do it at the age of 26 is unbelievable. It's an honour that I cherish and to be leading my country out at Old Trafford for such an important game will be extra special. Everybody knows that I have been a Manchester United fan since I was a boy, so you can imagine how proud I am to be captain.'

A win would ensure England's place in Japan and South Korea in 2002. Germany, who were playing Finland at home, knew that bettering England's result would mean they would top the group instead. The result in Munich had been as crucial as it was emphatic.

After 36 minutes, Greece took the lead through Angelos Charisteas. England's response was strong, but they found a stubborn visiting back line unwilling to give an inch. It needed the intervention of Teddy Sheringham – who flicked in a Beckham free kick in the 68th minute, less than a minute after coming on – to restore hope. Attention turned to the score in Germany: still 0–0. England, who would qualify if results stayed the same, shot themselves in the foot immediately when legendary Greek forward Demis Nikolaidis scored less than 60 seconds after parity had been restored.

The following 20 minutes were surreal. The preceding 70 had been decorated by Beckham popping up all over the pitch, desperate and determined to drag England over the line. The closing stages introduced a growing intensity and sense of occasion. Free kicks were awarded in various areas outside the box

– Beckham had one, two, three, four, five efforts. Occasionally they'd get closer. It was beginning to feel as if it was slipping away.

In the 88th minute, Beckham won another free kick. 'At times,' said Sky Sports commentator Martin Tyler, 'it feels as if this is a one-man band.'

'If ever they needed their skipper, then my goodness the moment is now,' said Andy Gray, sitting alongside him. The kick hit a Greek defender and went out for a corner. Four minutes of injury time were announced; after the first of those, a roar came up from the Old Trafford crowd which made it obvious that the game in Germany had ended, and with a result which would help England if only they could score another. Beckham, almost exclusively parked on the right-hand side now, bent in a magnificent cross that no England player could get on to. Thirty seconds later, a long ball was punted towards Sheringham; the tall forward was nudged in the back. Free kick. The protests from visiting defenders fell on deaf ears, but they did manage to get the ball moved back a further few yards. This, however, was perfect for Beckham.

'For players like David Beckham, you do feel there are certain moments of destiny,' Tyler said as the whistle blew. There was a cinematic feel as Beckham struck the ball perfectly; it powered over the wall and into the top corner of the goal in front of the Stretford End, an area he'd hit with relentless accuracy time and time again in the past. England were going to the World Cup.

First on the scene was Emile Heskey, who jumped on Beckham's back. 'It's hard to explain the feeling, but it's something you can only get in football,' Heskey says. 'We hadn't even won the game with the goal, but the prize is bigger than that. We're going to the World Cup. I can only say that if it felt like a movie for fans, that's exactly how it felt for us too. I watched it go in and for two seconds or so you just take it in. It's like slow motion. The moment pauses. After that I rushed to him.'

As far as Heskey was concerned, it was a fitting end to a game where Beckham had almost run himself into the ground: the perfect example of his powerful influence from an area where he had no right to exert it in such a way. 'They say games are won and lost in midfield … but I'd never witnessed anyone dominate and control a game the way he did from the right wing,' Heskey explains. 'It baffles me even to this day. He was phenomenal, covering every blade of grass, up and down the pitch, putting in tackles and dictating the play. He was unreal.'

For the *Express*, Jim Holden described the afternoon as 'one-man total football'.

'For too long,' Holden wrote, 'Beckham's detractors have argued that his celebrity lifestyle and marriage is a millstone around his neck. The truth is the opposite. It is precisely because Beckham can handle the pressures of fame that he scored the glory goal here … It cannot have been in manager Sven-Göran Eriksson's tactical plan for Beckham to perform so individually; dribbling past hordes of opponents, playing on the left flank as much as the right, and being the essential driving force through central midfield as well.'

Eriksson – who might well have seen his job on the line with defeat – praised Beckham's timely intervention. 'He wanted really, really hard to win this game, and he showed once again that he is a big player and a big captain for England,' the manager said. 'David really deserved his goal because he played one of the best games I have ever seen him play, running all over the pitch, and I am glad that it was him who scored the crucial goal. He did everything he could to push the team and try to get the result we needed.'

Beckham was in dreamland – literally. If Roy Keane had Turin, and Ryan Giggs had Villa Park, then David Beckham finally had a moment of his own. It would take a harsh revisionist to remove Selhurst Park in 1996 from the selection, but this was precisely the environment the England captain operated in. He was constantly under pressure to replicate the sort of magic which had earned him celebrity status. Under pressure to weave emotional narrative into success stories.

'This is the kind of thing I have dreamed of,' he admitted after the game. 'It was unbelievable. But I never imagined I would have a free kick in the dying seconds to get a result like this one. They say that dreams don't come true, but today I proved that, for me and the rest of the lads, they do. To score a goal like that, as captain of England, the goal that gets us to the World Cup finals and at Old Trafford – it is all quite unbelievable.'

Was it unbelievable, though, really? Or was this the most prominent case of practice making perfect? When the dust had settled, on the second round of press conferences, Beckham was asked, 'Do you still practise free kicks now?'

'Yeah.'

'When was the last time, David?'

'Friday. I hit quite a lot on Friday and they all went in.'

This was not an unusual occurrence. Beckham – now 26, with five league championship medals, a Champions League medal and the most famous name in football – continued to do just what he had done ten years earlier. Then, he was following the example set by his father and the likes of Eric Cantona. Now, he was setting the example. Not everyone got the message. Heskey recalls that some of the England contingent would just sit and watch him after training rather than join in. They enjoyed the spectacle.

'There was never a case of being worried about him missing those earlier free kicks against Greece, even though he was,' Heskey says. 'Instead it was just a very weird confidence that the next one would be the one. We'd seen him do it in training every morning. He was unbelievable in training. Every one in the top corner. The accuracy was superb. We would sit and watch him in fascination, striking the ball over the mannequins and into the net.

The goalkeeper would always look at him in frustration. Beaten every time. There was never any worry. Some players would join in, others would watch with interest, but Becks would always be there, and that never changed from the first day I trained with him to the last. There was a relentless dedication.'

England were going to the World Cup with a famous qualification moment to boot; it was a free kick seen around the world, bringing praise from the biggest names in the game. 'From my point of view, Beckham is a very important player for the team,' Brazilian legend Pelé said. 'He works very hard, he has good vision, good movement and good delivery. But you must give him freedom. Some coaches might try to put him in one position. I would not. I would organise the team and let him free. He knows what to do and where to go to make things happen. Beckham reminds me of Gerson, my team-mate in the 1970 World Cup finals. He is one of those rare players who can always get in perfect crosses with deadly effect.'

Beckham continued to inflict punishment on the poor Greeks by netting the opener against Olympiakos in a game that had been rescheduled due to the terrorist bombing on 11 September in New York City.

Once United were back on Premier League duty, there was a tremendous fanfare for the homecoming. Their next game was against Sunderland, whose representatives could not wait to effusively praise Beckham.

'Put it this way, I wouldn't like to play against him every week,' defender Michael Gray said. 'If you are not on top of your game, you know he is going to get by you and put balls in the box or score goals or set goals up. You have got to be right on your game to try to stop that. I would be very happy if he wasn't playing.'

If that wasn't enough praise, then what about this from Peter Reid, who said: 'If there were a general election and David Beckham stood, he'd be elected prime minister.'

Reid's comments were indicative of the esteem Beckham was now held in. The Sunderland boss had a good relationship with Sir Alex Ferguson, which made the United manager's reaction very curious. 'The media circus surrounding him was over the top as usual,' Ferguson said. 'The media don't care a stuff for us – it's all about selling newspapers. I have to pick up the pieces, pick a team and bring players back down to earth.'

On the morning of the game, journalist Martin Samuel considered Ferguson's response. 'Ferguson knows his [Beckham's] worth,' Samuel wrote in his weekly *Express* column. 'For all his talk, he didn't leave him out of the match with Olympiakos. He didn't even take him off and was rewarded with another exemplary 90 minutes and the vital first goal. Maybe this irks the manager. Just as Brian Clough was infuriated by the lack of foibles in his captain Colin Todd because, psychologically, it made it hard to get a reaction (although he got round this famously by insulting Todd's wife at a club dinner), so the control freak in Ferguson is frustrated by a player who doesn't need controlling. What is he to tell Beckham? Not to drink? Settle down? Work harder? Practise more? Dedicate yourself? Here is a quiet family man with no record of excess, who has to be dragged off the training ground most days. He ran 10 miles during the match last Saturday, while still having the energy to nail a last-gasp free-kick. The one time the pair did fall out, almost two years ago, Beckham's reaction to a public admonishment by Ferguson (who dropped him for a vital match at Leeds) was to knuckle down and take his punishment. What a nightmare for a manager, eh? And, of course, Ferguson deserves plaudits for helping create such a man. Just as his decision to play Beckham in Europe this week was proven correct. But it is King Canute-like to command the tide of Beckham praise to go back.'

Clearly, though, the United boss was intent on proving a point. Beckham would be rested for the next two league games, including that visit to Sunderland. His replacement there was rookie Luke

Chadwick, who played very well in a 3–1 win. 'We see Chadwick train every day and he is a handful, even for our players,' said a presumably vindicated Ferguson. 'He got into the game right away and showed just the right appetite. David Beckham only ended up on the right side of midfield because we did not have anyone else at the time. He is really a central midfielder, but we had just sold Andrei Kanchelskis and Keith Gillespie. Young David was brought into the team to learn the game and now he is the best, but it is nice to know you have Chadwick as back-up.'

One could look at this a number of ways. You could take the comment at face value. There was nothing untrue about it. You could be cynical, read between the lines and suggest this was a bit of a ploy from Ferguson to test Beckham's resolve – to ensure he wasn't taking his position at United for granted. You may consider Chadwick, a promising youngster, to be unfortunate collateral damage. Chadwick himself insists he did not see it this way – 'I was just delighted to be playing minutes for United,' he says, in an interview for this book. 'Looking back, I'm sure sometimes I was used to sharpen Becks up, but he was a very energetic player, and if he needed a rest I was delighted to be chosen. I couldn't believe I was playing, to be honest.' Chadwick's modesty isn't completely representative of his status: the youngster was used and trusted in some important games, which gives a little indication of how he was perceived by the manager. Still, he wasn't David Beckham, so it is easy to see this as a classic Ferguson trick.

Against Bolton at Old Trafford the following week, Beckham was left out altogether again. It seemed as if Fergie's point had been proven when Juan Verón scored a fantastic early free kick. But the visitors turned the game around and won – this time the gamble had somewhat backfired. It was a poor month in the league for United, who needed a last-minute equaliser from Ole Gunnar Solskjaer to get a draw against Leeds, but could not muster any inspiration – despite a decent Beckham goal – in a comprehensive defeat at Anfield after which the manager questioned the hunger and desire of his players. Beckham, incidentally, had started both of the games against the better opponents.

The final international break of 2001 came at an opportune time for United to catch a breather, but Ferguson's criticism of his team was met full force by accusations from the press that it was in fact the manager who had lost his edge, with his forthcoming retirement cited as the reason.

It was inevitable that Beckham would be pushed on the issues at Old Trafford now he was on England duty, and it was interesting to see the position he took, defending Ferguson resolutely. 'Alex Ferguson is always intense as a manager and he always has that hunger to win things,' Beckham said. 'And that shows through with the way he is and the way he talks to players. In fact he can be quite scary. But I think we are all frustrated, every single United player. The manager is frustrated because we are not playing as well as we can do. There is not a problem in the United ranks, though. People might be saying it is a crisis, but there is supposedly a crisis every week at United whether we win, lose or draw. I am sure we have been tired rather than lost our hunger, but if the manager has said that, then all the players can do is respond in the right way and prove to him we are still hungry. The desire of every one of the players has always been massive. That comes from the manager. People have asked if the manager is still hungry for success. I don't think anybody can question how hungry he is in football terms. People question whether we are as hungry before the start of every season when we have won something the season before, and we have always proved people wrong, and it is up to us to continue to do that. The fact that it is Sir Alex's last season has hyped it up all the more. Sir Alex hasn't changed – he is still the same person he was when I arrived at United as a 16-year-old. In fact, he will never change. We want to go to the Champions League Final because it's such a big occasion, especially where it is next year [Glasgow]. We want to repay everything Sir Alex has done for us at this club.'

Beckham was doing the firefighting to repair the public front of the relationship, but United's form went from below par to catastrophic after England's 1–1 draw with Sweden, and Ferguson was not about to give the England captain any leeway. A 3–1 loss at Arsenal was followed by an excruciating 3–0 home defeat to Chelsea. Ferguson had tried to shore up his defence by moving Roy Keane to centre-half alongside Stam's replacement, Laurent Blanc, but it imploded with severity. With United 2–0 down, Ferguson made a bold move by withdrawing Beckham in the 76th minute.

'David Beckham was hauled off for the second time in four Premiership games, while Juan Sebastián Verón once again failed to impose himself on the big stage in the manner you could reasonably expect from a man who cost £28 million,' Richard Tanner concluded in the *Express*. 'Beckham can't trade forever on the national hero status earned for his last-gasp free-kick that handed England their ticket to Japan. Apart from a good performance against Olympiakos, when he was still on an international high, Beckham has been off the boil for Manchester United in the last two months.'

It was Beckham, and not Verón, who would be sacrificed against Boavista in the Champions League. Verón played from the right in a comfortable 3–0 win, but Luke Chadwick was brought in from the start of the next league game against West Ham. Ferguson's team again struggled – and although Beckham was brought on for Chadwick with the scores level after an hour, the team's confidence took another hit when the Hammers scored through Jermain Defoe. Three league defeats on the spin, and six before Christmas, meant hopes of retaining the title again were very slim indeed.

There was some consolation for Beckham that weekend as he was named BBC Sports Personality of the Year. With a requirement to speak publicly, the player again insisted he was committed to United, and tried to put a positive spin on his recent exclusion. 'I have been on the bench for a couple of matches, but you have to accept that,' he said. 'You have to accept what the manager does. I'm not going to question the manager for whatever he does. It's his decision and I do respect that. Deep down, I think I did [need it]. I wouldn't have admitted that to anyone else – not even to myself – but, yes, deep down maybe I needed a rest.'

Reporters were not convinced. The *Daily Star* went big with an exclusive on 15 December – their front page had the headline 'BECKS: I'M READY TO QUIT'. This sent United into brief mode; stories of niggling back and groin problems came into the press the following day, along with fresh reports that terms were in fact close to being agreed on a new contract worth £100,000 a week. Beckham was in Zurich, as the favourite with some bookmakers to win the Ballon d'Or again. But Michael Owen of Liverpool was the victor, whilst the United star finished second to Luís Figo in the FIFA World Player of the Year award. Pushed on his contract situation whilst in Switzerland, Beckham said, 'I don't think it's fair to go into details over my contract talks. All I can say is that I don't think they will be sorted out before Christmas, like we wanted to. But, hopefully, they will get sorted out. Hopefully when I'm fit again I will be back in the team. The club gave me this weekend off because of my back.'

Ferguson was in more conciliatory mood. 'He knows he hasn't been playing his best and he wants it sorted out,' said the boss. 'Rest is the best thing. There's no doubt he reached a point where it all caught up with him. He apparently ran 10km in the game against Greece and he hasn't been the same since. His work-rate has been absolutely phenomenal, but I think he's paying for it now.'

It didn't help Beckham that his rest coincided with an immediate upturn in form from the team. United recorded handsome wins at home to Derby and Southampton and a crucial victory at Middlesbrough before David was back in the fold, named on the bench against Everton on Boxing Day. He came on in the 56th minute and, 20 minutes later, created the opening goal for Ryan Giggs. Another away-day contribution – a stunning free kick at Southampton which turned out to be the winner – helped put United top of the league for the first time in the season. United's number 7 was in the early stages of a truly inspirational run of form: the perfect riposte to any reservations his manager may have had. In fact, despite the indications previously suggesting otherwise, there seemed to be a fair few statements put on record to insist that there was a rosy Old Trafford future for all. First of all, Verón – who tabloids had suggested had fallen out with Beckham, and that tensions were simmering after Argentina had drawn England in the World Cup groups – dismissed talk of a fall-out, saying he had a 'great relationship' with Beckham.

In early February, Sir Alex intimated he would reverse his decision to retire and was privately urging the club to sort out Beckham's contract. The news of the manager staying on was celebrated with a 5–1 win over Nantes, in which Beckham opened the scoring for United from yet another free kick. After the game, David spoke to the press. 'This is the only environment I've known – it's difficult to imagine how I might react to anything else,' he said. 'The best thing about the manager is you know he will never distance himself from the players when there is a problem. If you've got a problem, he's one of the first people you think about. We all trust him and we all trust his judgement on just about everything.'

Ten days later, Beckham scored two in what the *Express* described as an 'inspirational' performance in a 4–0 win over Spurs. The following weekend, it was reported that a basic wage on a new contract had been agreed, but there was an impasse over image rights. A week after that, and another Beckham brace – the first a sublime clip over David James, on the run – at Upton Park helped secure another 5–3 win in London.

'Today we saw the David Beckham we all want to see,' Ferguson said. 'His first goal was marvellous, so delicate. I am sure that break has done him good.'

Hammers boss Glenn Roeder couldn't help but praise the England captain. 'If you look at a video of every one of David Beckham's passes or crosses today, every single one was a winner,' he explained. 'Every one of them could potentially hurt you badly. His goal was only half a chance, but he beat David James hands down. I had a word with him as he came back down the touchline. I can't repeat exactly what I said, but I told him it was unbelievable and only he could have done that.'

Beckham's second was a penalty – he scored again from the spot as United secured their qualification for the next round of the Champions League in a routine win at Boavista. It was reported that terms had finally been agreed on a new deal; the news was not made public.

It could not be said that United had a goalscoring problem this season; but they occasionally had moments where it seemed like they might never score. There had been a huge rotation in strike options. Ruud van Nistelrooy had emerged as the number-one striker at the club, and Ole Gunnar Solskjaer was the preferred partner for him; that was when Ferguson played 4–4–2, but these days he was more inclined to try a 4–4–1–1 with Paul Scholes and Juan Verón in the same team. That meant Dwight Yorke and Andy Cole had followed Teddy Sheringham through the exit door. Ferguson had signed Diego Forlan in January, but the Uruguayan had not scored for the club yet, and his struggles were summed up when he was brought off in the 83rd minute of a 1–0 home defeat to Middlesbrough. The loss meant United had only a one-point advantage over Arsenal, who had two games in hand.

There was a strong response at Elland Road ten days later. Beckham didn't score, but was fantastic in a 4–3 win; his influence was much more evident, though, against Deportivo La Coruña at the Estadio de Riazor the following Tuesday. Just 15 minutes had gone when Beckham received the ball from Roy Keane. The Deportivo defenders stood off him – perhaps because he was too central to attempt a cross, they felt they could afford the distance. Beckham, though, seized the opportunity, and was able to set himself up perfectly to strike the ball just like he would a free kick. The shot was simply magnificent; it flew over the goalkeeper, Molina, who could only watch the ball sail into the top corner. His personal catalogue of greatest hits – comparable with any player in history – now had a new addition. It was the type of goal that only he, particularly in the United side, could score, the arching direction and accuracy of the strike feeling like it had come straight from the training pitch. Practice made perfect.

A second goal from Van Nistelrooy had put United in command of a tie which was as comfortable as the two-goal cushion suggested, and as otherwise uneventful as the manager had hoped. That was until the second minute of injury time, when a shocking tackle from Diego Tristán right on Beckham's ankle was serious enough for Ferguson to use his last substitute to bring his player off. Serious enough, too, to keep him out of the weekend trip to Leicester, with a race against time for the second leg against the Spanish side the following week.

He made it, but wished he hadn't. Just 15 minutes had been played of the return when Pedro Duscher's reckless tackle on the United star took him out of the game. Beckham stood up, but immediately knew the damage to his foot was more severe. United's chances of silverware this campaign, just like England's World Cup hopes, were immediately plunged into turmoil; David Beckham's season was over.

Leaving Home Again

THE EVENING of Wednesday, 10 April 2002 introduced a new word into the footballing lexicon: *metatarsal*. This hitherto unmentioned, and presumably therefore undiscovered, bone was broken in David Beckham's foot, thus making the England captain a trendsetter in sport, fashion and medical science.

Facetious nostalgia aside, it was a relatively rare break due to the small size of the bone – but significant enough, nonetheless, to mean the player would not play for Manchester United for the rest of the season. That much was obvious, but it was also of secondary concern to the newspapers of the nation, who began researching and calculating recovery times almost before the player had been stretchered off the pitch.

United manager Sir Alex Ferguson saw his side win 3–2, making it a 5–2 aggregate win, but probably knew the post-match press conference would be dominated by talk of the injury. 'That's doubtful,' he responded when asked if he thought Beckham would be fit in time for the opening game of the World Cup, against Sweden on 2 June. 'He has a broken metatarsal bone in his foot. It will take six to eight weeks. You could see the pain he was in. But he's young; he will play in the World Cup again and play in the European Cup again.' The blow was the last thing United needed. They were already without Roy Keane for a few games – he had failed to recover from a hamstring injury picked up in the first leg. Ferguson would participate in a fairly public difference of opinion about whether Beckham should go to the World Cup. More on that to come.

The newspapers suggested the nation was in a state of mourning. The front page of *The Sun* on 12 April carried the headline 'BECK US PRAY'. There was an image of (presumably) Beckham's broken foot with the words 'Lay your hands on David's foot at noon and make it better'; the player was due to undergo a scan which would reveal the extent of the damage.

Meanwhile, it was convenient for tabloids that the villain of the piece was an Argentinian international defender. Aldo Duscher had originally been uncomfortable taking any blame for the incident, telling reporters on his exit from Old Trafford after the game: 'I haven't spoken to him. Why should I? Would anyone bother if it was one of us that was injured?'

On quick reflection, Duscher was apologetic but still defensive. 'It was a hard tackle and I'm sorry Beckham is injured,' the Deportivo star told *Marca*. 'I know how important he is for Manchester United and England. I hope he gets better soon and plays for England. The reaction to this has been like I killed someone, and all I did was go for the ball, just as I always do against any opponent. I feel bad for what happened to Beckham, but my conscience is clear. It was a normal incident – a 50–50 ball, the type you see a dozen times in any match. But because of everything which Beckham represents in his country and the fact I am an Argentine and we are playing each other in the World Cup, many have thought terrible and different things to what actually happened.'

But Duscher admitted he had phoned Beckham and would send him a 'get well soon' card. 'Obviously I'm sorry,' he said.

'I never thought it would have such an impact. I didn't do it intentionally.'

United's season ended in underwhelming fashion. They were eliminated from the Champions League semi-final on away goals against Bayer Leverkusen. And in the league, they not only finished without the title for the first time in four years, but also had to make do with third place, behind Liverpool of all teams. Beckham had confessed his frustration about not being able to influence the run-in. 'The focus seems to have been around the World Cup, whereas I have been thinking about the United games I will be missing,' he said soon after his injury. 'The season has been building to a great finish and I wanted to play my part.' (In his autobiography *My Side*, though, Beckham did confess that he had thought, even whilst laying prone on the pitch, *'What about the World Cup?'*)

It was estimated that Beckham would miss six to eight weeks of action. FIFA told the FA that Sven-Göran Eriksson could name the player in the initial squad on 9 May and fly in a replacement on 30 May if he failed late fitness tests whilst out in Japan and South Korea.

Somewhat bizarrely, Gary Neville and Danny Murphy both missed the World Cup completely because they too broke metatarsals in their feet, and their later dates of injury meant insufficient time for recovery. It was even suggested that Beckham's place ought to have gone to a fully fit member of the England periphery. This is not a theory that was supported by the England party, in particular, Emile Heskey. 'That place was his and he had deserved it. He was the one who got us there,' Heskey says. 'And for what he had achieved and, for what he could potentially bring to the team, we had to take him with us. You're talking about your captain.'

That Beckham was England captain presumably had some bearing on why the newspapers were as hysterical as they had been. Beckham was experienced enough to understand the cycle and not be distracted by the hysteria, and as far as Heskey is concerned, 'That's the reason why you shouldn't get too close to newspapers. You go from them printing dartboards and effigies one minute to declaring you the best thing since sliced bread the next. And then the whole country needs you, depends on you. Setting you up for the cycle. Today it's a lot easier for players to call that out, to admit they are struggling and say they need help. Back then you just dealt with it. And David dealt with it very well. He went from rock bottom to sky-high in the eyes of the newspapers.'

Beckham was selected and even made it through the final cut, with Eriksson prepared to take the chance. The skipper was hugely popular with the dressing room at international level, not only for what he gave in terms of leadership. 'He was a great guy. Really forthcoming,' Heskey recalls. 'This was a guy who was well on the way to becoming a world star but he would sit and talk to you all day, no problem. He's the same now as he was then. People are surprised by how down to earth he is. He was not only one of the group, but he made an effort to be. I remember at the 2002 World Cup, he was sponsored by Armani at the time. He came in to the dressing room with a big box of Armani gear and threw it into the middle, saying, "There you go, lads, take what you want." Everybody dived in! There were times we were cooped up in the hotel. Becks asked us all – he'd ring the room or knock on [the door] – if we wanted to go out and get something to eat. We didn't think it would be possible but he arranged it with Sven and we were allowed. He sorted it, no problem.'

It's fair to say that Beckham would have walked over hot coals to make this World Cup in particular. After the way the previous one had ended, you'd have been given long odds on him being the captain going into the next one. Eriksson decided that he would play Beckham from the start against Sweden – despite the player having had no football for six weeks.

'To lead out not just any England team, but this England team, is going to be a special moment for me,' Beckham said on the eve of the game. 'Never in my wildest dreams could I have believed four years ago that I could get back up to this level. The turnaround for me over the last four years has just been amazing, and I think this team is definitely better than '98. Even though we have had replacements, there is no one making up the numbers. They are all so young and talented, and while there were times in the past when players may have gone on to the pitch feeling nervous, there are no nerves at all with this team. When you are young you don't worry. With the talent in this squad you can just go out and play.'

In an impressive stadium in Saitama, Beckham led the England team out to the soundtrack of camera clicks and frenzied support. In a tight game, the United midfielder did little to impose himself on the fluid pace of the match, but his importance to this team was underlined in bold when his corner was headed in by Sol Campbell midway through the opening period. When Beckham was brought off in the 62nd minute – a precautionary measure, the England public hoped – three minutes after the Swedes had levelled, the game petered out into a stalemate. Campbell's goal had promised, falsely, that better was coming. 'England celebrated and Beckham began to exert his influence, knitting moves together and linking midfield and attack with short and long range passes,' wrote Phil McNulty for the BBC. 'But the hope was short-lived, and Beckham's anonymity after the break was grim evidence of his lay-off. It was no surprise when he was substituted by another recent crock, Kieron Dyer. Now Eriksson must hope his gamble on Beckham has not failed.'

The England boss was defensive of his use of the captain. 'It might have been dangerous for him to play for more than an hour,' he said. 'He did well for 35 or 40 minutes, but then he was tired. We hope he can play more than one hour on Friday.'

There was absolutely no way Beckham would miss that one – the eagerly anticipated clash with Argentina. Facing the press, the captain explained that his ultimately subdued outing against Sweden was due to ring rust. 'I feel 90 per cent fit,' he insisted. 'Obviously for a couple of months there's still a risk of breaking the bone again. But I'm fit to play … My lungs and legs just went on me. When I came off at half-time I felt fine, but when the match restarted I just couldn't get going. That had never happened to me before. I'm one of those players who likes to run around for 90 minutes.'

The bigger question was: would he be able to hold his temper in this time around? 'I would definitely not do that again,' he smiled.

Curiously enough, the subtext in the press ahead of the match was a theme of revenge – somewhat ironic, considering how the ire associated with the incident which apparently necessitated said avenging was cultivated by these very reporters. Of course, though, the idea of 'revenge' is one much more frequently used in footballing parlance than even 'metatarsal' these days, as it was in those days too. At the top level, such a mentality is often dismissed by professionals who insist their mind is on the game. Just before the break in a keenly contested encounter, England were awarded a penalty, permitting Beckham the very prominent opportunity to write his own storyline.

'Before big games, players don't usually like talking about revenge for a previous incident, just in case it doesn't go right on the day,' Emile Heskey says. 'They play it down as if they're not thinking about it. But I know for sure that David had 1998 on his mind when he was playing against Argentina. Definitely. There was a lot of emotion in that performance. So getting the opportunity to take the penalty would have been very sweet.'

Beckham remembered thinking, 'Everything else I've done in my life, everything that's ever happened to me: it's all been heading towards this.' 1998, Simeone, effigies, Duscher – *Argentina* – he was not wrong. Just for a certain sense of mischievous pantomime – although a little more sinister than that – Diego Simeone chose now of all times to bury the hatchet and offer the hand of friendship to Beckham.

The penalty kick, by his own admission, was not the greatest strike in the world, but it was hit with conviction, carrying the weight of all that past as it struck the net and gave England a lead they would not relinquish.

After the game, Beckham understood the significance. 'It is a fantastic feeling,' he said. 'This is probably the sweetest moment of my whole career. It is a victory for the whole nation. When you play one of the best teams in the world, to score the goal that wins the game is very special. I may have scored the goal, but everyone in the team was fantastic. Nicky Butt came in and he was superb. He kept things going in midfield and put some great balls through. As soon as Michael went over, I knew it was a penalty. And I went up to him and he said, 'Do you want it or shall I?' And I wanted it, so I took it. We had not decided it before the game. Before I took the penalty, I took a few deep breaths. I needed to – at one point, I had nearly stopped breathing. I needed some breaths badly then. I don't know what Diego was trying to do or to say. I didn't look at him. He was literally trying to shake my hand. I didn't want any eye contact because I was concentrating on what I had to do. I was trying to blank him out to be honest, because there were a few antics going on – which we knew there would be anyway. I had to shake hands with him afterwards. A lot of things have gone on and a lot of things have been said, but we're sportsmen and professionals at the end of the day.'

Beckham admitted he was aware of the situation he was putting himself in. 'In my mind in that instant there were flashbacks from four years ago – the red card, that first game back at West Ham when, to be fair, some of the crowd were clapping me,' he explained. 'But as soon as it went into the net I went blank. I've thought about it since and I couldn't sleep that night. It was such a close thing between being a villain or a hero. If it had gone wrong it would probably have been back to square one for me. Before we came out here Victoria said, "Please don't take any penalties."'

England got through the group stage and comfortably negotiated the second-round tie with Denmark – Beckham's corner headed in by Rio Ferdinand for the first goal in a 3–0 win. After the game, the England captain confessed he was in some discomfort – the first thing he did after the final whistle was to remove his left boot.

Whilst England were winning, it was worth the sacrifice, or so it seemed. If Beckham's contribution was relatively sparse, there was no doubting that he was the star attraction of the tournament in the eyes of the public. As ever, there was a continuing conversation about how the World Cup might affect the domestic game in the Far East, and Beckham was asked if he would consider spending some of his career there. 'You never know,' he said. 'I might play over here at one point, possibly at the end of my career. My popularity out here is amazing. I was expecting it a little bit because I've been over with Manchester United and it was pretty manic then, but it's been absolutely mad. Popularity-wise it's the biggest thing I've ever experienced. I've said before that I'd like to open a soccer school when I finish, because I enjoyed them so much when I was young. I could open one here, that's an option. Opening a soccer school here would be something special.'

Clearly the sight of Beckham taking his boot off did not set alarm bells ringing in the same way as seeing him prone on the turf, but it was clear that he was still struggling when England took to the field against Brazil. Michael Owen opened the scoring, but Rivaldo equalised just before half-time. 'The looks on the England players' faces said it all,' Beckham recalled. 'We're knackered. We've got nothing left.'

He might well have been speaking for himself: he was unable to influence the game at all. Ronaldinho scored from a long-range free kick which deceived David Seaman in goal, and England could not recover in confidence or energy. These depleted reserves were evident as Eriksson rung the changes but insisted on leaving Beckham on the pitch, in the hope of a set piece. Clearly a Beckham on one leg was a better gamble than another player with two.

'His injury was probably noticeable against Brazil,' remembers a sympathetic Heskey. 'There are some players you want on the pitch regardless of how fit they are; if they are capable of getting on the pitch and turning it with a moment of magic you're as desperate for them to play as they probably are. David fell into that category. But then everyone expects something from you and sometimes you are not able to provide it because of your injury. David would never have said he didn't want to play. We would always say we wanted him on the pitch. But sometimes the decision has to be taken out of your hands. It's difficult if you're not able to do yourself justice … that desire can sometimes help, like against Argentina. Other times, it can be sensible to sit one out or be more pragmatic. Having a player like Beckham on the pitch, just his presence and a reminder of the standards he expects from others and delivers himself, it makes you up your own game, it sharpens your own focus. It makes you feel that everything will be OK. We had it with Michael Owen at Liverpool.'

Beckham spoke like a captain after the game, saying England had a young team who could bounce back. He also jumped to the defence of a player likely to receive the majority of the criticism. 'If anyone tries to make a scapegoat out of David Seaman, I think it will be an absolute disgrace,' Beckham said. 'It wasn't his fault, it was a fluke goal.'

The skipper had been here every time England had been eliminated from a tournament, so he knew the drill. Perhaps Tord Grip, assistant to Eriksson, didn't get the memo, as he was more than happy to speak to a mischievous reporter asking questions about Beckham being unfit. 'We thought he would get better and better,' Grip admitted, 'but he was almost the same as against Sweden. It's difficult to say how fit he was; we didn't have time to test the player. But he was under 100 per cent. He only had the games to work; between games it was impossible. You need to be up there [fitness-wise].'

England were out, but Beckham was still leaving an impression, with two of the great past and present players moved to comment. Diego Maradona was quick to downplay the contribution of the United star. 'Fame is gauged on what you do on the pitch,' he said. 'Beckham scored a penalty that shouldn't have been a penalty and England went out in the quarter-finals. That's no reason to go out and buy a Beckham shirt.'

It was unlikely to stop anyone doing so. Or getting a Beckham haircut. Or having their own strange hairstyle to mark the occasion. Brazilian striker Ronaldo shaved a bizarre triangle shape at the front of an otherwise bald head, but insisted, 'It's a joke. I don't want to take Beckham's place. I try to look the way I want. It's that bad, is it?' (Yes, it really was!)

* * *

Sir Alex Ferguson wasted no time in reigniting the row with the Football Association when the time came for club managers to be of interest to the newspapers again. In early August, he reiterated his belief that David Beckham should not have gone on a 'pre-tournament bonding session' in Dubai.

'They wanted him in Dubai and my opinion is that was wrong,' Ferguson said. 'I tried to argue against it, but they wanted him. He should have been training under our control. It would have been better if he had remained in Manchester. I don't think he was on the ball enough. You just saw bits of him here and there, but he wasn't the dominant part of the team.'

Beckham insisted he took a step back from this particular argument as he wanted it sorted out by the respective managers, but wondered if the result – country over club – 'finished him' in the eyes of Ferguson.

That certainly didn't seem to be the case in the first few weeks or even months of the season. Beckham had his place in the team without question and, when Roy Keane was both injured and suspended (a hip injury came at the same time as a ban for comments made in his autobiography), he was even named as captain. His form was steady but not spectacular. He missed the last-ever Manchester derby at Maine Road through suspension; City won 3–1, causing Ferguson to make a peculiar criticism about his team.

'We are playing far too much football,' he said. 'At the moment we don't have the killer instinct because we are playing the extra pass all the time. If you look at the statistics, we have the best possession of any team in the league. You know, we had 70 per cent of the ball against City last weekend – and we still lost. Jesus Christ! You don't get that much possession against schoolboy teams. What we have to do is mix it up with more effective football, and that's something we have already discussed within the club. Teams don't contest for the ball against us now. They just sit back and leave us with the ball. What happened is that because we have had such a long run of success, there isn't a player in the game who does not know what the strengths of Manchester United are: our style of play, our set pieces, everything. We have no surprises for anyone. Eventually the penny drops with all opponents. They don't even bother to send scouts to watch us now.'

But United would have to do without the *depressing predictability* of Beckham's set-piece accuracy for a few weeks anyway, as he suffered a rib injury which was more problematic than initially hoped. During his time away, Ferguson deployed Ole Gunnar Solskjaer from the right, with convincingly positive results. Five goals were scored against Newcastle, and wins were recorded against Liverpool and Arsenal. When Beckham was fit to return, he had to make do with a spot on the bench against West Ham, where he watched Solskjaer open the scoring and Juan Sebastián Verón strike a remarkable free kick into the net two minutes later.

He was eased back into the team as a substitute in defeats at Blackburn and Middlesbrough; it was deemed necessary to bring back the number 7 for the visit of Birmingham on 28 December. The impact was impressive: he scored a fabulous lofted chip to secure three points in the 73rd minute. An even more crucial goal followed on New Year's Day – a late equaliser in a 2–1 win over Sunderland.

It was, so far, a fairly quiet season for Beckham, but one in which his status in the game had never been more respected. England played a friendly against Australia at West Ham's Boleyn Ground in early February, and even though the Aussies won convincingly, the captain emerged with some credit.

'Every time David Beckham scurried down the right wing at Upton Park last night, the name and the memory of Bobby Moore must have flashed in to his mind,' John Dillon wrote in the *Express*. 'It is emblazoned in giant claret and blue letters at the back of the stand attacked by England during the 45 minutes which properly mattered against Australia so Beckham couldn't help but see it every time he looked up. If the view was reversed and England's finest captain Moore was to be looking down and assessing the progress of his most celebrated successor, he would have to conclude that Beckham has a heart and soul more than big enough for the most coveted job in the game.'

The last 18 words of that sentence would feel fairly significant in the days which would follow. United had an FA Cup tie with Arsenal at Old Trafford at the weekend. Beckham and Giggs combined to create the game's best opening for United – a long pass from the number 7 was collected by his opposite winger, and the Welshman rounded a defender and the goalkeeper but fired over an empty net from the edge of the box. Edu scored a deflected free kick later in the half, but it was an early second-half goal which had Sir Alex Ferguson furious. The manager accused Beckham of a relaxed attitude to the run of Edu, who comfortably played in Sylvain Wiltord to secure the game for the Gunners. Both Giggs and Beckham – the regular supply line – were hauled off later in the game. United–Arsenal games are usually eventful enough to fill columns, but it was what happened after this match which was to generate the headlines.

Let us begin the story with Ferguson's recollection of what happened.

'As usual, with David at that time, he was dismissive of my criticism. It's possible that he was starting to think he no longer needed to track back and chase, which were the very qualities that had made him what he was. He was around 12 feet from me. Between us on the floor lay a row of boots. David swore. I moved towards him, and as I approached I kicked a boot. It hit him right above the eye. Of course he rose to have a go at me and the players stopped him. "Sit down," I said. "You've let your team down. You can argue as much as you like."'

Beckham's version of events isn't dissimilar. He, of course, rejected the insinuation that he didn't, or wouldn't, listen, but also insisted that he wasn't solely to blame for the goal. 'I felt like I was being bullied,' he said. 'In public, and being backed into a corner, for no reason other than spite. I was trapped. And I swore at him. Something no player, certainly no United player, should ever do to the manager.'

Ferguson apologised after the incident, but Beckham felt it was indicative of a bigger issue. He had felt ignored at team talks and recalled the manager telling him that he even questioned his commitment to the club. Beckham had instigated clear-the-air talks, but Ferguson had insisted there wasn't an issue between them. However, the boss admitted that he told the board in the days after the Arsenal defeat that 'David had to go'. 'David thought he was bigger than Alex Ferguson,' he said. 'There is no doubt about that in my mind ... that was the death knell for him.'

Beckham insisted that he didn't want to leave, but felt he was being pushed out. He referred to it as a period of depression in which he even contemplated retiring from the game altogether. This may well have been melodramatic, but it certainly proves that appearances of contentment had been deceptive. Now there had been a major flashpoint, something to focus on, Ferguson had a reason to exert control. The reaction to the fall-out only made him surer in his conviction. Beckham did not require stitches but did need steri-strips on the wound, which was still fairly visible. Almost as if accentuating it – and certainly with no desire to hide it – it was an Alice band and not a beanie which Beckham wore on his hair to training the following day.

At Manchester United, particularly under Sir Alex Ferguson, every game from February becomes a huge game, almost a cup final of its own. The next was no different – Juventus at Old Trafford was not an occasion the manager could hope to get through under the radar. Especially as European games come with an extra requirement for pre-match press conferences, which were inevitably dominated by talk of the weekend's clash.

Ferguson was in defensive mood. 'Contrary to a lot of reports, David did not have two stitches in his head – he had no stitches,' He said. 'It was a freakish incident. If I tried it 100 or a million times it couldn't happen again. If I could I would have carried on playing! There is no problem and we move on. That is all there is to say.'

The man of the moment refused to give the press what they wanted. 'It was just one of those things – it's all in the past now,' Beckham insisted.

He played from the start against Juventus and showed his importance by creating both of United's goals. After the game, Gary Neville faced reporters and insisted that the performance spoke volumes. Asked if he thought Beckham would be 'packing his bags', the defender said, 'Do I really have to answer that? You know the answer to that, though. In fact, you saw the answer from David on the pitch against Juventus. We've grown together down the years. We have had to deal with a lot of nonsense with United and with England. These things happen in football. The problem is that with this club the publicity is increasing more and more. There's nothing you can do about some of the headlines. You just come to the stage when you know all you can do is show that things are OK out on the pitch. David has proved that and so have the rest of the players here. He's shown a tremendous strength of character.'

The public face and the private one were summed up by Neville's memory of the time in his autobiography: 'Change seemed inevitable,' he wrote. 'Becks is one of the United greats, but I could understand why the manager – particularly our manager, who was so used to controlling his players – was put out by the attention from the press on one player. It was time to say farewell to my best mate.'

There was a definite phasing-out period. Solskjaer started crunch games against Liverpool, Newcastle and Arsenal. United won the first two and drew the latter (after the Arsenal game, David was approached by Thierry Henry, who couldn't understand why he wasn't playing, and said, 'You can come and play for us!').

Beckham had started in the first leg of the Champions League quarter-final against Real Madrid, but the Spanish side won convincingly, dominating the midfield. At the end of the game, Beckham shook hands with Roberto Carlos – the Brazilian defender he'd become familiar with in recent years of competition – and was seen on camera smiling. This did nothing to dampen speculation of a move away. Inter Milan had already been linked with a £25m swoop, and Madrid – with their policy of signing 'Galactico' players – were naturally part of the same conversation. The clash between the clubs gave the English press a convenient opportunity to get some quotes from the Spanish side's players.

Steve McManaman felt a move 'would be difficult as Luís [Figo] plays in the same position', but Zinedine Zidane was a little more forthright with his own thoughts. 'I'm not saying it's definite he is coming to Real Madrid, but when they say they want someone, more often than not they get them,' the legendary playmaker said. 'I doubt Manchester United would want to lose him. But sometimes when a bigger team makes their mind up that they want someone, the lure of playing for them and the financial rewards can be too strong. As a player, I have a great deal of time for Beckham. Can he fit in here? You can always accommodate a player like him. He is a tremendous star and the type of player Madrid would want. I know from experience that when Madrid come calling, it's difficult to turn them down. It is hard to imagine what would've happened if you didn't go. That could be a big problem, because Beckham will have to think very carefully before turning them down. Madrid are very persuasive, they make you feel as if no other club on earth is equal to them. They certainly made a case for me moving and if they went for Beckham, he would find it hard to turn down.'

Ferguson, though, had responded angrily to these comments and the surrounding speculation. 'It is totally out of the question,' he said. 'There is no way we'd sell him, or any of our best players.'

By the time of the second leg, it looked as if Beckham had played himself back into contention by starting in the win against Blackburn. United against Real Madrid at Old Trafford was shaping up as the biggest game of the season, and it was a genuinely stunning shock when Beckham was left out of the starting line-up. Ferguson could definitely justify his selection of

Solskjaer, but the Norwegian was starting up front – Juan Verón had been selected to run the right wing in place of the England captain.

The game is remembered for three things: United's exit, Ronaldo's hat-trick, and Beckham's cameo from the bench to turn the game around on the night to earn a 4–3 win. Ferguson's side were eliminated 6–5 on aggregate. Verón had not justified his place, and that was a decision made even more confusing in the wake of Beckham's stunning contribution, which included one of the finest free kicks of his career. How could the manager question the commitment, dedication and energy levels of a player who had turned such a game around in such a fashion? Ferguson may have grown tired of the 'circus' around his player, but he had poured oil on the fire with his selection.

Beckham's proposed exit was now reported as being practically as certain as United's exit from Europe. The *Express* got a line from Beckham's father, Ted. 'I don't think he wants to go anywhere,' he said. 'He loves it at United – it's where his heart is. David has never said a word to me about Madrid but my gut feeling is that he will stay. I am convinced he doesn't want to leave Manchester United. It would break his heart if he did go.'

As United closed in on the league title, Ferguson had been sufficiently compelled to reluctantly abandon his dreams of a 4–5–1 system with Scholes and Verón interchanging. He reverted to his 4–4–2 and deduced that his greatest chance of guaranteed goals was by playing Solskjaer up front with Van Nistelrooy. His greatest chance of a consistent supply line was Beckham over Verón. The England captain would at least play the last three games of the season.

Ahead of the first of those, at Spurs, Ferguson received a question in his press conference from a Century Radio reporter who asked if he was 'sick of the hype surrounding Beckham this week?'

Ferguson replied, 'You've been told not to fucking ask that. Cut that off. Cut that off. Fucking idiots, you all are. You do that again and you won't be coming back here. You fucking sell your papers and radio stations on the back of this club.'

Of course, it didn't stop the speculation. On the morning before United played at Spurs, it was rumoured that Madrid might offer Ronaldo in exchange; Beckham was involved in the crucial opening goal at White Hart Lane which helped his team get three points.

There was a growing sense of inevitability in the following week. First of all came the public Madrid statement of innocence on 29 April: 'There exists unconditional friendship between Real Madrid and Manchester United. There has not been any contact between Real and United over Beckham. Neither directly nor indirectly has there been any contact with Beckham. Contrary to the speculation, we have no intention of negotiating his transfer.'

Those words were treated with contempt by the press, who remembered a similar statement less than a year earlier when Madrid denied they were about to sign Ronaldo, before they in fact did.

On 2 May, John Dillon of the *Express* suggested that whether he did or didn't move, it was surely fated that David would eventually play in a corner of the world which had an emphasis on his profile. 'Beckham has served his time in the darkest stretches of the media jungle,' Dillon wrote. 'No footballer has been savaged as he was after the 1998 World Cup. He now knows how to manipulate his former tormentors exactly to his tune. You cannot blame him when the celebrity business is often so plainly mad and the media are so willingly conducted. When the music stops, Beckham will be the winner whatever happens. He will play for United or Real. The riches either of America or Asia will await further annexation. And right at the centre of this frantic whirlwind, he will still have his eye on the ball.'

On the same day, it was reported that a planned Beckham autobiography was being rushed into print. To ensure release wasn't delayed, a decision had been taken to not allow United or Ferguson to read it. The club had started to put clauses in contracts which allowed them to vet books after the controversy surrounding releases by Jaap Stam and Roy Keane, but this deal had been agreed prior to the new procedure, so Beckham and his team had no obligation to.

Eleven minutes had passed in the penultimate game of the season when Beckham cut in from the right and took an opportunistic shot at goal with his left foot. It was on target, and the deflection from a Charlton defender took it away from the goalkeeper and into the net. As he had done so often on impulse in the last five or six years, Beckham ran towards the quadrant of the East and South stands, where the away supporters were based. Whenever he scored a goal in front of the East Stand, he would automatically run there to revel in the frustration of those who had jeered him throughout the game. This time, though, he paused around halfway, and decided to celebrate in front of the United fans. In the second half, Beckham's cross-field pass was converted by Van Nistelrooy, who completed his hat-trick. Considering the history of imitation, there was an eerie similarity between this and Eric Cantona's last involvement in a goal at Old Trafford – the Frenchman had laid on an almost identical assist for Jordi Cruyff in the second half of his last game.

United could relax after a 4–1 win put them on the verge of the title – after the match, as the team did their lap of honour to thank the Old Trafford crowd, Beckham appeared to be waving goodbye. An Arsenal implosion the following day against Leeds at Highbury secured the Premier League championship for Ferguson's side.

In the week before the final game at Everton, Beckham insisted he wanted to remain at Old Trafford. 'I want to stay at United,' he said. 'My feelings for Manchester United, the club itself, the players, the fans and the back room staff, are as strong as ever. There's been lots of stuff in the media about me and my future, but I can honestly say that there has been no contact between either me or my adviser, with Real Madrid, or any other club.'

Nobody needed a reminder of his brilliance, but he provided it on the last day with a quite exquisite free kick delivered in that unique way that almost looked like a cross, with the tremendous whip Beckham would put on the ball. It set the tone for a comfortable 2–0 win in which United players were careful not to over-exert themselves before the celebrations began in earnest. Quizzed by reporters after the game, Beckham insisted this was the 'sweetest' of the six titles he had won. 'We have stuck together through thick and thin,' he said, but when asked about his future, he said, 'Well, you know.'

Beckham didn't, apparently. He should have felt reassured when the club unexpectedly proposed a new contract to him on 14 May that included a pay rise. But the player felt the contract had been offered in a manner that said 'take it or leave it' – a vast difference to the protracted discussions which had lasted almost 18 months prior to agreement in the summer of 2002. He went away on England duty and broke a bone in his right wrist in a friendly against South Africa, though he insisted he would be fine to go on United's pre-season tour of the United States. His appearance on the tour was seen as crucial to breaking into the American market, with his growing popularity in the US. On 9 May, he had been the central figure used in the promotional piece run in *USA Today*, which described him as 'the most famous athlete in the world (except in America)': 'He's the most famous man Americans don't know – one of the world's highest-paid athletes, a fashion pacemaker, married to a glamorous pop star, an idol of gays, teens and mothers alike – and gorgeous to boot. If David Beckham is relatively unknown in the USA, he is indisputably among the most recognisable sports figures elsewhere in the world, where soccer is the king of sports.'

After featuring for England, Beckham embarked on what was reported as a 'promotional world tour' which featured a stop in Los Angeles. He was quoted by the *Los Angeles Times* as saying, 'I've never said that I'd never move away from Manchester, and I've never said that I'd end my career there.'

At the start of June, Barcelona made their interest public – or, perhaps it should be said, Joan Laporta, who was campaigning for the presidency of the Catalan club, had included the signing of Beckham as part of his manifesto. A £30m deal had been proposed to Laporta, who said: 'I view this as a great price for Beckham. He is one of the few players in the world capable of earning the money back for you.'

Beckham responded to the speculation by brushing it off. 'About a month ago, it was Real Madrid and now it's Barcelona,' he said. But I'm a United player. I'm contracted to United for another two or three years, I think. As long as they want me, then I'll stay. But I've never said I'd never move away.'

On the evening of 10 June, Beckham (now in the Far East) was caught completely unawares – just as the rest of the world was – by Manchester United releasing an official statement.

'Manchester United confirms that club officials have met Joan Laporta,' said the club. 'These meetings have resulted in an offer being made for the transfer of David Beckham to Barcelona. This offer is subject to a number of conditions, critically to Mr Laporta being elected president on 15 June and Barcelona subsequently reaching agreement with David Beckham on his personal contract. Manchester United confirms that in the event that all the conditions are fulfilled then the offer would be acceptable.'

The player's representatives, SFX, responded immediately with a statement of their own: 'David is very disappointed and surprised to learn of this statement and feels he has been used as a political pawn in the Barcelona presidential elections. David's advisers have no plans to meet Mr Laporta or his representatives.'

On 16 June, Laporta told the press that he intended to speak to Beckham as soon as he was back from the Far East (the player was indeed now back in the UK). On the 17th, however, he had performed a remarkable about-turn. 'I did not promise to bring David Beckham to Barcelona,' he insisted. 'I said I had an agreement with United that contained conditions.'

Beckham exercised his right to a say in his own future. He had heard that Madrid were still interested, so he called their president, Florentino Pérez, to say he would be interested but that he did have a contract with United – and also to apologise for the disruption. This was on the eve of a crucial game at hated rivals Atlético Madrid, which Real needed to win to stay at the top of La Liga. They did – convincingly so, to quell talk of a distraction – and with United now very publicly willing sellers, Real were happy to step in and accelerate the move to steal one of the world's highest-profile players away from their biggest rivals in Spain. On 18 June, United issued a statement to the London Stock Exchange which confirmed they were selling David Beckham to Real Madrid for £24.5m: 'David Beckham has agreed personal terms with Real Madrid and expects to sign his new contract with the club on completion. The deal is expected to be completed in July, conditional upon approval by the boards of Manchester United and Real Madrid, and on the provision of satisfactory payment guarantees. The proceeds of the sale will be used to support Manchester United's business development, including continuing to maintain its playing success at the highest levels of the game.'

United followed this with more personal acknowledgements, starting with the manager. 'I've known David since he was 11 years of age, and it's been a pleasure to see him grow and develop into the player he has become,' Ferguson said. 'David has been an integral part of all the successes Manchester United have achieved in the last decade. I would like to wish him and his family every success in the future, and thank him for his service to the club.'

Beckham's own statement was equally cordial. 'I recognise that this is an amazing opportunity for me at this stage in my career and a unique and exciting experience for my family,' he said. 'I know that I will always regret it later in life if I had turned down the chance to play at another great club like Real Madrid, which also has world-class players. I would like to publicly thank Sir Alex Ferguson for making me the player I am today. I will always hold precious memories of my time at Manchester United and Old Trafford as well as the players, who I regard as part of my family, and the brilliant fans who have given me so much support over the years and continue to do so. I wish them the best of luck and led by such an inspirational captain as Roy Keane, I am sure they will continue to go from strength to strength.'

The transfer has gone down in United folklore as one of those which suited all parties. But that isn't strictly true. Nor does it feel as if it was inevitable. It is fair to say that if 'blame' is an accurate term to use, there was enough of it to go around. The key factor seems to be one of control: that being Sir Alex Ferguson's power in the United dressing room. It is likely that it is the accumulation, then, of incidents, rather than a specific individual event, which made things end the way they did. Being late for training, where opinion differed over excuse against reason. Swearing at the manager in a heated after-match blowout. Haircuts? Well, maybe not the first one, but creating a fuss intentionally after the first one when it would grind the manager's gears. It is fair to say, though, Beckham did eventually adhere to these unwritten or undeclared rules. He understood Ferguson didn't like the fuss; so, after the mohawk incident in the summer of 2000, he mostly either had 'sensible' haircuts or at least waited until he was on England duty. When he was challenged about spending time in London, Beckham ensured he would be closer to Manchester, even staying with Gary Neville when Victoria was away on her own promotional business. Whatever the hoop, Beckham would jump through it. Ferguson was growing tired of the new hoops.

There is no indication that really supports any idea that Beckham thought he was bigger than Ferguson or the club, but you could easily look at it from the manager's perspective and understand that the constant pushing of boundaries – whether the issue was forced by Beckham himself or because of his fame – effectively meant the same thing.

In a normal footballing relationship, one would understand the natural parting of the ways; but Beckham and Ferguson did not have that. This was a player who had eaten with the team he supported as a child. He was allowed to sit on the Manchester United bench as a young boy. It is no exaggeration to say that Beckham saw Ferguson as a second father. So when Ferguson says – as he did in his second autobiography – that David 'maybe … wasn't mature enough at that time to handle everything that was going on in his life', perhaps he has a point, but there was also definitely a time where Ferguson stopped being that parental figure. He had no obligation to be that, of course; his job, as manager of Manchester United, was to exert that control so that he had the right discipline in his squad. In years to come, the relationship improved, but this was a dramatic and desperately sad way for it to blow up.

Was it a good move for Manchester United? They received £24.5m, a fee which has been the subject of retrospective attempts by figures of the club to reflect a good payment for a player who gave such service. But two years earlier than that, AC Milan were willing to break the world record of £50m, and it was obvious even then that on marketing alone it would probably be a sound investment.

Beckham's departure left a space which was immediately filled by Cristiano Ronaldo, a very different kind of player, just as Beckham had been different to Cantona, and Cantona had been different to Robson. Just as Beckham had been different to Kanchelskis. Ronaldo was such a success, and a success story which required early development struggles in order to later thrive, that one can say the replacement was worth it. Looking at it another way: United lost bodies in a rapid manner over the next two years, particularly in the middle of the park. Beckham could finally have thrived in that area. Additionally, his set pieces were never replaced. Ferguson had sacrificed that reliability for unpredictability. There is a strong argument to say Beckham's quality in this area could not be replaced – and that each passing year brings a rubber stamp of confirmation that he was, in fact, the greatest when it came to set-piece execution that United, or English football for that matter, has ever seen. That, of course, is a testament to Beckham's individual brilliance and the unique attributes he brought to the team.

The move caused division within the United support, too. There were some who backed the manager, some who couldn't believe Beckham had been sold, and others who were just sad it had ended in such a way. There is a number, not insignificant, who believe the version of events which says that a move to Spain had been in the works for a year by Beckham, and that his shock at the move had been a facade designed to save face.

Terry Byrne, Beckham's friend and former manager, has since spoken to *Sports Illustrated* to explain what was going on behind the scenes. In June 2002 – according to Byrne – Beckham called him to tell him that he would be leaving his management group, SFX, and offered him the job. There was one condition, though: he would have to move to Spain:

'David then called me and said, "Look, I'm going to split with SFX. Would you consider you and your wife moving? I'm going to go to Real Madrid next summer and leave Manchester United. Would you come and live in Spain and just run my world?" I said, "OK, fine." And I can say this with my hand on my heart, I never took a penny of commission out of David. Ever. I took the same salary I was on at Watford. I said, "Look, it's not about money. I'll help you for a period, get your life sorted back out, and then there will be a time when I step away." I managed him for five years. Lived in Spain, loved it. There came a point where the England players asked me to manage them too. David wanted me to move to LA, and my wife and I didn't want to. Our baby had just been born, so I said to David, "Now is the right time for me to step away." So I chose at that point to extricate myself from it. I still speak to David regularly, and he'll ask my advice on whatever. But the friendship comes first and will always come first before business."

Adding fuel to this was a remark made by Peter Kenyon shortly after the deal was agreed. 'What does not make sense for the club is to let top players leave at the end of their contract on a free transfer,' Kenyon said. 'In David's case, our approach in mid-May to his advisers about extending his current deal, which had just two years to run, did not meet with an immediate positive response. We knew David was excited by the opportunity of playing abroad and we felt that if we could generate a substantial fee in a transfer deal, it would support our efforts to strengthen the squad for next season.'

Regardless of where you stand on that theory, and maybe this is a naive take, but it did not feel as if the position was untenable and certainly, at the time, it was not a popular move for Manchester United to make. Nor too, it transpired, for Real Madrid.

Galactico

IF FIRST impressions count for anything, then David Beckham was not making a positive initial impact on his new team-mates at Real Madrid.

It wasn't enough that his arrival had come right in the middle of their last week of the season; Beckham also made a faux-pas at his first press conference. 'Of course I would have been happier if the transfer had been done differently,' he said. 'But I don't want to talk about that side of it. I'm a Real Madrid player now and I'm looking forward to it.'

After some sections of the media took that as a statement of discontent about the move, the player was compelled to issue a quickly prepared comment: 'I understand reports are circulating that I was unhappy with some aspects of my transfer from Manchester United. That is not the case and I did not mean to give that impression in any way. I have publicly expressed my thanks and appreciation for the way the deal has been done by the club, my advisers and Real Madrid. The only thing I was a bit concerned about was the timing, bearing in mind the Spanish league had not finished. I want to apologise to the Real players because all this has not been caused by me and I didn't want it to detract from their last two games of the season. They're fighting to win the league and I didn't want anything to upset that. I wish them good luck.'

In an attempt to curry favour, Beckham also insisted he would not be looking to take the number 7 shirt from club legend Raúl. 'I would never think of taking that number off Raúl,' he said. 'He is the king of Real Madrid as far as I'm concerned. Whatever number they want to give me, I'm happy.'

It was a worthwhile exercise: Raúl's nose had been put out of joint (to put it mildly) to find that while he was at training, reporters and photographers had been camped outside his home attempting to question his wife Mamen about how they might get on with 'Posh and Becks'. The *Daily Star* said Beckham was 'Public Enemy No. 1 in the Real dressing room', which sounded like a huge over-reaction, not least because this group of highly experienced and highly professional athletes knew exactly what came with the territory and how certain elements were out of a player's control.

Madrid won 3–1 against Athletic Bilbao to seal the title, and the reaction from the players afterwards suggested they were going to be very welcoming indeed to their new colleague.

'Beckham will be very happy with us,' Ronaldo said. 'Also, I would not mind giving him my number 11 shirt if I can wear the number 9 next season. The signing of Beckham is a very important moment in the history of Real Madrid. Now this club really will be the very best in the whole world. If there is one piece of advice I can give Beckham when he joins us, it is this – just enjoy playing football. I have been at Real for one year and I enjoyed my first season a lot. I have scored goals and won titles and this is everything a player wants. His arrival will mean there is more competition for places, but this is good for the club as it will keep everyone hungry.'

Roberto Carlos offered an even greater sacrifice than his number – shared duties of free kicks! 'I'll let him take some of them – but only some!' he joked. 'He has scored some beautiful goals from free kicks, but he doesn't have to take all of them. Our president, Florentino Pérez, has shown he can sign the biggest players. Beckham is part of that group, and at Real Madrid you can never have too many good players. I am sure he will settle into the squad well.'

There would be a gentler acclimatisation than Beckham expected: hours after winning La Liga, Florentino Pérez ruthlessly sacked Vicente del Bosque and replaced him with highly rated Manchester United assistant manager Carlos Queiroz. Beckham was officially revealed to the Madrid public on 2 July, holding up a shirt with the number 23 – chosen because of Michael Jordan, the basketball player who Beckham described as his 'all-time sporting hero'.

Madrid sporting director Jorge Valdano responded to the controversy, such that it was, over the timing of the move. 'If there is embarrassment about all the fanfare caused by Beckham, it should be on the part of the media,' said Valdano. 'The timing of his signature was not ideal for any of us, but the need to finalise his signing was really pressing and I explained it to the dressing room before the deciding game of the championship against Athletic Bilbao. If you look at how the team played against them to win the title, you can say that Beckham's signing did not eventually affect their concentration, and we showed that we are a great team capable of focusing on big objectives rather than being distracted by the media. I admit the departure of Vicente del Bosque and Fernando Hierro plus the signing of David Beckham mean that winning the league has not been given the praise it merited. But that comes with the territory of being Real Madrid. People are now saying that because of Beckham's arrival we have to win every single game, but that is what they said last season when Ronaldo arrived. We are Madrid, we know how to live with such pressure. Some people say that Figo was an electoral signing, Zidane was to add beautiful football, Ronaldo was a risk which paid off and Beckham is simply to help our marketing, but that is inaccurate. Each of our stars has made our club greater and our team stronger. The only thing I know for sure is that the fans are ever more happy to pay for a ticket to come and watch this Madrid playing football. David Beckham and Figo are compatible because we envisage them swapping during a game. Bit by bit, they will learn how and when to do that automatically, so we become a team which is less easy for the opposition to predict or close down. Every game over here will bring different challenges for David, and we will use his skills in a way which fits with those challenges. As a footballer, Beckham will bring us great vision and passing skill. His ability to vary his passes is sensational, and that complements one of our shortfalls because in our team only Roberto Carlos is capable of hitting a brilliant 25- or 30-metre pass to a team-mate.'

Beckham would be going back to the Far East, and his adoring fans in China, for Madrid's pre-season tour. Meanwhile, Sir Alex Ferguson was faced with questions from reporters who were representing disgruntled fans in the north-west of the US.

'Any words for the people of Seattle who will be disappointed Beckham isn't here?' he was asked ahead of United's first friendly against Celtic.

'No words at all,' was the curt reply.

In early training sessions, Queiroz had to bring Beckham out of his shell and encourage him to play his natural game. Where once he had endured the harsh words of Eric Harrison imploring him to cut out the Hollywood passes, here, that sort of expression was not only welcomed but was clearly going to be necessary if Beckham wanted to leave his own impression on the team. There had been a rare moment of doubt from the former United star wondering where he might fit in, but that dilemma was resolved (and another caused) by the sale of French international star

Claude Makélélé at the end of August. Makélélé – a holding midfielder whose discipline and defensive nous made him an essential cog if the Madrid machine was to function – moved to Chelsea.

'During the years I was at Real Madrid, it was a selling club – not a buying club, as it had a target to reach, lowering the deficit to zero, which the president had promised club members,' Queiroz told *Tribuna Expresso* in 2018. 'The policy was basically: six Galacticos – all of whom were in midfield to attack – and the "Pavones" in defence. But in that squad, there was also [Claude] Makélélé and [Fernando] Morientes and both of them left. With Morientes, immediately after the Super Cup, I had a couple of words with him and said: "See you on Tuesday" and he replied: "Tuesday? Haven't you heard? I've been loaned out to Monaco." I had no idea. At least, I thought, I still had Makélélé and I could drop [Ivan] Helguera back into central defence, where he did well. But shortly after that Makélélé left to join Chelsea because he wasn't selling shirts and so that Beckham could play in the middle. Beckham's position was right wing, but when I joined Real Madrid that position was already filled by Figo.'

Beckham was immediately welcomed by the Brazilian contingent of the Madrid dressing room; but it seemed as if he would have to win over the legendary Zinedine Zidane, who reportedly quipped about the transfer activity of the summer: 'Why put another layer of gold paint on the Bentley when you are losing the entire engine?' Zidane, of course, had years of international experience alongside Makélélé as well as their time at Madrid, so was bound to have a strong opinion.

Beckham, then, had to work that little bit harder to leave an impression on his new colleagues. But here was a player not afraid of hard work – and, as that was contrary to the reputation of his celebrity image, not least remarks made by his former club manager about his commitment, the midfielder's energy levels in training did in fact impress some of the bigger names at the club. Luís Figo, ostensibly a rival for a first-team position, described him as a 'phenomenon': 'The image he has is totally different to what he is really like as a player and a person.'

Beckham enjoyed his first pre-season, and spoke excitedly about the opportunity to finally get a long run in the middle of the park. 'This experience with Real makes me want the season to start proper,' he said. 'It is nice scoring in the friendlies, getting my first goal and making my debut before that in China, but the big game starts when we get back to Spain. It is important to carry on the form we have shown and build on our fitness. There was a great team spirit at Manchester United and one that I enjoyed. I didn't know if I would find it here, but I have. There is one thing that I have been surprised about, though, and that is me getting the free kicks with Roberto Carlos on the pitch. It tells you how much I have been made to feel welcome.'

He had already started to turn around some initial reservations within the Madrid ranks; though it should be said that, despite the Galactico profile, there existed the natural hope that Beckham *would* prove them wrong. His first game on Spanish soil for Real Madrid was a friendly at Valencia, and he confessed to Queiroz that he felt very nervous. A 0–0 draw was not the glamorous first impression he had hoped for, and he would have been grateful for his beginner's grasp of the Spanish language. Beckham had proven to be his own worst critic – he said it 'couldn't get much worse', but even that awareness brought little sympathy. *El Mundo* said he did 'nothing, nothing at all', but *AS* really stuck the knife in, saying he had a 'stinker', showed 'incomprehensible passivity' and was 'little short of calamitous'.

Former Madrid winger Míchel could not have been more damning. 'Beckham looked like he did whenever Manchester [United] played in Spain,' he said. 'The Englishman couldn't adapt to the Iberian pace, passion, pressure – or greatness.'

His first official game came in the Spanish Super Cup against Mallorca. He set up a first-half goal for Luís Figo, but goals from Arnold Bruggink and Samuel Eto'o meant Carlos Queiroz needed an answer. That answer was to withdraw Beckham after just 53 minutes (to replace him with Makélélé, ironically enough, before his sale); the former United star booted a water bottle at his own dugout as he walked off. 'I was angry,' he admitted later. 'Any player who is substituted is angry. I am no different. I want to stay on the pitch for 90 minutes, so I am disappointed any time it happens. But it is the manager's decision. He has his opinions and of course, I haven't asked him for an explanation.'

The manager's reasoning was that he had to 'sacrifice' him; Madrid still lost 2–1. It was a much happier occasion in the second leg: goals from Raúl and Ronaldo turned the tie around, and, in the 73rd minute, Ronaldo's left-wing cross was missed by goalkeeper Leo Franco – Beckham took the opportunity to head in from 15 yards, and celebrated with the relief and joy you might expect from someone carrying such a weight of expectation. Beckham's contribution made it around the world – the Spanish equivalent of the Charity Shield was now newsworthy even on Fox Sports News in the US – and it quickly attracted the attention of broadcasters back in the UK. BSkyB hastily agreed a deal – concluded just 36 hours before the league kicked off – to show La Liga games for three years. Their first game, of course, would be Beckham's league debut against Real Betis at the Bernabéu.

The watching audience were given the moment they were waiting for after just 120 seconds. Ronaldo played a one-two with Raúl and squared the ball across the penalty area. Arriving in the six-yard box, with all the predatory instinct of those aforementioned forwards, was David Beckham to nudge the ball into the net.

On the big Bernabéu pitch, Beckham was able to spray passes around with ease, although there seemed a natural temptation to drift over to the right-hand side. That old habit was broken in the second half, as he settled into the middle: first unleashing a rasping drive from 25 yards which struck the crossbar, and then pinging one of those flash passes across to Zidane, who crossed for Ronaldo to make the points safe. It rounded off a man-of-the-match performance.

'I always work hard and try to create as many chances for players as is humanly possible,' he said. 'And I suppose it was a bit of a compliment that they started fouling me, as they were with Ronaldo earlier on. I know that there are critics out there who doubt my ability to succeed here and it is down to me to prove them wrong. Playing in this atmosphere will help me improve as a player. That is my whole philosophy of being here.'

Three official games in, and the England captain was learning the fickle ways of the Spanish press: *AS*, who were the most damning, now carried a quote from ex-Argentina goalkeeper Hugo Gatti, who said of Beckham, 'Perhaps his physical beauty forces him to show more than the other Madrid stars – but he is the best.'

Even accounting for these turbulent beginnings, one could comfortably describe Beckham's first few months in Madrid as a qualified success. Queiroz played a 3–5–2 formation, with wing-backs Míchel Salgado and Roberto Carlos, whilst Beckham played as the anchor behind Zidane and Figo. Ronaldo and Raúl were the strike partners. The goals came thick and fast – he was the taker of a clever free-kick routine between Figo and Roberto Carlos against Malaga, where the ball looked as if it might be teed up for the Brazilian, only for Beckham to strike it in much the same way as his last United goal at Everton. It turned out to be the winner in a 3–1 victory. He was congratulated in a manner which suggested he was very popular indeed. In the game before, there'd been an even more exciting flash of brilliance – Beckham had hit one of those diagonal passes, which was blasted into the net in stunning fashion by Zidane, in a 7–2 win over Valladolid. This was, officially, the football version of the Harlem Globetrotters.

There were plenty of players quick to help him settle, the first being English-speaking Míchel Salgado. 'I was the one to babysit David Beckham,' he told the *League of Legends* show. 'I did it a lot. It's because I was the only to speak English. But it was great with Beckham. He was alone in Madrid because his wife was travelling a lot, living in LA and England. So he would call me every day, saying "Let's go out." And my wife was really pissed off with the situation – but it was a great time.'

As time went on, Beckham found an affinity with the Brazilian section of the Real Madrid changing room, growing particularly close with Roberto Carlos and Ronaldo. That pair scored in a famous win for Madrid in the Nou Camp in early December – Beckham had expected some abuse from Barcelona fans for the failed move, but Luís Figo, having made the move between the Spanish giants, was still the subject of the greatest resentment.

'For me personally, those first four or five months of the season were as enjoyable and as satisfying as any I can remember in my career,' Beckham later said. He spoke excitedly about training – how the more technically gifted players like Ronaldo would still be trying to learn new tricks, and how that inspired him to do the same. The affection was mutual between the two biggest names in world football (Ronaldo as the headline act for Nike, and Beckham for Adidas).

'We are very impressed with him,' Ronaldo said in October. 'He has surpassed expectations. We knew before he was a good player, but we did not expect him to be such an influential player, to show such commitment to the team spirit. The way he runs for everything, the way he tries his best. He has everyone's respect. The great thing about Real Madrid is there is always room for another big-name player. Every player is given his space, his role. Our dressing-room spirit is a collective. We are all there together for each other. We have all been doing our utmost to make Beckham comfortable after he arrived. When I invited him to my house, it wasn't anything particularly special, I just wanted to welcome him as my team-mates had for me a year before.'

It was Beckham's old tricks, rather than new ones, which were most impressive. His new central role permitted him to dig deep into the archives for long-range spectaculars, but the muscle memory was intact against Albacete early in the season with a wonderful 25-yard strike into the top corner.

That said, it was not a season without its ups and downs. Beckham had endured incidents with Argentine defenders other than Aldo Duscher and come out of them with a nasty, recurring ankle injury, which, coupled with his first experience of a winter break, took a while to get right. His post-Christmas form was not perceived favourably. In the first leg of the Champions League second-round tie with Bayern Munich, Beckham had a subdued game, provoking renewed criticism, particularly from *Marca*, who viciously awarded the player no marks out of three, with their reports claiming that he added little to the team and should be replaced by Spanish midfielder Guti.

'It is slightly harder for Beckham at the moment, but there is an explanation for that,' insisted Real fitness coach Valter Di Salvo. 'He missed our last game before the winter break and then had his first-ever time off at the time of the Christmas holidays. To recover the level of fitness after the winter break, I stage a training programme, but because David had his ankle injury he was not able to benefit. This is the reason that he is a little behind the rest of the squad in terms of rhythm and fitness, but I believe he will need only another couple of games to hit full speed.'

Manager Queiroz felt the transfer had, so far, been a success. 'From my own experience living abroad, I especially remember my first two years. It is the first time David Beckham has lived abroad,' he said. 'For the moment he is doing very well. Much better, I must say, than I expected. When you move away, it is the food, it is the environment, it is the culture, it is the language on TV, friends. It is really very difficult. We hope, and I hope for him, that step by step he is settling his own life on a daily basis, because it will help him a lot to concentrate. Let's wait and see.'

He described Beckham's success in repositioning as 'amazing'. 'Of course David Beckham is not Patrick Vieira,' he said. 'He will never be. Guti is not Makélélé. And I don't want them to change. But if you want to play central midfield, you need to understand the basic tasks of that position.'

Beckham, for his part, insisted he was happy and looking forward to the future, despite speculation already hitting the newspapers that Chelsea owner Roman Abramovich was keen to take the biggest English name to Stamford Bridge. 'I am not looking to move,' Beckham said. 'Why leave? I will be a Real Madrid player next season. Why would I move when I am already happy?'

Never happier in that first season than after 23 minutes of the Copa del Rey Final on 17 March (on a sporting level, at least – David, like everyone, was devastated by the terrorist attack near Atocha train station on 11 March which claimed 193 lives). Beckham's tremendous free kick from 30 yards clipped the inside of the post as it opened the scoring against Real Zaragoza. The midfielder remembered thinking before the game that the way things stood – a cup final, league leaders and having got through the Bayern tie – he had a real chance of repeating his best ever season at Manchester United. He also recalled, however, that it was just a moment, and from that point everything seemed to fall apart. Zaragoza mounted a stunning comeback effort and won the cup in extra time.

Madrid then contrived to throw away a 4–2 first-leg lead against Monaco in the Champions League and were eliminated on away goals on 6 April. That was nothing compared to the collapse they saved for La Liga – a 5–1 win over Sevilla on 28

March looked like a significant step in securing the league title. But Barcelona won 2–1 at the Bernabéu on 25 April to start a dramatic run of form – defeats to Deportivo and Mallorca were followed by the last chance to do anything about the title in the penultimate game of the season at Murcia. But the hosts took an early lead, and when they were awarded a soft penalty in the 33rd minute, Beckham was so incensed that his argument with a linesman was met with a dim view by the referee. 'After all the jokes about me struggling to learn the language, I got a red card because of something I said in perfect Spanish,' he said sardonically.

Murcia won 2–1 – and Beckham was suspended for Madrid's final capitulation, a 4–1 home defeat to Real Sociedad, which marked five defeats to end the season. Carlos Queiroz finished fourth after having an eight-point lead, which ultimately cost him his own job. Beckham continued to ignore the speculation linking him with a move back to the Premier League – but English eyes would be watching, and expecting just as much as those Spanish fans, as the Three Lions headed into a tournament with greater levels of hope than *almost* ever before.

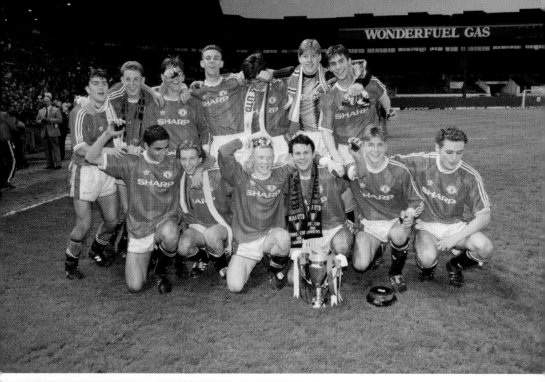

The first success of a glittering career, David celebrates with his class of '92 team-mates

On the opening day of the 96/97 season, Beckham's goal from the halfway line at Selhurst Park cements his place in footballing immortality

From fame to infamy; David is sent off after clashing with Diego Simeone at the 1998 World Cup

Redemption arrives on the national stage as Beckham, now England captain, takes his country to the World Cup with a free kick against Greece which is as dramatic as it is fantastic

Beckham finds ultimate retribution after a year of abuse from opposing supporters when he wins the treble with United

In February 2003, David is struck by a boot which is kicked by Sir Alex Ferguson in a dressing-room bust-up. He is soon on his way from Old Trafford

Galactico! Beckham's modest £24.5m transfer fee is recovered by Real Madrid in merchandise sales before he even kicks a ball for the club

After announcing his intention to leave, David is axed from the Real team, but returns and wins the league title in his last game for the club

A landmark day for US soccer as the world's most famous player signs for LA Galaxy

On loan for AC Milan, he makes his only playing return to Old Trafford and is caught up in controversy when he takes a scarf from a supporter which is being used as part of a protest against United's owners

Beckham and sons pose with the MLS Cup, won in his last game for LA Galaxy

… And again, Beckham and his boys with the Ligue 1 trophy as he calls time on his career with a short spell at PSG.

Spotlight

BETWEEN THE end of the domestic season and the start of Euro 2004, David Beckham continued to dominate the newspaper and magazine columns. Speculation about a move to Chelsea raged on, despite David's insistence that he would continue to play for Real Madrid.

He arrived in Portugal for the European Championship as David Beckham the central midfielder, although whether he would play there for his country was another matter. Sven-Göran Eriksson had a pool of talent in that area which was almost embarrassing – Beckham, Paul Scholes, Steven Gerrard and Frank Lampard to name the four most prominent players, all of whom were in the category ranked as 'world class'. For Eriksson, surely the biggest obstacle to England succeeding depended on whether he would somehow contrive to get that balance wrong. But history had already proven that Beckham would be missed so much on the right that it would not be sensible to play him anywhere else.

This was not, however it may have seemed, a concession of lesser talent. He went into the tournament with an endorsement from the legendary Holland and Barcelona playmaker Johan Cruyff, who had named Beckham 'man of the season'.

'In comparison to the others, he came with the maximum expectation,' Cruyff said. 'When he arrived in Spain he had to meet sky-high expectations. The season may have been a disaster for Real, but his season has been absolutely noteworthy. When he was full of energy and fit, he was keeping them high in the league and in all competitions, despite spending a whole season in a completely new position. That shows his indisputable quality as a footballer.'

Beckham was looking forward to the first game of the tournament – against France, and club-mate Zinedine Zidane – whilst reflecting on how he had dealt with his year in Spain. 'Lots of things have improved since I went to Real Madrid,' he said. 'People talk about another English player failing in Spain, but I don't feel I've failed, other than not winning anything yet. I know I've definitely improved as a player while I've been here. It's been a great, great experience for me to play alongside Zidane because, even at 29, I am always looking to improve my game and learn from other players. I've learned off players like Bryan Robson and Eric Cantona and now, to be in a team with Zidane, is amazing. I played a 50-yard ball to him this season and if he hadn't volleyed it straight into the bottom corner, then it wouldn't have made my pass look half as good. Playing with Zidane has made me a lot more confident. My touch and quickness of feet are better. It's been said about the whole team at Real Madrid that we haven't had a very good season by our standards. Apart from the start I made to the season, it's been said about me. It's been said about Raúl and it's been said about Ronaldo. Maybe it is being said about Zizou, too, but his bad game is everyone else's man-of-the-match game. There has not been banter between Zidane and me about this match – there's just respect from my side and his. He realises we have got a great squad of players, too. So we are looking forward to this match, because you have to put yourself up against the best – and they are definitely the best. I can sense that people are more excited about this tournament than any other I have been involved in with England. When people look at our squad – the mixture of youth and experience plus the talent – it puts a smile on their faces. We've got a great chance.'

It is incredible to look back at that England squad, the composition of it, and think they never really came close to challenging for a major international honour. Alongside Beckham there was the experience of the United contingent in Scholes, both Nevilles and Nicky Butt. The goalscoring prowess of Michael Owen; the capable technical ability of Owen Hargreaves, who would surely be challenging the likes of Scholes, Gerrard and Lampard for a place in the middle. The valuable, selfless play of Emile Heskey, the promising youth of Joe Cole and Kieron Dyer, and the unknown quantity of young Everton forward Wayne Rooney. There was the bouncing confidence of Sol Campbell and Ashley Cole coming in from an 'Invincible' season, and a defence so strong with Campbell and John Terry that Ledley King and Jamie Carragher had to accept their role as back-up. A name notable by his absence from that list was Rio Ferdinand, arguably the best defender of the bunch.

Ferdinand was, curiously, a self-inflicted omission by the FA. He had missed a scheduled drug test at Manchester United earlier in the season and was consequently banned from all competitions – including playing for the national side. The matter had provoked anger, especially from the United corner of the England dressing room. Led by Gary Neville, there had been the threat of a strike ahead of an important qualifier in Turkey. One newspaper reported that Beckham had arranged a meeting with Eriksson, with an 'insider' claiming, 'I could not believe what I was watching. I have never seen a player dictate to a manager like that. I can't imagine strong characters like Brian Clough, Alex

Ferguson or George Graham standing for something like that. They would have left Beckham in no doubt about exactly who the governor was.'

According to other players in the England dressing room, though, the matter was led by Neville, and not so much Beckham. Eventually the players relented and played the game. It finished goalless, but did not pass without incident. Beckham missed a penalty and was accused of spitting at, and headbutting, Turkish defender Alpay.

'No. 1, Beckham butted me,' Alpay said. 'No. 2, he spat at me. If his spit hit me on the head it wouldn't have mattered, but it hit the star and crescent on the Turkey badge on my shirt. I really wanted to retaliate, but I didn't. That's the only reason I am annoyed at him. I wasn't in the fight in the tunnel, and I didn't see anything. Maybe they started fighting because of what happened in the penalty area between me and Beckham, but how things have got to this stage, I can't believe it. I'm not going to apologise until Beckham apologises to the Turkish fans for spitting on my Turkish kit. The world worships Beckham, but 20 Beckhams wouldn't make one Emre or Hakan Şükür.'

But Alpay's claims did not seem to add up: everyone could see that the defender was first on the scene after Beckham's miss, yelling at him and confronting him, attempting quite clearly to provoke and antagonise him. The Turk played his club football for Aston Villa – but Villa chairman Doug Ellis terminated his contract after the incident, leaving nobody in any doubt where he stood.

England had qualified, and would have to compete without Ferdinand, but surely had enough strength to compensate; it certainly seemed that way as they took control against France. Beckham set up Lampard for a first-half opener and then stepped up to take a 72nd-minute penalty when Rooney was fouled. But Beckham missed, and England capitulated. First of all, Heskey gave a soft foul away and Zidane scored from the resultant free kick. Then, Gerrard hit a woefully short back-pass, which Thierry Henry seized upon. He was brought down in the box, and Zidane had inflicted a remarkable last-minute turnaround on Beckham's team.

The press had no shortage of scapegoats for this setback. It was surprising that Emile Heskey seemed to be the first choice, with his 'crime' being the least significant. England had only lost a game – not exited the tournament yet – so the haranguing was not quite as vicious as it could have been.

England recovered from this setback in spectacular fashion – Wayne Rooney scoring twice in wins over Switzerland and Croatia – but were then eliminated in their traditional manner, on penalties, this time to Portugal. Beckham missed the first kick, but it still went to sudden death, with Darius Vassell being the unlucky man this time around. England were out, and, as it would have been hugely unfair to put the blame on a squad player's shoulders, the finger was instead pointed at England's dysfunctional midfield. Paul Scholes had been moved to the left wing to accommodate Gerrard and Lampard in the middle. It had not been a resounding success as a partnership, but at least both had scored, which was more than could be said for Beckham, who was charged with having a below-par tournament.

'I like to look at myself in the mirror and believe that I have given my best. I believe I have done that,' he insisted to reporters the morning after the game. 'The people who ask me questions about whether I have done myself justice will write what they want to anyway. I always give as much as I can in games, and that is good enough for me. If it is not good enough for other people then so be it, but I will not let that affect me. I have had to play a different role here. I have never been one to go past players. I have always been a player who has gone out wide, and puts balls in. I agree I haven't put that many crosses in, but we have played different football and that's just the way it has been. I would probably give myself seven out of ten for effort. I want to stay as England captain, I want to stay an England player. It is as simple as that. As long as the manager and players want me to stay as captain, it doesn't matter what anyone else thinks. If they want me as captain, I want to be captain. I'd like to think there will be two more chances at tournaments for me. We will see how my legs hold up. Hopefully we will end up winning something, who's to know?'

There was the suggestion put to him that his profile as a celebrity had caught up with him. 'People say about the commercial activities, but I do one or two things every month and the commercial side has never got in the way of my football and never will,' he said. 'People have mentioned my adverts this summer, but that is the way it is. That part of my life has never come before my football. I will stand by that. The tiredness is down to the football, not commercial activities.'

The following day he gave another interview where he was more frank and contemplative rather than defensive. 'I'm not saying that this [Euro 2004] is one of them [low points in his career], but it's a big disappointment at the moment,' he said. 'I am man enough and strong enough to come through this, forget what has happened and move on. People are looking for something from me. I am not prepared to do it. I am not prepared to lie down and take it. I will take criticism, but I am the type of person who will fight back. People don't realise how strong I am as a person. If they want to write me off, I will keep coming back until I have won. I think situations always affect you, and when there is pressure on a person day in, day out, there does come a point when you have to say enough is enough – unfortunately that is my life. It's full of three or four cars following me wherever I go. People ask me about my commercial activities getting in the way of football, but the answer is they don't. People think I am just moaning. They just say, "tough". But I have got children and I want them to enjoy their lives.'

He also suggested that the different approach to training might have had an impact on his fitness at the tournament. 'I don't think we have done so much conditioning work at Real Madrid as we did at Manchester United,' he said. 'That's the way it is in the Spanish league. I didn't feel as fit in the second half of the season. Maybe that has spilled into this tournament, but I am not going to make excuses.'

That suggestion was put to Luís Figo, who strongly rejected it. 'I am fit,' he said. 'I do not agree with David on that point. This year we did the work we could do when you play every Wednesday and Sunday. With so many games, it is difficult to train more. You always feel you can do better, but physically I am OK. We are not the same as we were at the start of the season. But it depends how you think about it. David is my friend. After the game, I couldn't get in touch with him. I will see him on 16 July when Real Madrid report back for training. I am sympathetic about what happened to him and England, but one of the two teams had to leave and it was better for Portugal, and me, that it wasn't us.'

So ended England's greatest chance for success with their so-called 'Golden Generation'. On the balance of the history of his relationship with the press, Beckham could consider their reaction this time around reasonable, if not a little personal.

Emile Heskey – who, remember, had received just a little taster of what Beckham had been through – believes that his generation was conditioned to accept it. 'It is what it is, it's part and parcel of playing for England. I didn't get anything like what David got. It was still over the top, but you almost have to come to expect that it's part of playing for England,' he says. 'Who polices the press? They can do whatever they want. Now, with social media, you have a player like Raheem Sterling who can highlight the hypocrisy, and it is shown for what it is. But it still happens –

people can say what they want and they're never held accountable. We as players learned to live with it, but should we have had to?'

Heskey's comments scratch at the surface of a more serious problem, a problem which has never gone away, and one which really has escalated out of control in recent years with the evolution of social media. 'It helps, but it is a hindrance,' he said. 'You have the platform to address things but you're also there 24/7, available for people to say whatever they want without a filter. Look at the abuse Jesse Lingard gets. Would you be happy for your child or a family member to go through that? People who have the spotlight of the media are expected to behave differently to the standards expected of other people. You're expected to be the bigger person. But people behave differently to you. They hurl abuse in the street in the way they wouldn't to anyone else, just because you're a footballer. If you were living life normally and did that, you'd expect to get a punch in the face! People think they can say and do whatever they want, and because footballers by and large don't respond to it, they think they can carry on. They think there's no impact. But there is. Look at what happened to Caroline Flack [the British television personality who committed suicide in February 2020]. And no one cares. Don't get me wrong, the attention you get online is largely positive. But that which isn't positive can be vicious. And that can affect people in ways you can't imagine. Everybody is different, people react differently. What if David had been more vulnerable in 1998? What if social media had been around in 1998 and went in on him? It is dreadful to say, but it is not impossible to envisage a repeat scenario due to the way the media is, and then who knows what might happen? People are suffering from mental health issues, and football players are people. Look at what happened to Chris Kirkland when the supporter ran on to the pitch and punched him in the face. That affected him badly. It is so unpredictable. It's a social responsibility, but within that, the media have a large part to play.

It's fuelled by them, after all. They'll say something and people believe it. The negative part might be a front-page headline; the apology is usually hidden away on an inside page somewhere. Who reads that?'

Beckham had continued to endure that extra baggage during his first year in Spain. Out of sight but never out of mind; speculation about his private life, about his safety, about his future, usually conducted with an air of malevolence, preying on that general uncomfortable relationship some of the public have with envy and jealousy.

'If he got a new haircut, the thousand or so people watching us at training for England would have the same style,' Heskey recalls. 'We'd walk around with six security guards. Two for us, four for him. It was bizarre sometimes, and I didn't think anything of it other than it was sometimes quite funny. I've got a friend in Leicester who owns a black hair salon. When David got his braids, their business went through the roof. I'm not joking. All people wanted to do was to copy him. That's what he brings. But he was a brilliant captain and a brilliant footballer. It's fair to say he became more mature as a player when he moved to Madrid. Players improve with experience anyway, usually, so it could have just been that, it could have been moving to a different country, it could have been moving into the middle of the pitch, where you have to be more responsible with your passing. As for when it came to England, we had so many good central midfielders, but we didn't have anybody who could cross it like David, so for me it always made sense for him to be playing from that side. For me, he was among the best, if not the best. There was nobody better. Beckham's passing ability was second to none. On dead balls he was phenomenal. He wasn't given the credit he deserved. I think, without getting the credit for it, he changed the way people think about wingers. Wingers were players who would run up and down the side of the pitch, get to the byline and cross it. Becks didn't need to do that. His technical ability to cross the ball effectively from anywhere was something nobody else could do. All he needed was the space to do it, and he was a master at finding it. At Leicester, I can remember Steve Guppy learning to copy the technique.'

There would be further failures for England, but this was the one which stung the most; the one where it seemed as if success was a reasonable expectation. And so it is reflected upon that this group of England players underachieved. Heskey rejects this, either as a description of the squad, or of Beckham as an individual.

'One thing you could never say about David Beckham was that he was an underachiever,' he says. 'He was always a player that could be counted on to stand up and perform when we needed him. Did we underachieve as a group? I'd have to say no, we didn't. I think what we achieved was a fair reflection of our quality as a squad. In my age group, playing for France, you had Thierry Henry. Nicolas Anelka. Robert Pires. Petit, Lizarazu, Barthez, Desailly, Thuram, Zidane. They won the World Cup and European Championship. You have to be honest with yourself. Yes, we could have achieved more, and we did play very well at times, but we just weren't good enough. That said, for me, David was up there with the best: he could hold his head high for what he contributed.'

To justify that position in most people's eyes – and his own – Beckham would have to win something with Real Madrid.

Reputation

IN THE eyes of his birth country, David Beckham was deemed to be of strong enough stature that he was not held accountable in the long term for England's exit at the European Championship. A goal and an assist in a 3–0 win over Ukraine in August had *Express* journalist Niall Hickman saying the captain had 'won the fans back'; a fickle lovers' tiff, then, which had lasted all of eight weeks.

There was a resurrection of some discontent with the press when Beckham confessed to deliberately getting booked in a game against Wales; he had already scored a fantastic long-range goal before he hurt his ribs in a challenge with the combative Ben Thatcher. Knowing he would probably miss England's next game, and remembering that he was one yellow card away from a suspension, he went in on Thatcher, deliberately picking up a caution. 'I'm sure people think I haven't got the brains to be that clever,' he said. 'I have got the brains. I could feel the injury, so I fouled Thatcher. It was deliberate. I knew I would be out for a few weeks, so I thought let's get the yellow cards out of the way.'

England World Cup hero Geoff Hurst was aghast. 'I cannot possibly imagine such a thing would have happened in my time,' said Hurst. 'I come from a different planet when it comes to the modern thinking about this. Never mind what Bobby Moore would have made of it, what would Alf Ramsey have thought if our great captain had deliberately got himself suspended? It's really poor and I am very disappointed. I think Alf might have said, "That's it. Thanks very much. We won't be seeing you again." But we played in a different era.'

It had been a peculiar start to the season for Beckham in Spain. José Camacho had taken over the reins as coach, and the England star scored the first home goal of his tenure, a free kick from distance in a 1–0 win over Numancia. Ten days later, there was a sense of groundhog day: an almost identical free kick in a 1–0 victory against Osasuna brought the first home victory for new head coach Mariano García Remón. Camacho had been ruthlessly dismissed after defeats to Espanyol and Bayer Leverkusen. But Remón was also on the brink after a 3–0 November humbling in the Nou Camp – and was dismissed following a 1–0 home defeat to Sevilla. Vanderlei Luxemburgo became the third man to try to steer Madrid to glory, but things merely stabilised for them to finish in second place – comfortably ahead of Villarreal in third, but never close enough to threaten Barcelona, who could afford to draw their last three games.

Luxemburgo, like his predecessors, was treated to an early Beckham free kick in a win at Numancia in January; if there was no real time for the midfielder to leave a lasting impression on his coaches, he was at least winning over reporters. Earlier that month Real had recorded an emphatic 3–0 win at bitter rivals Atlético.

'El partido con Atleti was mucho mejor para todo,' Beckham told a stunned group of journalists, who impulsively responded by applauding. 'Siete puntos es mucho mejor para jugadores. Vamos mejorando pero tenemos que seguir trabajando juntos.'

In English: 'The game with Atlético Madrid was much better for everyone. Seven points is much better for the players. We are getting better but we have to carry on working together.' Clearly 'footballspeak' is a language that translates well.

On 15 March 2005, David realised one of his ambitions when his first soccer school was opened next to the Millennium Dome in Greenwich, London. 'This is a long-term project for me,' he said. 'This is what I have always wanted to do when I finished playing football. Hopefully, these will run for many, many years. I want to continue playing as long as I can until my legs are too old. Then I will devote all my time to the soccer schools. Management has never appealed to me. I am just one of those players. I have two more years on my contract at Real, and I would like to carry on beyond that.'

Beckham had only suffered through two full seasons at United without silverware – 1997/98 and 2001/02 – but now looked set to do so in his first two years at Madrid. 'I am not used to not winning anything in my career,' he admitted. 'There is always talk when teams like Real don't win. They are supposed to win. But I am happy there. I would love to stay as long as I can. England is where I started. I might end it here, but who knows what will happen?'

Beckham was certainly right when he referenced his intelligence after the booking against Wales. He had been around the block long enough to know the value of using the press when it was necessary – and, let's face it, if anybody had earned the right to use the media to boost his image in certain respects, it was him, and he was only exercising the opportunity to benefit where others had attempted to take away from him.

He would still have no shortage of takers if he wanted to go back to the UK – Chelsea were still reportedly very keen – but it seemed clear that the 'here' in his remark meant Spain. He was reluctant to move back to England, and if the reason is obvious then it was probably two-fold. Yes, there was very much the public image of him being a devoted Manchester United player. He had already witnessed Paul Ince and Peter Schmeichel return to England after moving abroad, and returning to play for hated rivals no less. Could Beckham really do that and move to Chelsea, a club with which he had shared a tempestuous relationship to say the least, and a club now emerging as United's biggest rivals? The other way of looking at it is that even if he did, he would know that it would still be perceived as a backwards step, a concession of failure; that he had not made a success of his move to Madrid, and he would have had to return to England to a club with a lesser profile than the one he had grown up at. There was, realistically, nowhere to go after the ceiling of United and Madrid. It stands to reason therefore that he had always spoken positively about 'breaking' America; where the stature of the club would be relatively insignificant, as it would be about Beckham himself.

In mid-2004 he had again talked up a move in the future after he had been the cover star of *Vanity Fair*. In May 2005 he was back in the USA: England were playing a friendly in Chicago, and the captain was in the country as he planned to launch his second soccer school out in LA, although he would miss the game with an injury.

'No English footballer has ever really made it big over here,' Beckham said on 30 May. 'I would love to be well known in America. I'd love to be recognised over here. The American people are so patriotic about their sports, more so than anywhere else in the world. I like the way their people are. I like the way they look up to people like Michael Jordan and Tiger Woods. I'm sure that they criticise, but not to the extent that they are putting their own people and own sport down. That is what is nice. The American people love all their sports – basketball, baseball and American football. Soccer is not one of their major sports. I'm surprised that football has not made it here, because the facilities are amazing and the women's team are doing very well. But I don't see why in the future it can't change. It is another challenge for me to get noticed.'

Whilst other British players had played in the NASL (North American Soccer League) – United legends George Best and Gordon Hill among them – Beckham had a point, as he was referring to that transcending effect players need to have in order to take soccer into the mainstream. Hill, for example, was and remains an icon of the North American game, as well as the British, but whilst he is a hugely respected youth soccer coach, he hadn't dragged the sport into the American mainstream in the way Beckham was discussing.

At the launch of the DB Academy on 4 June, Beckham arrived to find hundreds of journalists and TV crews, with many young fans wearing England and Real Madrid tops outside the building.

'I want to give kids the chance to pursue their dreams like I did mine,' he said. 'I've not been as popular in America as I have in other parts of the world. Having this much attention is amazing.'

After a difficult calendar year in 2004, Beckham was seen as having something of a renaissance in the year he turned 30, perhaps helped by the increase in the number of Brazilians in the dressing room that summer. Luxemburgo was overseeing a big turnover at the club. Notably out of the door were Luís Figo, who moved to Inter Milan – thereby increasing Beckham's importance in the middle of the pitch – and Michael Owen, who had moved from Liverpool and now to Newcastle after a single year.

In his 2019 autobiography, Owen revealed that he and Beckham had not been close in Spain. 'As much as we ended up living close to David and Victoria Beckham and were two English families living abroad in the same city, there wasn't much in the way of social life as far as them and us were concerned,' he said. 'Given that both Louise and Victoria were quite lonely and both looking after young kids, they'd occasionally see each other while we were training. That was the extent of the friendship, however.

This perhaps wasn't a surprise given that, by the time we found ourselves in Madrid together, David and I had even less in common than we ever had. I certainly didn't like wearing the trendy gear or mingling among socialite company. David and Victoria on the other hand, were both bona fide superstars in their own right. They were operating on a completely different stratosphere from a social perspective. I never once got the impression I was on the inner circle of David's group of friends.'

Given Owen's admission that he still held some resentment towards Beckham for what happened in the 1998 World Cup, it isn't surprising that there was no relationship, though one could contend that the discussion about that was only one way.

Owen was replaced by Brazilian sensation Robinho, who had a very different relationship with the England captain. 'Beckham was always hanging out with the Brazilians,' Robinho recalled in 2017. 'He was part of our group. In fact, there was even a little jealousy among the Spanish players because he could speak Portuguese better than Spanish, so he used to spend most of his time with us. He's a very humble man – I'd say the most down-to-earth player I've met. He's amazing.'

Sevilla were ravaged for Julio Baptista and Sergio Ramos, whilst another Brazilian, highly rated full-back Cicinho, arrived from São Paulo. These players would all fit into Luxemburgo's new tactical masterplan, which he described as 'the magic rectangle': an extremely narrow 4–2–2–2 formation which proved immediately unpopular with the Madrid fans. 'Forget about the bandas [wings],' the manager told *AS*. 'The only bandas [bands] I want to see play music.'

But condensing the space in the middle of the pitch made it more difficult for Beckham and Zidane to influence games as they usually could. Beckham was one of the furthest-back midfielders. This unfamiliar shape resulted in some terrible results – a narrow opening day La Liga win at Cádiz was followed by three consecutive defeats: two in the league and a crushing 3–0 reverse at Lyon in the Champions League. Luxemburgo was saved only by a club belief that there was a conspiracy against them by referees – a couple of decisions had gone against Madrid in the opening weeks, and it was thought to be a consequence of Florentino Pérez voting against the sitting president of the Spanish Football Federation.

Robinho – perhaps predictably – also defended his manager and the tactical system. 'Vanderlei has won a lot with this system. We are still getting used to it, but we will soon adapt,' he said. 'The new players still have to settle in. We are doing what he asks of us, and he is confident in his system.'

Beckham, too, came out in support of the boss: 'I hope the same thing that happened last year to the manager doesn't happen again. We need stability. We want to keep the manager, but you never know, sometimes things are done differently here.'

A run of four consecutive emphatic wins suggested a corner was being turned; but it was a false dawn. In the third of those, Beckham had been involved in a running spat with Mallorca defender Sergio Ballesteros. In one altercation, a challenge from Ballesteros sent Beckham to the floor; the England star had appeared to stamp on his opponent, causing a reaction. 'I fell into Beckham's trap,' Ballesteros said. 'He was craftier than me, because his stamp on my foot was not noticed, but my slap was seen by everyone.'

Beckham was suffering through a difficult October – though, to be fair, that was just following on from the theme of September's troubles. He had to delay joining up with the England squad ahead of a World Cup qualifier against Austria, as his son Romeo had gone to hospital.

England, like Madrid, had not enjoyed the easiest of Septembers. A 1–0 win in Wales had seen Beckham majestically playing as a 'quarterback'. 'I enjoyed the role because I am on the ball all the time and always free,' he had said. 'I'm comfortable passing the ball, and that role gives me a lot more satisfaction. Playing there means I give extra protection to the centre-halves. Rio said he felt it was a lot more steady and felt a lot more comfortable. If that's what that role can give the central defenders, it's great. I get more of the ball there, and that means I can play different passes like the ones to Shaun [Wright-Phillips], who has pace to frighten defenders, and Joe Cole and Wayne Rooney. At the end of the day, it is playing for England, so I am happy to go anywhere. But I have made no secret of my feelings about playing in the centre. I feel I am comfortable playing there.'

The England captain had played peacemaker, to no avail, with a fiery Rooney in Northern Ireland a few days later. Rooney was sent off for sarcastically applauding the officials and furiously argued with referee Kim Milton Nielsen – remember him – whilst Beckham tried to calm him down. Rooney, who had now moved to Manchester United, told Beckham to 'fuck off'; the captain very quickly defused the situation after the game. 'Of course there is no fall-out,' he said. 'Me and Wayne have talked a number of times in the last week. The whole thing has been blown out of all proportion. Wayne is not just a team-mate of mine in the England side, but he is a friend. I'd like to think I can be an example. Wayne respects all the senior players in the England team, and all the senior players respect the younger players. And he's got experienced players at United like Roy [Keane] that he can look up to. That's the sort of person he needs to follow. I am sure Sir Alex has got the situation in hand – he gave me a lot of support, as did the players and the fans at United. I have always said that in terms of the support he needs, he couldn't be at a better club. Alex Ferguson doesn't need me to tell him how to handle players. That's what he's good at, he looks after his players.'

But Beckham himself was sent off against Austria; this time it was for two bookable offences. The referee who sent him off this time was Luis Medina Cantalejo – whom Beckham had previously criticised after a 2003 Copa del Rey tie: 'The referee lost his head a little. He had been showing cards to both teams without apparent reason … It couldn't happen in England.'

But it did. Sven-Göran Eriksson defended his captain, who had claimed an unwanted place in history. 'I thought both decisions against David were harsh,' the England boss said. 'He won't be proud of becoming the first England player to be sent off twice, but you have to remember that he has played 85 times for his country and that is a lot of games. I don't want to believe that the fact that this referee has sent him off before was the reason for some bad decisions. If you think that, it is very serious. But I don't think the referee had any such intention.'

Further indiscipline before Christmas, though, suggested there was more to it – even if that was a sense of opportunism from opponents and referees to make a name for themselves. First, Beckham was dismissed in the 87th minute of a home defeat to Valencia, channelling his inner Rooney when he sarcastically applauded referee Arturo Daudén Ibáñez. Real appealed – and were successful – on the grounds that although the act took place, it was not done in a confrontational manner.

In a November international friendly against Argentina, Beckham was the target for what the *Daily Star* described as a 'battering' on the evening he would captain England for the 50th time. He had admitted before the game that history would be dredged up. 'Unfortunately that will always be the case with games against Argentina until I retire,' he said. 'I really don't know why it is. My first season at Real Madrid, every tackle, every booking, any problem, turned out to be an Argentine player, which was bizarre. There has always been a great rivalry between the two teams and, even though friendlies aren't taken as seriously as normal competitive games, Argentina is always going to be a tough match.'

Beckham was fantastic in a 3–2 win, but back in Spain, matters went from bad to worse. Barcelona won 3–0 at the Bernabéu: an incredible victory described as the 'perfect game' by Barça star Ronaldinho. Beckham's performance was described as 'rudderless' by *The Independent*, whilst the dominant criticism and observations from most outlets was centred around the premature demise of the Galactico era.

This time, Luxemburgo would not be able to escape the full force of the blame, which would cost him his job. He would be the fourth coach to be sacked during Beckham's short time with the club, just over two years. 'It is all going off again now, with a lot of different things and even talk of a new manager,' said Beckham. 'The missing ambitions in my career are to win something in Spain and to win something with England. Really, I didn't expect things to turn out in Spain the way they have. When I joined Real it was all about the club and the Galacticos we had. I thought the games would be easy, but they are not. When Barcelona are your closest rivals and they are winning the league, it is hard for the city of Madrid to take. They play beautiful football and have team spirit as well. It wasn't just Ronaldinho who beat us the other night. It was their whole team. Every one of their players ran a lot harder than ours did. Barcelona are strong and have togetherness, which is good for them. The Brazilian national team have that as well, and they have also got five or six other players like Ronaldinho.'

Beckham had reiterated his desire to extend his spell at the club, and even suggested he would retire there. In 2015, he revealed that a deal to continue had been agreed – but in January 2006, Florentino Pérez resigned as president.

'I had a contract for four years and had talks to renew for another four, but Florentino left and there was no agreement with the new president,' Beckham said in 2015.

'I wanted to stay, but when Florentino left, everything went wrong.'

Luxemburgo's last game in charge was actually a 1–0 victory over Getafe. Beckham was remarkably sent off yet again – this time in the 56th minute for a rash challenge following a tussle with Getafe player Riki. 'I think Beckham is having a bad time at the moment,' Luxemburgo said. 'He reacted mistakenly. But to suggest he was seeking a red card is another matter. Perhaps he is trying to do things the wrong way.'

By the end of the evening, the Brazilian manager was out of work. The new coach was Juan Ramón López Caro, who had previously been handling the Madrid 'B' team.

There was a renewed uncertainty about Beckham's future, which seemed to play into speculation in the early part of 2006. The player had given an interview to *Four Four Two* magazine where he said: 'I've always said that, if I had to go back to England, the only club I'd want to go back to is Man United. I started my career at the club and thought I'd end my career there. I'm happy at Real Madrid but you never know what could happen in the future.'

Around the same time, Sven-Göran Eriksson had been the victim of a 'sting' by a Sunday newspaper, which had set him up with someone claiming to be a Sheikh looking to buy Aston Villa. The fake Sheikh said he wanted to hire Eriksson – the Swede had allegedly told him that if he did, he would be able to persuade David Beckham to join the Midland club. Arsenal boss Arsene Wenger also hinted he would be interested if Beckham was available, describing him as a 'wonderful player'.

The midfielder was concentrating on impressing his latest new boss in Spain. And he did just that – scoring a spectacular free kick in a 3–1 win over Cádiz, and earning a rating of '12 out of 10' from López Caro. In February, Beckham spoke about how the new manager had improved the morale and togetherness, but it seemed inevitable that it would be another short-term stint after a 6–1 defeat to Real Zaragoza in the Copa del Rey.

In the second leg, there was a moment of hope. Real were on fire from the first whistle, scoring within 60 seconds and then again in the fifth minute. In the tenth, Beckham provided a sublime pass to Ronaldo: from deep inside-right, the ball was arrowed like a heat-seeking missile, and when it completed the 40-yard journey, it was almost a tap-in for the legendary forward.

In 2020, Ronaldo held an Instagram Live conversation with Beckham where he paid the England midfielder the highest praise.

'For me, and this is the truth, you were one of the best of all time with the centre,' he said. 'The way you would touch the ball, the way you could put the ball wherever you want, and without looking at me, I was just moving and the ball came. I should thank you for the many balls you gave to me.'

On the night, Real made it four but couldn't atone for the first leg. That embarrassment was followed by a Champions League exit to Arsenal. Another second-place finish in La Liga meant three years as bridesmaids. In the last game of the season, Beckham scored two goals at Sevilla, but his team lost 4–3; David was actually substituted early in the second half. According to *Marca*, Beckham 'did not even look at the coach on his way to the locker room'; López Caro would be replaced by Fabio Capello within weeks.

'It's an unusual and strange situation, as it's something that's never happened to me before in my career,' Beckham said in May – standing on the turf of the new Wembley Stadium, which was due to finally open over the coming months, ahead of the 2006 World Cup. 'When I was at United, there was only one year we went without winning anything [it was actually two]. It is a strange feeling, but it also gives you that push to want to go on and try to win something again. I've said that I want to stay in Madrid. I'm happy with my life there, and I just want to win a trophy now. There is always the determination in me to win something. This summer with England would be perfect for that.

We're going to do what we can. The perfect scenario would be returning here to Wembley as world champions. The confidence we've got in each other, and the manager and the players we've got, makes me believe. Possibly it's fair to say it wasn't like it is now in 2002. This time the competition is in Europe, so that's better physically for the team. We have a lot of young players, but also a lot of experienced players who have delivered great performances in big games. That's where the belief comes from. I feel different going into this tournament than before. Physically, I'm going in without any doubts, and no broken bones or anything like that. Mentally, I feel perfect. I am at my peak. Even though we haven't won anything as a club, I've played well this season and have been happy with my own performances. There is more to come from me. There are four or five years left in my career, and that will be as an England player as well as a Real Madrid player. You never know in football, but I would love to think there will be another big tournament for me after this one. I'm going to enjoy this one and, hopefully, be successful in it. But I still want to be playing for England for as many years as possible.'

Beckham had claimed this could be his 'best ever' international tournament and had support, and pressure, from his former manager at Manchester United – who was actually attempting to deflect pressure from Wayne Rooney, who was going into the World Cup with an injury. Sir Alex Ferguson actually spoke with the belief that Rooney would not be going when he said: 'I definitely think there was too much put on the boy's shoulders. Now the emphasis changes. So step forward, Steven Gerrard. Step forward, Frank Lampard. Step forward, Joe Cole – because these guys have all the experience and are older. David Beckham, step forward. These guys have huge experience, David in particular. He's played in World Cups. He's the captain. He's played in a European Cup Final. So Beckham and the others have got the opportunity now to make an impact for England. And it's not a forlorn hope for them. You couldn't say one player was going to decide everything, because a young player can have a bad game. They can lack consistency at such a young age. Therefore the older players have now to step forward.'

They did, but those earlier insinuations that Eriksson did not have the balance of discipline right in his dressing room were returning to haunt him. The January sting had caused the manager to announce he would step down after the tournament. That revelation had come before a friendly against Uruguay at Anfield – Beckham had reacted to the report by telling journalists, 'I was England manager before Sven came, an … er, I mean, I was England captain. Oh, God. I can see the headlines tomorrow!'

Prior to the World Cup in Germany, ITV commissioned Rio Ferdinand – he who missed the previous tournament – to make a television show where he would play practical jokes on his team-mates. The captain wasn't exempt. Beckham's ordeal – and the word is chosen carefully – saw him live his worst nightmare. He was picked up by a car, with the ruse being that he would be chauffeured to a promotional event in Manchester, only to be 'kidnapped'.

Rewatching the footage is an uncomfortable experience. David gets in the car and hides down in the back behind the driver's seat. In one of his many books, he explained how he would do this with his children and say it was a game to not make them fearful. Once the car is on the road, he feels comfortable enough to sit up, but becomes agitated and frustrated when it is clear that the journey is not going to plan. He is sufficiently concerned to jump out of the car at a traffic light in Moss Side and run for his life. There, he is confronted by Rio, who is laughing uncontrollably. Beckham wears a smile – and will respond with dignity when recounting the story for the press the following day.

'It has never happened before, and I hope it never happens again,' he said. 'It was funny once I realised it was Rio, but I never thought for one minute that I was being kidnapped. I just thought I had a real pain-in-the-backside security man. I had a driver taking me somewhere, but the security guy was telling me how he had been arrested that morning and had to go and pick his documents up from the police station on the other side of Manchester – the opposite side to where I was going. On another day I would have said "Not a problem", but I was rushing around trying to get the kids some presents and I was getting annoyed – and then he wouldn't stop the car. So that's when I decided to run for it. We were going through Moss Side and a couple of times he should have stopped. I'm thinking, just turn around. He was saying, "No, no, no I can't do that." It just made me more annoyed. Then I looked behind and there was a camera crew. In Spain that happens all the time. When it's not paparazzi, it's a film crew. I thought that if I got out and ran, they wouldn't catch me. There were two taxis on the other side of the road going into a petrol station, and I knew I had my chance. The car was still moving and I thought "Sod it", so I jumped out and ran across the road for the black cabs. I heard Rio shouting and running behind me, but when I looked back a car must have gone across him so I didn't see him. I just kept running, considering I was in Moss Side! It was funny when I realised it was Rio. Thankfully, an attempted kidnap has never happened to me before and hopefully won't again. There was never a moment when I thought I was actually going to be kidnapped ... but I did say sorry for my bad language. I always thought I would know when it was a set-up, but not this time. Me running for a black cab? The last time that happened was when I was in digs in Manchester.'

One can only imagine what Ferguson would have made of this if the pair had still been team-mates at Old Trafford; it was certainly one of the more ill-advised publicity stunts from Ferdinand who, at 27, could not use immaturity as an excuse. The candid sight of David's genuine concern is deeply unsettling.

To Beckham's credit, he took the incident in good enough humour and did not use it as an excuse to derail his concentration. If this was another tournament that nobody came out of with much credit in the eyes of the press, then Beckham could at least hold his own head high, with arguably his best contribution at a World Cup. It was his free kick after just three minutes of a sweltering opening-day victory over Paraguay which earned England a 1–0 win, even though it was later registered as an own goal.

It was the best way to respond to a remarkably disgusting article written in the German newspaper *Bild* by journalist Tobias Holtkamp, who made disparaging remarks about Beckham's entire family – his kids, his mum and even his sister were considered fair play for insults.

'How could anyone drop that low?' Beckham said. 'I don't really want to give people like this any more publicity than they deserve. It is sad that someone has sat in a room and thought of this stuff. I have come to terms with people having a go at me as a footballer, but when it comes to family, it is one thing I will never take. For some reason, one person has found it funny to criticise my mum, sister and children. I find it sad. I have had a lot of things said about me since the World Cup in 1998 and am prepared for anything. But I can't tolerate this kind of thing about my family. I am not going to let it put me off my football, especially so close to the next game. There are some people out there who are just like this. I am prepared for this type of thing, and I refuse to worry about it. I have always had a great relationship with the German public.'

Holtkamp was quickly backtracking as he faced criticism himself. 'I didn't mean to offend,' he claimed. 'It was a joke. I wasn't calling Beckham's sister a pig, it was a play on words.'

Back to the football. Despite making the crucial contributions in the tournament – that winning goal, and creating the first goal in the win over Trinidad and Tobago which ensured qualification for the knockout stages – Beckham was accused of having a 'patchy' tournament by a reporter who challenged Eriksson about the captain's position in the team. 'I am not married to David Beckham, even if people think I am. I am not even engaged to him,' said Eriksson. 'If I think he's not doing the job, I would leave him out. It is the same with him as all the other players. If I see things are going wrong, I am prepared to do whatever I need to do. Most people think he should be in the team. I've taken him off before. He is the captain, but he is treated the same as all the other players in every way – at the dinner table, on the bus, tactically, in training, in a match. He doesn't have any favours just because he is the captain.'

In the third group game, England drew with Sweden, a game mostly remembered for Michael Owen breaking down with injury after just a few minutes. Owen – who had missed much of the previous season with injury – had confessed that he felt 'incapable of going out and taking any of these games by storm' and that he was 'completely undercooked'.

Beckham, meanwhile, insisted that he was the same as he'd always been. He was once more playing from the right as Eriksson persisted with the Gerrard and Lampard combination in the middle. 'The way to get the best of me is to give me the ball,' he said. 'If I get the ball and I have got a yard of space, I will deliver it to someone to score a goal. I have done that for years – that's my game and that's what I am good at. If I am given the ball, then 99 per cent of the time I'll put it in the right space for people to score goals. I am not going to talk about my form, because I am in a team that are very talented and have a great chance of making the quarters. We're not kidding ourselves. We've lost players and we have had some situations that have not gone right for us. But we are right as a team. The togetherness just could not be any stronger. Barring injury, everything is perfect. There are no excuses this time. And I would not say that if I did not mean it.'

Against Ecuador in the second round, Beckham scored the only goal, and this time it was credited to him: a fine moment for the captain who became the first England player, officially, to score in three World Cups. But he was suffering from heat exhaustion and vomited after scoring, before being brought off in the 88th minute.

There was a premature end to his tournament as a whole in the next game. England were facing Portugal in a repeat of their clash two years earlier. The score was 0–0 in the 52nd minute when Nuno Valente crunched on the ankle of the England captain. Beckham was visibly in tears as he had to be replaced by Aaron Lennon.

Ten minutes later, England's realistic chances of progress were dealt another blow when Wayne Rooney was sent off for an alleged stamp on Ricardo Carvalho. Eriksson's team held on for their perennial penalty-kicks exit.

The morning after the game, Beckham made an emotional announcement to journalists – that he would be resigning from his position as England captain.

'It was the greatest honour of my career, fulfilling my childhood dream,' he said. 'Now, almost six years later, having been captain for 58 of my 95 caps, I feel the time is right to pass on the armband. It has been an honour and a privilege to have captained our country, and I want to stress that I wish to continue to play for England. I came to this decision some time ago, but I had hoped to announce it on the back of a successful World Cup. Sadly that wasn't meant to be. This decision has been the most difficult of my career to date, but, after discussing it with my family and those closest to me, I feel the time is right. I would also like to thank the press, and of course the England supporters, who have been great. Finally, I have lived the dream. I am extremely proud to have worn the armband and been captain of England, and for that I will always be grateful.'

In a scene which would have been simply unthinkable eight years earlier, Beckham stood and left the room to applause from the reporters.

The promise of 2004 felt much more hollow in 2006. It was already clear that Gerrard and Lampard did not appear to have the compatibility which enabled either to replicate their club form – Paul Scholes had retired from international duty too. Goalscoring hopes were placed on the injured legs and feet of Michael Owen and Wayne Rooney. Beckham had predicted better days in 2002 and hoped for them in 2004 – but the truth was that, if he had learned anything by the age of 31, nothing of the future was certain.

Out of the Wilderness

THERE WERE new beginnings on almost every single front for David Beckham as he looked forward to the last year of his contract at Real Madrid. First of all, Fabio Capello arrived at the Santiago Bernabéu, becoming the fifth manager to take charge since his arrival.

The Italian was hired by new club president Ramón Calderón; and this was a new era indeed, as Zinedine Zidane had announced his retirement following the World Cup. Capello was given a handsome transfer kitty and used it to lure some players who were more functional than glamorous – veterans Fabio Cannavaro and Ruud van Nistelrooy still came with lofty reputations after remarkable careers in Italy and England respectively.

There would be some justification for optimism about Beckham's own future, then: as the usual provider of goals for Van Nistelrooy at Old Trafford, he could reasonably expect to be given the chance to repeat the trick. 'Firstly he is a great player, secondly he is a great person and thirdly he is an amazing goalscorer,' Beckham said. 'There was a lot of speculation about him coming to Real Madrid, which always happens. All great players get linked to big clubs all around the world, but it is great to have him here. He is one of the best goalscorers that I have ever played with. He scored many goals from me, and it was great to play in the same team as him at Manchester United. I think that it is good for the team that he is at Real Madrid, and also good for him.'

That good news was swiftly followed by a significant blow. Beckham had insisted he wasn't closing the door on England, but new manager Steve McClaren had made it his first major act to axe the former captain completely – a more bitter blow than it might have otherwise been, considering McClaren's familiarity with David at both club and international levels. John Terry would be the new captain.

'I spoke with David last Monday, and notified him of my decision and said I was planning for the future to change things and go in a different direction and that David wasn't included in that,' McClaren said. 'He was a fantastic captain and still is a great player. He took the news well. He was disappointed, but I got the reaction I wanted. That was for him to continue to fight for a place.'

Beckham later conceded he was devastated. 'I'm gutted not to be part of the England set-up any more, and I was surprised when I got the phone call,' he said in September. 'I am disappointed. I wouldn't lie about it – and it hurts me to watch the England team without me being in it. But I've watched them because I believe in these players and this team. They are an amazing team and an amazing set of players. To be part of that for so many years was an honour. Nothing gets better than pulling on an England shirt and being captain.'

There was, apparently, better news at club level, when Ramón Calderón took it upon himself to announce to journalists that talks on a new contract for Beckham had been concluded. 'His renewal is agreed,' said the new president. 'He's happy here and he wants to continue at Real Madrid. It will be a two-year deal.'

A spokesman for Beckham quickly corrected that statement, saying that talks would continue into September, but things were looking good for an extension. If you're reading between the lines, though, you might have already noted a significant disparity: the length of the deal had been revised from four to two years, which would have surely concerned the player and his representatives.

Noises continued to be positive, but actions spoke louder than words: in the third game of the season, Beckham – who had been playing as a right-winger in Capello's new shape – was dropped and replaced by on-loan José Antonio Reyes, the left-footer who had usually played as a left-sided forward for Arsenal. Reyes scored from a free kick against Real Sociedad before coming off for Beckham in the 70th minute; the English midfielder then gave a timely reminder of his own talent, scoring a breakaway goal in injury time to secure three points.

It was not enough to get back into the starting line-up. Capello's team won at Real Betis and drew at home with Atlético before a defeat at Getafe: all games which Beckham had to watch mainly from the bench. The last game had some significance, as Capello had urged for '50 days' before the public judged his team. Fifty days were up, and even goalkeeper Iker Casillas called the loss to Getafe the 'worst Madrid performance I can remember'.

Despite being used so sparingly, Beckham tried to keep a positive outlook when talking to Spanish media outlet *La Razón* about the new regime. 'It has also been difficult to have had six different coaches in three years,' he said. 'I like Capello because he is the most similar to Ferguson. He is strict in training, in the team hotel, in everything. That is how I like things to be.'

A week later he also spoke about his future: 'I am happy here. My family are happy here. At the moment I play for Real Madrid. Let's hope it carries on. If it gets to January and nothing changes, I am not leaving. I am not going anywhere in January. I want to stay because I believe we can win something this season. My lack of games for Real Madrid is not a reason for me to worry since it's only a question of five or six games at the moment. It will be necessary to see what happens if I go without playing 12 or 13 games.'

Game time was being more and more scarce for the midfielder, though. It was widely tipped that Ronaldo would be allowed to leave in the January transfer window (he did) and that Beckham wouldn't be far behind. He started just two games before Christmas, with no indication that he was seriously back in Capello's plans as a starting player.

Was Beckham truly in decline, and even if so, was that so marked and rapid that it warranted such a public exile for club and country? If he had been below par for Real Madrid since Vanderlei Luxemburgo was hired, then surely he had been as much a victim of the peculiar formation as anyone? Certainly there had been a regular enough supply of free kicks to say he was as capable as he'd ever been; and it was no secret that his game did not depend on pace, and he had not suffered any major injuries, so did not show any real wear and tear. Perhaps Capello had been influenced by McClaren's statement. After all, if someone who had worked with Beckham on and off for more than seven years now deemed him to be not even worthy of a squad place in the national team, could he really be good enough to start for Spain's most glamorous club?

As far as McClaren was concerned, Beckham was an obvious choice for the axe, even if just the merest scrutiny would make the decision seem perplexing. A bold new start was needed to move on from the 'Golden Generation' era, but Steven Gerrard was 26 and Frank Lampard 28, so neither of them would really feel under threat – but McClaren's promising start quickly gave way to underwhelming performances where England didn't score or even really look like scoring in World Cup qualifiers against Macedonia and Croatia. In Croatia, McClaren tried a 3–5–2, and had Lampard, Scott Parker and Michael Carrick in the middle from the start, before he introduced Shaun Wright-Phillips late on. None of the above were able to create anything of note as England lost 2–0.

Meanwhile, Real Madrid's last game before the Christmas break had been a deeply concerning 3–0 home defeat to Recreativo de Huelva. If you were a betting man, you would have surely laid money on Capello being out of a job instead of winning the club's first league title in four years. There had been no upturn in performance that justified dropping Beckham, although it has to be said that there was also no public clamour for his recall, either, even if there were one or two murmurs back in England that McClaren might have been a little bit hasty.

With his contract due to expire at the end of the season, and Madrid still not having agreed anything despite saying it was close, Beckham would be entitled to speak to other clubs and even agree a deal from 1 January. Speculation was rife, if not always logical. Some rumours were based on the idea that Beckham would need to return to England to win back his place in the national team. It was a plausible theory, so even some of the stories floated which look ridiculous in hindsight looked as if they might have something in them at the time. No fewer than seven Premier League teams were rumoured to be interested – Spurs and Arsenal were obvious names due to their location, while Aston Villa, Everton and Bolton seemed unlikely – not as unlikely, though, as West Ham and Liverpool, who both reportedly made enquiries.

Inter Milan were apparently ready to offer £110,000 a week, but a move to Major League Soccer (MLS) in the United States seemed unlikely according to Jane Clinton of the *Express*, who shared this anecdote about the Beckham family's most recent experience in Los Angeles: 'At one party to celebrate Beckham's LA Soccer Academy, the reality of their diminished status hit home when the guests comprised at best C- and D-list stars.

"Victoria was incandescent when she realised the guests were far from stars," added one fellow party-goer. "It was a blow to her that they could not attract bigger names but given her networking skills she will be trying to remedy that as quickly as possible.'"

The start of January came and went; it was as late as the 10th when news quickly began to escalate. It started with speculation of a 'crunch' meeting with Real officials that day, where it was suggested a new deal would be agreed. But it was also revealed that MLS had amended their salary structure specifically to permit the recruitment of players such as the former England skipper – this change was even pointedly dubbed the 'Beckham Rule'. It quickly became apparent that there was more to this than just paper talk.

On 11 January, Beckham issued a statement via his representatives which still managed to catch the football world off guard:

'This week, Real Madrid asked me to make a decision regarding my future and the offer to extend my contract by a further two seasons. After discussing several options with my family and advisers to either stay here at Madrid or join other major British and European clubs, I have decided to join the Los Angeles Galaxy and play in MLS from August this year. I would like to thank the supporters and people of Madrid who have made my family and I feel so welcome in my time here, making this an extremely difficult decision to make. I have enjoyed my time in Spain enormously and I am extremely grateful to the club for giving me the opportunity to play for such a great team and their amazing fans. I am proud to have played for two of the biggest clubs in football and I look forward to the new challenge of growing the world's most popular game in a country that is as passionate about its sport as my own. For the rest of this season I will continue to give 100 per cent to my coach, team-mates and fans as I believe Fabio Capello will bring this club and its supporters the success they truly deserve.'

The day after the announcement, he was on the ABC network's *Good Morning America*, where he insisted that the move was not financially motivated. 'Of course, it's a huge amount of money,' he admitted. 'It's what most people have been talking about actually, over here and in Europe. It's an amazing amount. Some people laughed at me, but I said this move for me is not about the money. It's about making a difference in the US with the soccer, and that's what I'm going there for. I'm going for the life, of course, for my kids to enjoy it and my wife to enjoy it. But the main thing for me is to improve the soccer and improve the standard and be a part of history. I think soccer can be a lot bigger in the US.'

The hype was enough to make David Beckham a renewed figure of interest – certainly in the US, where the reaction was significant and almost universally positive.

Galaxy head coach Frank Yallop (who had previously enjoyed a long career in the UK with Ipswich Town) was excited about the prospect of Beckham joining his team. 'To be able to manage and coach him will be a dream come true for me,' he said. 'He is going to do very well here. He is coming here at the peak of his career. He is ready to make a real impact on and off the field, and we are going to enjoy it. I see him playing centrally in our league. We have to get him on the ball as much as we can, making us tick. It's an athlete's game here, played at a little less pace than the Premiership.'

Timothy J. Leiweke, president of Anschutz Entertainment Group (AEG) – the sports and entertainment company who owned the Galaxy – said: 'David Beckham will have a greater impact on soccer in America than any athlete has ever had on a sport globally. David is truly the only individual that can build the "bridge" between soccer in America and the rest of the world.'

The MLS commissioner, Don Garber, spoke on the transfer. 'Beckham's decision to continue his storied career in Major League Soccer is testament to the fact that America is rapidly becoming a true "Soccer Nation" with Major League Soccer at the core,' he said. 'As importantly, David's enormous success as a player and team leader will serve as an inspiration to millions of soccer players and fans in this country, and his global popularity will help take MLS and the sport of soccer in this country to an unprecedented level of excitement and popularity here and abroad.'

Rodney Marsh – who, remember, had doubted whether Beckham would even match Steven Gerrard or Michael Owen – was now performing an about-turn: 'Becks will be like the Pied Piper. It will be like the Harlem Globetrotters or whatever you care to name. He will be the Pelé of the new millennium. He is a world icon, and in America they love their stars. They already love Beckham, and they will grow to love him more. It's an unbelievable coup. I've heard some people suggesting that he's not well known in the States. That's nonsense. They adore him. They might not know say, Alan Shearer for example, but they know Beckham. We are about to see David Beckham's face everywhere in America.'

British players who had already made that journey had mixed feelings. Paul Dalglish, son of Liverpool legend Kenny, could not have been more encouraging. 'Some of the players might say he shouldn't be getting that money, but I think he is worth every penny,' he said. 'David Beckham has proved himself at the very, very highest level. He is the biggest soccer star in the world, and if you want to promote your league and there is one player you can pay more than everyone else, then David Beckham is the person to get. One thing you can never accuse David Beckham of is a lack of effort. He works harder than anybody the moment he steps over the line, and I'm sure he'll do the same in America. LA is a great city, and the best thing for David Beckham is that it's probably the only place where he can go and blend in, because there are that many superstars there and he can live a normal life.'

It was surprising, then, that when there was a dissenting voice, it came from someone who used to share a dressing room with him. Terry Cooke – a member of the youth team at United which followed the class of '92 – described the financial aspect of the move as a 'disgrace'. 'Obviously it's good for him, but we have a salary cap here for each team … for a roster of 28 players,' Cooke explained. 'I love Becks to bits. He's a great player – we lived together in Manchester – and it's not his fault. I heard that the salary cap might be raised by a few hundred grand for next season. But even so, it doesn't matter who it is: you can't justify paying one player that sort of money [around $6.5m a year, which didn't count towards the salary cap].'

That is where the cynical opinion came in. Maybe MLS and the Galaxy could justify it – but, according to *Los Angeles Times* columnist Bill Plaschke, it would be in somewhat bad taste. Plaschke wrote: 'You want to sell soccer in America? Vend it like Beckham. Arguably the world's most famous athlete is coming, but there's something you should know. David Beckham is not joining the Galaxy as an athlete, but as an advertising campaign. He is coming as soccer swag, a walking Super Bowl commercial, a big-haired billboard. His job is not to win, but to give his sport one last chance to work in the biggest place where it doesn't.'

The *New York Post* carried an image of Beckham on the front page, whilst the *Boston Globe* stated: 'Not since the Beatles has there been a British invasion of this magnitude.'

Whatever the motivation, there was already a significant impact – television rights for MLS reportedly jumped from just £100,000 to over £10m overnight, according to the *Express*. The American public apparently could not wait for the chance to see Beckham play football. That appetite was not shared by Real Madrid boss Fabio Capello and president Calderón, who were so furious with the player's decision to not only leave, but make the announcement on his own terms, that they initially insisted he would not play again for the Spanish club. 'The decision of the player is to go to Los Angeles,' Capello said. 'He is a great professional, but he has such an important contract with another club, and therefore he will continue to train with us, but he is not going to play.'

Asked if Real would be willing to permit Beckham to leave sooner than the end of his contract, Capello said pointedly: 'You will have to ask Beckham. He must decide what to do until the end of the season. I have never had the smallest problem with Beckham, but I believe one cannot have the same desire when you have another team.'

Capello would have presumably expected a similarly smooth exit plan for Beckham as he had experienced with Ronaldo. They were the two remaining Galacticos (Roberto Carlos technically qualifies, but this was a term used for the superstar signings of the era), survivors of a laboratory experiment which started spectacularly but spiralled out of control – arguably the two players who personified the worst of the era, objectively speaking. Ronaldo was signed after a stunning World Cup in 2002, but was not the player he had been four years earlier when it seemed he may go on to be the best ever.

And, at the time of his signing, Beckham was deemed – even by the existing Galacticos – to be a signing of style over substance. Ronaldo went and Beckham was left as a wonderful dichotomy. Still the highest-profile name in world football (there were two young stars at Manchester United and Barcelona about to battle for that distinction), and yet something of a relic, an anachronism – the last remaining example of Real's dysfunctional recent past, a present reminder in the dressing room of the reason for recent failures. Not for the first time in his career, Beckham was suffering by reputation.

By any measure, his time in Madrid had not been as successful as his spell at United. The trophies, of course. But performance, too. In every full season he played at Old Trafford, he scored at least eight goals, but his most productive in that regard at Madrid had been seven in his first season, with just four and five in the seasons since.

There was some resentment in Madrid. Beckham was supposed to leave gracefully and on Real's terms. Ramón Calderón didn't hold back when he gave a speech to university students that was broadcast on the radio station Cadena COPE.

'His representatives have toyed with us for the last two months,' he said. 'Whenever his representatives met Predrag Mijatović [Real's sporting director], they never informed him or the club that he had agreed a contract with another club. They never told us that Beckham had made his decision. I don't feel that it's right and I certainly don't like it. I don't like the way Beckham has acted, publicly announcing that he was going to another club, doing it with a video conference. David Beckham will be an average cinema actor living in Hollywood. The proof that our technical team was right in not considering his continuity has been ratified by every single technical team in the world, because no one, with the player having been free, has wanted him.'

The Galaxy, and MLS, had made such a significant financial commitment – rumoured by Forbes to be a five-year contract worth a total of up to £125m in salary and endorsements – that a transfer fee to buy him out of his remaining contract was out of the question. Madrid, their pride hurt, were not about to be benevolent, so it was decided that Beckham would see out his contract in Spain. If he wanted to play again, it would need a turnaround of epic proportions. Luckily, David had form for such matters.

It was also fortunate that Beckham remained a hugely popular figure in the dressing room. Calderón's comments were met with anger from the Real players, and the president was forced to hold a meeting with them – led by Raúl – where he apologised. He later said sorry on Real Madrid's official television channel too: 'I want to apologise a thousand times to anyone that might have been offended.'

'Everyone came out with a good feeling, although some team-mates felt more upset than others,' said Raúl. 'We want the problems to be resolved internally, so that there are not different messages, and everything that needs to be said to improve things is done so internally.'

The resolve of the players left an impression on Capello. The manager conceded that he may have been hasty to dismiss the former United player from his plans completely. 'We have to see,' he said. 'The idea that we have now is the one that you know. It is necessary to be flexible sometimes. Beckham is a great professional who always trains with a great desire. Ideas can be changed.'

David was carrying an injury, so might not have been available for selection anyway, and Mijatović told the press that the number of promising young players at the club might restrict his chances when he was fit. But Beckham's cause was certainly helped by Real's results after the Christmas break. Defeats to Levante and Villarreal put the pressure on.

When Capello took his team to face Real Sociedad, Beckham was not only back in the squad but back in the team – and, better yet, back on the scoresheet. Sociedad were leading 1–0, when Madrid earned a free kick around 25 yards out. To the right of goal, this was a position Beckham had scored from many times before; this time, the execution was not quite as spectacular, but the value of the technique was evident and the result was the same. Goal. Once more for David Beckham, it was a case of years of practice making perfect at just the right time.

'This is almost fairy-tale stuff,' said former England and United midfielder Ray Wilkins, commentating on the game, as the Real team flocked around Beckham in celebration. 'Look at the players. That's the reaction you're looking for when you've been left out of the team. If you're causing a few problems at the club, players won't come anywhere near you. They couldn't get to him quick enough. He's obviously a very popular character.'

Real won 2–1, and Beckham's popularity was tested, and proven, again the following week. Capello – whose own position was under threat – confessed that Beckham was now back in the fold. 'At first we doubted that he could train and play with the same desire after having signed such a big contract,' he said. 'But a few weeks ago I started to see that he was working hard. This week he has trained perfectly. He has been better than good. He has always had the support of his team-mates, and he has behaved as a great professional.'

Asked if he regretted saying he would never pick the midfielder again, he said: 'Intelligent people are those who are able to make good a mistake.'

David was in from the start against Real Betis, but the game ended 0–0. He didn't last the 90 minutes – this time his ejection from the field was caused by the referee. Beckham believed he had been fouled on the edge of the area and reacted by scything down José Isidoro. Referee César Muñiz Fernández immediately sent him off. Proving Wilkins' theory, though, the club immediately backed the player. 'The sending-off of Beckham was a clear passage of play,' said Predrag Mijatović. 'We received a clear foul, and it turned into a sending-off for our player. A [Betis] player, on a yellow, elbows Robinho and the referee, who is half a metre away, does nothing. I don't know what has happened, but I have the feeling the referees are against us. There were plays and cards that I did not understand, nor does anybody. We are not going to complain, but it is necessary to highlight it. We have always remained quiet, but the time has come to say something.'

Mijatović was talking about Beckham again ahead of the Champions League game with Bayern Munich. 'His exemplary behaviour made us reconsider, and now he's playing again,' the sporting director said. 'He does everything he can to help the team. We're counting on him until the end of the season.'

Beckham was outstanding against Bayern – one of his best games in four years, setting up two goals in a 3–2 win. The performance caught the attention of Steve McClaren, who suggested the exiled star would be considered for upcoming qualifiers against Israel and Andorra. 'We have four weeks before the squad is announced, and we will see what happens,' the England boss said. 'He is performing well for his club – obviously that's a problem I would rather have than not have. He has always bounced back from every adversity in his career. It's pleasing to see that a month ago he would never play for Real Madrid again and there he is starring in a game against Bayern Munich and being man of the match.'

Just when things were looking up, adversity struck another blow – this time in the form of an advertising board. Beckham smashed into one during Real's draw with Getafe, damaging his knee ligaments. He would be out for a month.

In the meantime, the Los Angeles Galaxy were preparing to kick off their MLS season, and Beckham's presence was being felt even though he was thousands of miles away. His image was used on tickets for the opening game of the campaign against FC Dallas, even though it would be a few months until he was able to play for the team. The Galaxy had also announced that they would be changing their club colours – their traditional green and gold outfit would be replaced with an all-white one, mimicking that of Real Madrid. 'Given that David's arrival is a major chapter in the club's history and knowing his reputation as a metrosexual, it has been decided that the club kit should have a whole new look,' a 'team mole' told the *Express*.

Beckham was back on the bench for the visit of Valencia on 21 April; coming on to replace Gonzalo Higuaín as the right-sided attacking midfielder in a 4–2–3–1. Within six minutes, he created the winning goal for Sergio Ramos. The contribution earned a recall to the starting line-up against Athletic Bilbao the following week, and this time the Beckham–Ramos connection opened the scoring in a 4–1 win. An accumulation of yellow cards meant a one-match suspension, but Beckham was straight back in, and back to business, with another assist in another win, this time for Robinho, as his team won 3–2 at Huelva.

With three games remaining, Real had pushed themselves back into the title race. And Beckham had pushed himself back into the England squad.

'His form is good,' McClaren said on 27 May. 'I know that David can help us win in Estonia. You can never close the door on anybody. You can't do it to David or the likes of David James, Sol Campbell, Nicky Butt, Paul Scholes, etc. You always have to keep an open mind, because you might need these players.'

McClaren said that Beckham had come back into consideration following a defeat in a friendly against Spain in February: 'We reassessed where we were after that game. We felt things needed changing, and David came into the reckoning then for the next games against Israel and Andorra. Unfortunately he got injured, so it's certainly not a panic measure to bring him back.'

The England boss was asked if Beckham was a better player now than he had been when he was dropped. Now 32, of course, the point was there was nothing new to know about the midfielder, whether that be praise or criticism. 'It's a good question,' McClaren admitted. 'It's subject to opinion, subject to people's eyes, how they view it. The most important thing is me picking a squad with players capable of beating Estonia.'

He was asked again, as the diplomatic avoidance route was not accepted. 'I wouldn't go back on my decision to leave him out at the time,' he insisted. 'I did say that the door was left open and I meant it. David will bring experience. He has played for Real Madrid with a great attitude and hunger. He looks fit and is performing well. He was disappointed to be left out after the World Cup, but he has fought back by being professional.'

The international recall presented an unexpected complication across the Atlantic. The Galaxy believed they had acquired a player whose England days were behind him – now that they weren't, it was suggested that the different time of the football season in the US (running from spring to autumn) would mean that Beckham might have to return to Europe to play regularly in the winter, and to also play at a higher level.

LA Galaxy president, and US soccer legend, Alexi Lalas, insisted that there were no issues – although his stance did already seem a little optimistic. 'I don't think fitness is a problem. I would argue it is much more physically taxing than other leagues,' he said. 'Having said that, we understand we are still a developing league. But I refuse to think a player cannot come to Major League Soccer and develop as well, if not better, than in other leagues in the world. If he is lucky enough to be called up while he is playing with the Galaxy, I believe England will be getting a player who is physically and mentally fit and going through a unique experience that is ultimately going to make him a better player. But he probably can't win either way. If he misses a cross or doesn't score a goal, people will say it's because he is playing for the Galaxy. If he does do well, people will say it is because he is a brilliant player and it doesn't matter where he is playing. From a business perspective, it is not the greatest news, because we are selling the team with David Beckham and a lot of people are excited to see him play with the Galaxy. We will deal with it from a business perspective, but for us to say one of our players is representing England internationally is a great thing. I don't want to stand in the way of a player representing his country, but we have to be prudent and understand they have to be the appropriate games. I would think they would have to be competitive matches. If it works out scheduling wise, we would be happy to let him go.

But he has a responsibility on and off the field to our organisation and to our support. He recognises that responsibility to the Galaxy and to the sport in the United States. I represented my country and I know what it means. It is something above money, it is something you take with you for ever. I would never stand in the way of a player doing that as long as it is reasonable.'

Before the game with Estonia, England were christening the opening of the new Wembley Stadium with a friendly game against Brazil. Beckham started and gave a performance worthy of the headlines he was stealing – first hitting a free kick narrowly wide, and then creating a goal for new captain John Terry (who, before the game, had revealed that Beckham had called him one or two times a week to give support). Brazil levelled late on to get a draw, but this was Beckham's day – he was substituted in the 77th minute to a standing ovation.

He was outstanding against Estonia, too, setting up a goal in a 3–0 win before coming off injured in the 68th minute. He faced a race against time to be fit for the penultimate game of the La Liga season against Real Zaragoza, but made it; Capello's team knew that if they at least matched Barcelona's results, they would win the title. Ruud van Nistelrooy scored a late equaliser in a 2–2 draw – they were relieved to hear that Espanyol had done the same at the Nou Camp to earn the same result. It was a crucial moment in the destiny of the title. A win for Madrid on the final day of the season would see them finally regain the title they had last won in 2003.

Beckham looked forward to what was sure to be a memorable occasion, whatever the outcome. 'My last game will be on Sunday,' he said. 'There is no clause in the contract with the LA Galaxy saying things could be changed. Everyone knows my last game is on Sunday. In four years here, the people and the fans have been incredible, but I had to make a decision because after my contract expired on June 30, it was not going to be renewed and my option was to go to the United States. I could have stayed at Real Madrid for two or three years, for the rest of my career, but things happen. I have lots of respect for the president and Capello, who is one of the best coaches in the world. I respect him, but my Real Madrid career will be over on Sunday. Many things have happened since I signed for LA Galaxy, many things have happened since I signed for Real Madrid. There have been a lot of presidents, a lot of managers and a lot of players. But I will never criticise anyone. Things have happened here that are different to Manchester United, many things are different to those at Manchester United, but Real Madrid is the biggest club in the world and it has been an honour. Hindsight is a strange thing – my life and career six or eight months ago were different to what they had been before and to what they are now. I was told I would be leaving, and I made the decision to go to Los Angeles. I said I would end my career at Real Madrid, but I also said I would never leave Manchester United: things change in football and in life. This has possibly been the most difficult year of my career both on and off the field. 1998 was difficult, but this season I have experienced things I never thought possible, not to be involved in training and matches, and to have people saying things that were not true. But I will be sad to leave and it will be emotional on Sunday. I've had a lot of friends, not just my family, not just my English friends, but I've had a lot of other friends who have given me so much support while I've been at Real Madrid, and especially this season. I haven't won anything in four years and, hopefully, I can change that. My best memory so far was signing for Real Madrid. I'm hoping that will change when my memories here will be taken to another level by winning something.'

Close friend Roberto Carlos was also being allowed to depart that summer. He had enjoyed considerable success compared to Beckham (though he had arrived at the club much earlier) – three league titles, three European Cups and two Intercontinental Cups

– but had of course shared in the drought of the last four years. 'David's as sad as I am about leaving the best club in the world,' the full-back said. 'He's a great player and a wonderful human being. No words can describe what he has done for Real in his time in Spain. His contribution in the last couple of months has been vast and has got us to where we are today – 90 minutes away from being champions. David has been struggling with his injury. I'm no doctor, but I know he will play. He won't contemplate not playing one last time. We all want him to play. We are desperate for David to leave Real Madrid with the piece of silver he deserves. It's very hard to make me cry, but I feel myself and David will shed a few tears when we both say our goodbyes to the Real Madrid fans.'

And Raúl – the alpha club legend who had, in those early days even prior to Beckham joining, experienced the increase in attention that he would bring to even Real Madrid – now spoke with fondness too. 'We have to say goodbye, and we want to join the fans in enjoying watching him play for one last time in a Real Madrid shirt,' he said. 'And for him to leave the best way possible – winning the La Liga title. That's what David deserves after all he has done for this great club.'

Finally, you could add Fabio Capello to those who had perhaps been guilty of an incorrect presumption. 'He has been, and is, a great player, but in the last few months he has recovered his mental and physical condition and without doubt he is among the best players I have trained,' the Italian said. He went on to discuss the matter further with *AS*: 'We all made mistakes over Beckham. The sporting staff decided things, and I'm responsible for that section of the club, but the truth is, we got things wrong with him. It's a shame he's going. He has now recovered his best physical and psychological form. He is a great player and is now playing as he did when he was at Manchester United.'

There was a real sense of occasion at the Bernabéu for the final game. Movie star Tom Cruise was in attendance, providing a response to those pre-Christmas 'D-list' jabs by the press. This might have been a farewell for Roberto Carlos too, but Beckham was the main target of affection from the Madrid fans – his name was cheered the loudest as it was announced that he would be starting, and there was a banner which urged him to 'Get divorced and stay at Madrid'.

The drama of the sport took over. Barcelona raced into an early lead at Gimnàstic, scoring three times without reply in the first half. Mallorca, who clearly hadn't read the script, scored in the 17th minute. There was the indication that Beckham – as he had done against Greece – was warming up to have a significant say in proceedings. Within 60 seconds of Real falling behind, Beckham had a free kick saved. Early in the second half, another shot struck the crossbar. He was just finding his range when, on the hour mark, he began to succumb to the ankle injury which had been causing him such discomfort. In the 66th minute, he could continue no more.

He was replaced by José Antonio Reyes, who scored twice (and should arguably have been sent off) as Real mustered a second-half fightback with the sort of backbone they had been accused of lacking in recent years. Barcelona won 5–1, but it wasn't enough: Capello's team won 3–1, and had won the title.

'I couldn't have dreamt it any better,' Beckham generously said afterwards, presumably referring to the title win rather than the evening. 'It's been about winning the title for the last six months – and we've deserved it tonight. It's been an incredible experience, but all I remember now is the great things. Winning this tonight now puts to bed everything else.'

The success might not have been enough on its own to recalibrate the entire story of the past four years, but it was enough to ensure Beckham's spell in Spain would not be written off as a failure. There was also a certain significance in the manner of the league title victory. David had outlasted the other Galacticos, and the ethos of the club had changed with a frustrated desire to become the best team in Spain again. The title had been won by showing determination and perseverance when all seemed lost – qualities that Real Madrid were not really renowned for. Qualities Beckham possessed in spades, but which had gone overlooked for years because of unfair judgements based on his reputation and profile. At the ages of 31 and 32, he had shown incredible professionalism to come back and play a crucial role in Madrid saving their season, when it was expected that he would coast through the remainder of his contract.

In many ways, this six-month journey to repair his own reputation was more crucial to Beckham than the period after the 1998 World Cup. Then, nobody doubted his quality. Now, he had been effectively written off. The news of him moving to America had been welcomed even more than it would have been, as the transfer was so much earlier than would have been expected – to buck the trend of facing accusations of being over the hill. It would therefore be a major coup for MLS. That, however, had backfired, due to Beckham's marginalisation from first-team action for club and country, and even if that small matter would have been glossed over by the excited Americans awaiting his arrival, there was a small matter of personal integrity. That integrity *was* the difference between the perception of the move – that Beckham was edging into semi-retirement with patronising well-wishes – and the reality that there was a raised eyebrow as if to say, 'Wait a minute, you still have so much more to give.' And not only more to give, but you also still possess a rare quality nobody else at the highest level can replicate as consistently as you can.

Madrid officials conceded that they had looked into options for cancelling the transfer; but, as expected, the Galaxy and MLS were not willing to play along. That in itself was a sure sign indeed that the Los Angeles side had secured themselves a bona fide world superstar.

Top to Bottom

FROM CHAMPIONS of Spain to struggling at the bottom of the table. That was the realistic scenario facing David Beckham as he arrived in the United States to finally play for the Los Angeles Galaxy.

The Galaxy had been founded in 1996 and had a strong reputation as one of the west coast's top teams. They had finished in first place in the Western Conference five times, won two MLS Cup finals and reached a further three (the MLS Cup Final is the league's title decider, coming at the end of the play-offs). Their location alone made them the glamour franchise in the competition, but in 2007 there was a desperate need for that position to be justified. If there was a famous name in US soccer worldwide, then surely the New York Cosmos were it; they were defunct after the NASL folded, but there had been enquiries made by the New York/New Jersey MetroStars, before they became the New York Red Bulls in 2006, to resurrect the old Cosmos name. Peppe Pinton, de facto owner of the Cosmos brand, rejected these enquiries but was eventually encouraged to kick-start the club into a rebirth. There was a pressure on the Los Angeles Galaxy to step up a gear.

David Beckham had only been transferred once in his career. That transfer took place between the two football clubs with the highest profiles in the world, at a time when he was the highest-profile player in the world. There was an argument that all three entities remained that way in 2007, which made Beckham's decision to move to the United States a confusing one indeed. He was 32, and naturally fit.

A move to America had long been tipped for him, encouraged and facilitated by Beckham himself. There were the promotional world tours, and even comments made to that end back in 2004. 'It's one thing I've always said I would like, to go to America, and play in their league,' he had said in a television interview for ESPN at the start of his second season in Spain. 'It would be nice to do that.'

There could be no doubting the sincerity of his words or intention, but it would have been considered a more normal move if he had been older. A number of incidents aligned to accelerate the move. The more obvious and recent ones included his marginalisation from the first team at club and country levels. For the first time in his career, Beckham's confidence had been hit by the implication that he was not good enough to start. This had followed from the blow of Florentino Pérez leaving as president of Real Madrid. The informal agreement on a contract extension would have been made official in early 2006, long before David was free to talk to other clubs. Pérez was gone, and so was the contract.

But the first event to set the wheels in motion was even earlier than that: in the summer of 2005, when David opened his soccer school in Los Angeles. That was done in association with AEG, the Galaxy's owners – according to Alexi Lalas, there was hope of a future working relationship.

'None of it happens without groundwork,' Lalas says. 'Some of it is time and some of it is people. So the relationship with David Beckham – and when I use the term "David Beckham", it is not just the individual, it's the machine, if you will – started early on with the Anschutz Entertainment Group where we facilitated his camps. That was an initial relationship which was fostered with the ... I don't know if I would call it an understanding, but definitely a hope, that at some point the stars would align and we could create a seminal moment not only for the Galaxy but for the league and for soccer. Then it was just a matter of timing. There were three major players – Phil Anschutz, because none of this gets done without money. Then you have Tim Leiweke, who was a visionary. He had a belief that it needed to be done and that it could be done. The third was a man named Shawn Hunter who went about establishing and enabling the "Beckham Rule", which became the Designated Player Rule but started with David because the mechanism for doing something like that just didn't exist. We knew his time at Real Madrid was coming to an end and they were looking to do something big. We were there with a lot of money, but also an emerging market that from a brand perspective must have been appealing. That was the setting for it. We got lucky in terms of where David was in terms of his career, and also because it was a time when European teams didn't look at the Galaxy as any type of competition.'

This was a shot in the arm to Beckham: the shock of the move, coming at a time when there was still an active conversation about how wise it was for him to be axed from his respective teams, and also with the move happening much earlier than would have been expected – these elements combined to generate an even greater buzz. Some of it was negative – there was, inevitably, the suggestion from some that he was entering a forced, early retirement – but this was answered by his form in the last few months in Spain, so that when he did move to MLS, the Los Angeles Galaxy were not acquiring damaged goods. They were getting the real deal – David Beckham, the world's most well-known footballer, when his stock was high and there was an even greater appreciation for his usually unsung contributions.

'We needed to do something big and bold for the team and for the league. I still maintain to this day that there was nobody who could do that in the way that David Beckham did, and there's nobody today who could do that,' Lalas explains. 'Even if we were to sign Messi or Ronaldo, as big as they would be, David transcended the actual game. We had people interested in our team, in our league and in our brand, who had never been interested in soccer, let alone Major League Soccer. We paid for it and it was worth every penny.'

Worth more than every penny, some might argue. The coverage of the news led to sensational interpretations of how much David would be paid. Much of this was exaggerated, but as far as the Galaxy were concerned, the more outlandish the reports, the better. 'It wasn't a charity mission, and nor should it have been,' says Lalas. 'We were looking to secure that level of stardom and therefore the value that comes with that. We knew that it was going to cost us. We weren't going to complain about the numbers that were being reported, because that made us look good. It was always about a fight for relevancy, and when you are talking about these types of players and numbers, your relevancy increases. It wasn't all about the money, but it was an important component, certainly in terms of what it represented, domestically and internationally.'

There were some concerns – one was that Madrid might try to destroy that relevancy before it had come into being. Lalas confirms that the Spanish club had shown 'reticence' over their decision to allow Beckham's contract to wind down, and that they had even tried to discuss the matter with the Galaxy, but David himself had reassured officials at the American team that he would not go back on his word and he was looking forward to it.

Lalas, having played 96 international games, was as qualified as anyone to make a serious assessment of Beckham's ability and the type of player he was. Would his style of play be sufficient to genuinely attract supporters to the spectacle of soccer? 'It was, honestly, a concern,' Lalas confesses. 'David would be the first to admit he wasn't the greatest player to ever play the game. He didn't dribble a ball like a Ronaldo or Messi. He did some things spectacularly well. His work ethic was never in question. He was never a problem from an off-the-field perspective or in the locker room. There was a question of whether he could do those spectacular things on a regular enough basis to get supporters into and on the edge of their seats. He wasn't an individual who was going to dribble through an entire team, he wasn't a massive goalscorer. Some of the things he was going to do were going to be under-appreciated.'

Beckham was likely to make his debut for the Galaxy in a friendly against Chelsea in July. Jose Mourinho, manager of the Blues, spoke about the impact he expected David to make: 'Americans can answer better than me. What I do know is the objective is to bring soccer in the US up, and they couldn't choose a better player for that. David Beckham is more than just a player in terms of what he means to the world of football. He brings a lot of attention behind him, so if the objective is to improve the Galaxy team, then for sure, he is a better player than what they have. I tell you, I would love to work in this country. It is amazing. It is a big challenge to help soccer become more important in this country. This is a sports country, for sure, but everybody else knows that the "hand" games are in front of the "foot" games. Basketball and so on, everything is in front for cultural reasons. This is a big challenge, but he is the one to do it, the best one. European football will miss him, because he showed more than enough quality to play the European game. But for the objectives of him to come here, he's the perfect player. I believe other players will follow him. In 20 years this could all be different. He is at the end of his career as a player; at the end of my career as a manager I would love to come here.'

Mourinho's prediction had already come true. Abel Xavier, the former Liverpool and Everton defender, had joined up with the Galaxy, and it seemed that there was a key reason for that. 'Beckham can make the difference, because David is a huge figure, not just in England but in Europe,' Xavier said. 'Everybody is very excited. I am very excited because I played many times against him. I spoke with him to make a decision to come here, and I am very pleased. I have already been here for three weeks, and I have a very positive impression. But, of course, with the arrival of David, everything will be maximised – the expectations of the fans and the media. I thought to myself, "If David Beckham makes a decision to come, why shouldn't I?" It's very simple to analyse. When you want to have good feedback, the player is very important, and David knows the place. He has seen it a few times, he knew the people here and he was basically positive about the lifestyle and the project. When he said, "I'd like you to join," it was an easy decision.'

The attention given to the transfer had given some preparation for what was to occur when David Beckham finally arrived in the country, but *some* was not enough. 'There was the sports and the mainstream press all covering the story from January, and David wasn't even there,' Lalas recalls. 'So it was the likes of me talking to journalists about the move in the best and most positive of lights. When he actually arrived in the middle of the year, that was a whole other level of craziness the likes of which our league had never seen, and certainly our team had never seen. That's when our lives started to change. It was unlike anything you could experience. It's like a hurricane. Brand Beckham was like a storm, and every single person at the Galaxy – the team, the coaching staff, the office – this was new to us. There was some collateral damage. Some got fired, myself included. My priority was the brand of the Galaxy. But then the brand of Beckham came in that is not only as big and important, but even more so. The balance was difficult to achieve and maintain. There's no road map, nobody you can call. I made a living from kicking a ball, but also because of an image and aesthetics. I understood from an early age that I was a performer and I was in the entertainment business. I could only marvel at, and appreciate, and respect, the way David was able to manage and maximise that aspect of it. I looked at it as a positive. As far as getting the bang for our buck was concerned, as soon as he got off the plane in Los Angeles he knew his responsibilities were greater than just kicking a ball. He never shirked them.'

One of those responsibilities was to make it on to the field against Chelsea on 21 July. He had still not recovered from his ankle problem, so could only make the bench, but was determined to ensure the 27,000 capacity crowd at the Home Depot Center got to see their new man in action. It had been a miserable MLS campaign so far – just three wins from 12 games saw them second bottom of the Western Conference. But against one of the best teams in Europe, the Galaxy put in an admirable performance, losing only 1–0. Beckham made what could comfortably be described as a cameo appearance in the 78th minute, but was clattered almost straight away by new Chelsea midfielder Steve Sidwell, who was clearly equally keen to make an impression. 'Obviously I knew it was him, but it was just like any other tackle for me,' Sidwell said after the game. 'I went into it fully committed. When he went down and stayed down, there was a slight skip of my heartbeat, but I didn't really touch him so I wasn't really too worried. We got up and had a little laugh and a joke afterwards – there were no problems. I don't know about nailing him. It could have been worse. We were not told by the gaffer to take it easy on him. We've come out here to win the game, which we've done. That means to be fully committed in every challenge and every pass.'

Beckham was relieved to get through it unscathed, but did not complain about Sidwell's competitive edge. 'I saw him coming and I jumped just in time,' he said. 'My foot wasn't actually planted when he hit me, but you expect that in games whether they're friendlies or not. He's a competitive player, a good player who has done well in the Premiership, and now he's playing for a club like Chelsea so you know he's going to want to smash some people along the way, even if it's in friendlies. Unfortunately it was me tonight, but it's fine. That's part of being a footballer. The ankle has swollen up slightly, but that was going to happen anyway.'

David admitted that he hadn't even had time to properly meet his new team-mates. 'I haven't trained all week or kicked a ball all week,' he said. 'The decision to play was made this morning. I came in and we decided there was no way I could start. I'd play some part in the match, but, with me not training all week, not even kicking a football and not even really running – all I've done is deep massage and treatment – the decision was really late on. It was just nice to be out there with the lads and to get this game over and done with. I've enjoyed it. I wanted to be out there tonight. The reaction to me when I took my top off or kicked the ball has been incredible. It makes me feel a little bit embarrassed sometimes when I get that sort of reaction. But it's incredible. It was very emotional.'

Jose Mourinho felt that the Galaxy players had raised their game for the occasion. 'LA played the game with a lot of passion; I think maybe they wanted to show David Beckham they have a team,' he said. 'They were highly motivated and they gave us a hard game. I think this is the correct attitude to play football. If they continue doing this, they will get results and they will improve.'

John Terry, scorer of the match-winner, said he believed that Beckham would be 'one of the first names on the squad list' when the next international squad was announced. That was something the Galaxy were keen on, too – they felt Beckham playing for England would be a 'positive in our push for relevancy'. But more immediately, they were eager for their new star to settle in.

'He came in injured, which was a problem for a number of reasons,' Lalas says. 'There was a pressure and anticipation and a desire to live up to the expectations. There could never be a question about David's work ethic once he gets on the field. The other players were quick to realise that this player could provide them the ball in a way that others were not able to. This guy who could open up our game in a way we have not been able to before. The free kick part of the equation is legendary, but the accuracy of his passing and his long-ball game were extra benefits. He was coming to a new culture, a new way of life, a new dressing room, and to his credit he saw the responsibility to adjust as his. Perhaps the Real Madrid experience, where he was a stranger in a strange land, helped him. We didn't want him to be something that he's not, but at the same time, the locker room wasn't going to change for him.'

The game had undergone significant changes since Beckham made his professional debut in 1992, and even since 2003, when he moved to Real Madrid. He had been an unsung pioneer of one of those changes, which was in attitudes to training and self-improvement. Double sessions and staying behind were now the norm; maximising your potential in an increasingly athletic sport was seen as one of the basic common-sense requirements. Lalas: 'David did extra work, as did everyone. He wasn't doing anything we hadn't seen before, or anything extra to anyone else. If there was an awe about him, it was his ability and his accuracy, but from his fitness and attitude there wasn't a marked impression that any of the players hadn't seen before. That's not a knock on him, by the way. That's just the way the game had evolved and attitudes had changed.'

This much is corroborated by Bryan Jordan, who joined the Galaxy in 2008. 'In training, David was just one of the guys,' Jordan says. 'Although he was quiet a lot of the time, he did really well mixing and mingling with all the groups of players, the older and young alike, which I thought was pretty cool, and different than a lot of other big players I came across. He worked hard in training in the way in which a starter would ... I would say maybe not as hard as me, but that's just the kind of player I was, and I was usually trying to win a spot. We practised in the heat often, with shorter practices, so it had to be short and sharp. I would say he definitely stood out in possession drills and with the skilled stuff. As far as staying after practice ... a lot of the young guys at that time would come early and leave late. He would, from time to time, stay after, but when Bruce Arena was our coach we would focus a lot on set pieces at the end of training and especially at the end of the week closer to game time. That's when David would take tons of free kicks as we worked on marking, walls and clearing the ball. So I would say a lot of David's free-kick training time was almost incorporated into our training.'

There were small things he was doing to make an impression. He still arrived half an hour earlier than expected when meeting his new team-mates for the first time. There was some apprehension on all sides, not least because of how the financial disparity might impact relationships. Beckham's $6.5m yearly deal might not have been as big as was reported, but it was still more than three times the $2.1m salary cap in place for the entire rest of the squad. But the figures were more remarkable than that. For example, Alan Gordon, a forward who played a few hundred times for different MLS clubs and a couple of times for the national team, was on a salary of $30,870 (around £15,000 on the exchange rate at the time) a *year*. In the Premier League, a player of a similar standard could expect to comfortably earn more than that in a single week. Beckham would be moving to Beverly Hills. There were instances of some Galaxy players having to house-share just to be able to afford to live in the city where they worked.

The biggest change for Beckham was the culture shock of playing in a team well below the standards to which he had become accustomed. He was still unable to play a full game, but was named on the bench for the SuperLiga game with Guadalajara at the Los Angeles Memorial Coliseum. The Mexican side won 2–1, with striker Alan Gordon insisting that, despite not playing, Beckham showed some passion. 'I sat next to him on the bench and he was emotional about the game,' Gordon said. 'It is good for us to see that he is really caring about it. We were all a little upset by the calls on the pitch, and he was sharing in that. He is a competitive person, and that is going to continue. He is not taking it easy at all.'

Three days later, the Galaxy – with Beckham again on the sidelines – defeated FC Dallas in a game for the ages. The Galaxy had been 4–0 up in 18 minutes. Dallas pulled it back to 4–3 with goals in the 43rd, 78th and 82nd minutes, before a Landon Donovan goal in the 84th seemed to give momentum back to Frank Yallop's team. Remarkably, there was still time for three injury-time goals, with the Galaxy coming out triumphant 6–5.

On 15 August, Beckham made his first starting appearance, against DC United in the SuperLiga semi-finals. He had made his MLS debut a week earlier against the same opponents – DC already had a first-half lead, and just before Beckham was due to come on in the 67th minute, Kyle Martino was sent off, forcing Yallop into a reshuffle. David came on three minutes later, but couldn't influence the game. He didn't travel for the fixture at the New England Revolution on 12 August, to the disappointment of the 35,402 who turned up for Gillette Stadium's biggest crowd since the 2012 MLS Cup. But, finally making his first start in a Galaxy shirt, Beckham made up for lost time by influencing the game in the best way he knew how. In the 27th minute, the

Galaxy were awarded a free kick 30 yards from goal – the stage was set, and David duly obliged to act out the script accordingly, striking the ball into the top corner. He then set up Landon Donovan for the second in a 2–0 win before being taken off in the 63rd minute. The combination was significant: after training the previous day, Donovan had magnanimously bestowed his captaincy of the team to Beckham.

'David Beckham, starting for the first time since he limped across the Atlantic Ocean on a sore left ankle last month, scored a goal, orchestrated another and saved soccer in America on a sweltering summer evening in Carson,' wrote Helene Elliott in the *Los Angeles Times*. 'OK, he didn't save soccer Wednesday. Not yet, anyway. But he might have saved the Galaxy's season. He certainly showed what the fuss over his arrival was all about, a $250-million man turning a ragged, 39-cent field into his personal playground with the kind of savvy performance the Galaxy and MLS are praying is the first of many. He made the 2–0 victory a night to remember, displaying his storied ability to bend a ball to his will and energizing a team that had sputtered and stumbled and was in danger of falling apart before he could get his new career going.'

Beckham was pleased with his contribution. 'It was very important for me to actually get on the pitch and play some minutes … I was happy to get an hour, I didn't expect to,' he said. 'Once I'm on the pitch I know I can play well and help the team, and that's all that was on my mind, helping the team get to the final and getting our season going. It was a great team performance, and it showed a lot of character to play like we did.'

Landon Donovan was full of praise: 'If this was him at who knows what percent of himself, I can't wait until he's fully healthy. I thought our attitude was great, and I think David in there brought a lot out of a lot of guys … I'm not stupid and I'm not naive. I know he's been captain of England, one of the best teams in the world. I'm going to play the same whether I'm wearing the captain's armband or not. It made him an immediate part of the team … I think guys looked at him different and he could say things differently. He was a great leader, and I think he's going to help us.'

Beckham was not captain of England, but he was recalled into the national squad, and put straight back into the team, for a friendly against Germany at Wembley. 'David has trained and looked very good,' England manager Steve McClaren said. 'There is no problem with him at the moment, of course it is worth him flying over. Anybody would want to be involved for their country and David's attitude, being willing to make the trip, speaks for itself. I don't see how rest can benefit him. He needs to play. He hasn't played for a while, he is just returning to fitness from an ankle injury and he needs minutes on the field. He needs minutes and if we can give it to him, that's going to benefit us in three weeks' time against Israel.'

England lost 2–1, and David seemed to be an unlucky charm whether playing (as he did against New York Red Bulls and Chivas USA) or not (as he didn't for the next few games). Including David's debut against DC United, Yallop's side had lost six consecutive games, and even though their form improved towards the end of the year, that was mostly without Beckham playing. Fatigue and the ankle injury were cited as reasons, but a major blow followed in the SuperLiga Final against Pachuca in the week after the Germany game. The Galaxy fell behind in the 29th minute when Peter Vagenas put the ball into his own net, but less than a minute later their problems went from bad to much worse when Beckham chased a loose ball. The defender got there first by a split-second, planting a foot to ensure first contact, and Beckham also hit the ball, but the collision caused his knee to extend as he fell to the ground. He knew instantly he would have to come off.

As he waited for the results of a scan, he admitted he did not expect to be fit for England's European Championship qualifiers. 'It doesn't look great,' he said. 'It's a ligament strain, which could be four to six weeks, but if the scan comes back and it's not so bad, maybe I've got a chance. It's frustrating. I'd been given rest to get my ankle right and it felt better. Now it's gone from one problem to another. Maybe it's a sign I should just rest to get things right. Maybe when I went into the tackle I was compensating for the left ankle, which everyone knows isn't right. Maybe I've gone in a bit weaker than I would have fully fit. I'm devastated to have been hurt again. I've gone from one problem to another. I wouldn't have thought I'll be flying to England now. If I had six weeks' rest, it would clear up completely. But that isn't possible.'

David's problems continued into his personal life: his father, Ted, suffered a heart attack, and David flew straight from LA to London to be with him as he recovered.

Coach Frank Yallop faced increasing pressure after the Galaxy failed to make the play-offs. He had previously conceded he was struggling with the extra attention Beckham's arrival had given the team. 'It's not been easy because of the spotlight thrust on us,' he said. 'You try to imagine the hysteria surrounding his arrival, but when he's here it's so different. It's not been easy. It's been kind of testing, to be honest.'

After the Galaxy had lost the SuperLiga Final (they equalised in injury time, but lost on penalties), Yallop allegedly said in the dressing room, 'Everyone's fucked, everyone's fucking knackered and we are fucking spent.' His public response to the defeat was more conducive to print, but carried much of the same message: 'There are six-hour flights after matches. You need to rest players. But you can't, and this is one of the reasons you see a drop-off in quality when the squad gets thin. When David trained on Tuesday, it was only his third session here. But we rarely get to train anyway because of the fixture schedule. He shouldn't have been playing on Wednesday. We have needed him, though.'

Beckham missed all but the last two remaining games of the season, coming on in those games for a combined total of around 50 minutes. In all, he had managed just 360 minutes since arriving in America.

The appearances were enough to get him a place in the England squad for the friendly against Austria and the crucial European Championship qualifier against Croatia. In the first game, Beckham started, and set up the only goal for Peter Crouch; but for the match of real importance, McClaren decided to play Shaun Wright-Phillips. Beckham's recall to the national side had not been met with favour by the British press, who saw it as a desperate gamble from McClaren. The former Manchester United coach was certain to lose his job if England failed to qualify for the following year's tournament, and gambling on a veteran to save him when his first public decision had been to axe that very player was likely to come with a price. 'His achievements have never quite justified his global fame,' Mick Dennis wrote, rather unfairly, in the *Express*. 'His renown has more to do with his looks – and the golden generation have always looked better than they were.'

England were 2–0 down at Wembley within 15 minutes. Their midfield of Steven Gerrard and Frank Lampard was being bossed on the big pitch by Luka Modrić and Niko Kranjčar. At half-time, McClaren made his final gamble, bringing on Beckham for Wright-Phillips. It was David's 99th cap – England hoped for, and almost expected, another qualification rescue act. In the 65th minute, it seemed as if it would be coming. Lampard had already netted a penalty before Beckham's exquisite delivery was converted again by Crouch to level things up. But McClaren's side paid the price for their abysmal first half when Mladen Petrić scored a late goal to seal a win for the visitors. Croatia, and not England, would be going to Euro 2008.

'Without a doubt, I'm not retiring,' Beckham said afterwards. 'I said that the moment I was taken out of the team and the moment I came back into the team, and I'm not stepping down. We're disappointed as a team, and obviously the nation will be disappointed about not qualifying. If you don't win games you don't qualify. We just didn't perform, and that's the end of it.'

It certainly was for McClaren, who was sacked as a result. And it was the end too for Frank Yallop, who moved to the San Jose Earthquakes to become their head coach. For David Beckham – whose name had once been a byword for consistency and reliability – this sort of turbulence was becoming a regular occurrence.

Impression

FABIO CAPELLO was the man hired by the English FA to succeed Steve McClaren. David Beckham, then, presumably breathed with relief, considering their recent relationship at Real Madrid. A friendly against Switzerland at Wembley in early February 2008 would seem like the ideal occasion for Beckham to get his 100th international cap.

Only one problem. When Capello named that squad, Beckham wasn't in it. The reaction of the press was predictable, but the Italian was keen to assure them that this was not a repeat of what had happened in Spain. 'The reason that David is not in the squad is because he has not had any real match practice since playing in November,' the new man said. 'When I spoke with David, I advised him that he is still part of my plans, and once he is playing regularly in America we will look closely at him again.'

Capello was better than his word – Beckham only had to resume his pre-season training with the Los Angeles Galaxy to be back in the conversation, and on 21 March – some nine days before the MLS season even kicked off – the former captain was named in the squad to face France in Paris on the 26th. Beckham started at the State de France; the result was a 1–0 defeat, and

David was brought off in the 64th minute, but it took little gloss off the day for the Beckham family, including Ted, who was in the stands watching. He would have undoubtedly shared in the immense pride from the standing ovation given to his son, a reminder of just how far he had come in ten years.

Back in the US, David was keen to put right a very difficult first few months in Los Angeles. He had come to terms with the new soccer calendar, but was still finding some aspects challenging. 'For the first time in his life he was playing on a mediocre team,' Alexi Lalas says. 'He was playing in a league that celebrates manufactured parity. He was playing for a team that was historically one of the better teams in the country, but in terms of being an elite super-club like he was used to, it was an adjustment. We knew very quickly that the team was not great. He wasn't the first and won't be the last person to get a healthy dose of reality like that.'

Netherlands legend Ruud Gullit had stepped into the breach as head coach of the Galaxy following Frank Yallop's departure. The logic was sound. Gullit, a technical master with one of the most respected profiles (if the owner of a mixed managerial background which included some fall-outs with major players), could understand Beckham's profile. Not that he was going to make any special accommodations for it.

'He is a very well-known player, I know him personally,' Gullit said of Beckham on his unveiling as coach. 'But when we are on the pitch, he has to do the same things that the other players have to do. As a coach, we try to use his experience, because that is the reason why he came here, and of course his ability as a player. He has a role of helping other players to understand the game a little bit better, so he is going to be a link with the other players, but as a person he will be treated as equally as anyone else.'

There was a humorous contrast in how Gullit saw Los Angeles. As one of European football's most recognisable figures, he could be stopped anywhere to discuss the game. In LA, he could walk around and relax.

Gullit, like Beckham, faced an uphill battle dealing with the relatively low quality of the squad in general. A hard reminder came on the opening day of the MLS season when the Colorado Rapids – led by Terry Cooke – crushed the Galaxy 4–0.

Hope was restored in the first home game of the season when Beckham and Landon Donovan scored in a 2–0 win over the San Jose Earthquakes – a crucial factor being that the pair assisted each other's goals.

'We see the game the same way,' Donovan said. 'It makes it easier for both of us. Having time to train together has made it even easier, so I know how he wants the ball and he knows how I want it. He also knows if he puts it in a good area I have a chance to get to it.'

Beckham conveyed the same message: 'It's great to score a goal, I'm usually on the other end, assisting. I'm happy, but I'm more happy with the team performance than anything else. We've got some young players, and after the defeat in the first game it was important that we won tonight.'

Gullit talked up those inexperienced players, knowing that he would be counting on them to raise their name every week just to provide the platform for Donovan and Beckham to continue to influence games in a positive way. Indications of the struggle they would face came in consecutive home games against Toronto FC (a 3–2 defeat) and the Houston Dynamo (a 2–2 draw). Often it was Landon Donovan getting the Galaxy out of jail (when possible) with goals in the opening games; the defensive frailty was exposed again at Real Salt Lake when the hosts went into a 2–0 lead, their second courtesy of Kenny Deuchar. Deuchar, then 27, so in the prime of his career, had risen to prominence in a spell with Scottish side Gretna, where he scored prolifically. He had failed to make an impact in a loan spell with Northampton

Town, but had just moved to MLS to see if he could make an impact. This was just one of three MLS goals for Deuchar, but his profile is mentioned to give a perspective on the disparity in quality Beckham faced in his own team and in their opponents.

On this evening, Beckham provided the rescue act. He scored with an effort in the 36th minute which was almost certainly a cross, but then equalised in the 40th with a 30-yard free kick about which there could be no mistaking his intention. He had salvaged a 2–2 draw, but even that paled into insignificance by the time he was next on the scoresheet. The Galaxy were leading 2–1 against the Kansas City Wizards at the Home Depot Center, with the game moving into injury time. Kansas City goalkeeper Kevin Hartman decided to join the attack when his side won a late corner. As the Galaxy cleared their lines, the ball fell to Beckham on the edge of his own box. He took three touches to compose himself – the first two seemingly with the intention of firing off one of those long-range passes. The third, however, was different. Hartman was running back, but there was no way he was going to get anywhere near his own goal. Beckham had a target of an empty net. He was some ten yards further back than he had been at Selhurst Park in 1996, but the odds were in his favour, if only he could depend on his accuracy. Of course, he could. The ball didn't sail straight in – it finally crossed the line on the second bounce – but the result was the same. The Galaxy, and MLS, finally had a headline moment that would be beamed around the world.

Mike Magee – who had played for the New York Red Bulls in their win at the Galaxy a couple of weeks earlier – had confessed to only really knowing Beckham the celebrity. But the goal against Kansas City had a telling impact. 'MLS needed that. The media needed that. It was perfect,' he says. 'Without a goal like that from him, there was nothing from the league that would catch the world's attention. I didn't know what to make of it. I had no clue the effect it would have on our league. Not until he came to play against us and 90,000 fans showed up did I begin to understand. He was brilliant. The American fan base had no clue how good he was. The little intricacies of his game and his passing is what made him great. At that time, American fans only saw speed and goals.'

There was delight at the immediate consequence of the goal – it secured the points in a crucial victory – but also a palpable sense of relief in the boardroom at the Galaxy. 'The goal was a magical moment *because* it was scored by David Beckham,' Alexi Lalas says. 'It would have still been something to see if it had been scored by any other player, but it takes on new meaning when David Beckham does it. You want these high-profile players to be involved in great and magical moments that the world can see. In this day and age you want it to go viral. There are two components to it: how special the goal is, and the identity of the scorer. If a kid from Bakersfield, CA, had scored that goal, it would have been great, but it was important that David scored. From David's personal perspective, he put a lot of pressure on himself to deliver. He wanted to be successful, he wanted to give people what they expected … When it wasn't going well, I think he took it personally. It wasn't exactly validation, because he didn't need that, it was a moment of living up to expectations.'

Lalas says that this early-season form was strong enough to suggest Beckham had proved that he had the substance to match the style. He wouldn't score from the halfway line every week, but he had only done it once in Europe, so for MLS to have been the setting for such a goal was a big moment. Lalas won't be drawn into specifics about the reports of broadcasting revenue which estimated a change from $100,000 to $10m in television rights before Beckham had even arrived, but says, 'Whether it was broadcasting revenue or ticket prices, everything increased, and dramatically increased.'

Bryan Jordan, one of the forwards, loved playing alongside Beckham. 'My first experience playing with him, during my first year, he played central midfield while I played up top or on the wing,' he says. 'I think he liked me 'cause he loved to serve the long ball into the channels, and me being a speedy guy, I would run them down all day long. Feed me, I'd say! Whenever he wanted to send it my way, I told him I won't let a turnover go down on your stats … So I guess we had a bit of a connection when it came down to that. He was also a hard worker and kept the ball pretty well, so I was always very confident playing alongside him.'

Despite the hope that Donovan's goalscoring consistency, and Beckham's delivery and capability for the spectacular, could lead the Galaxy to an unlikely spell of success, the reality of a weak squad hit home, and a poor run of form through the summer meant that the team would fail to reach the play-offs again. There was in fact a run of 11 games without a win, which meant Gullit's team would finish second bottom of the Western Conference and the overall standings. The Galaxy could claim the highest scorer – Donovan, with 20 – and the highest average crowd, at 26,009: almost 6,000 greater than the gates at Toronto in second place, and 10,000 higher than the league average.

The arguments about style over substance continued, and Gullit paid the ultimate price for that conflict. After a defeat to San Jose, Gullit resigned amidst rumours of a dressing-room 'revolt'. General manager Alexi Lalas was dismissed from his position at the club on the same day as Gullit's departure.

The Galaxy's leading players were tasked with talking to the press about Gullit's exit, and you can easily see the difference in how they addressed the point.

Beckham had his politician's hat on, attempting to dampen the talk of unrest in the camp. 'Obviously it's disappointing,' he told the *Los Angeles Times*. 'But he's taken the decision to move on because of family reasons, and everyone knows family always comes first, so good luck to him. It's disappointing to lose somebody who's a good coach and a good person. But it happens in football clubs and it's happened here. Maybe it happened too early, but we wish him good luck in whatever he goes on and does. When there's troubles in clubs, it can have a good effect, it can have a bad effect. Hopefully, it will have a good effect on us where we come together as a team and we go out there and put in a performance. We can only put it right on the field.'

Landon Donovan, however, spoke in such a blunt fashion that it was impossible to deduce anything other than that there was no smoke without fire. 'At times he [Gullit] was a little disrespectful and that bothered me,' Donovan said. 'From Ruud's standpoint, I think it's been difficult for him. If you've been in a certain way of soccer for 40 years and you come somewhere where you can't get the players you want, you can't do the things you want, you don't have an unlimited budget, you have other issues around you that affect things, then it makes it very difficult. It's not easy, and not a lot of foreign coaches have done well here for that reason.'

US soccer legend Cobi Jones became temporary coach, with mixed results. He would be replaced by another icon of the North American game, Bruce Arena, but before the season was out, Gullit was having his say on his experience in the role. He complained about the rules, the weather, height and humidity, and claimed the cultural differences would make it impossible for Beckham to turn his spell into a success.

'David is more than just a football player, and I think he does extremely well to give football here a lift,' Gullit told Reuters. 'But I doubt if they [the US soccer organisers] really want that. I think they are afraid of football because it's so popular everywhere around the world. I think they will just control it so it doesn't become more popular than their American sports. So it is very hard for him. They will never allow that, and in some ways I can understand it as well. I have my doubts if they really want to make it popular. Some sports already have had a bit of a dive, so they don't want American football to become less popular, or basketball or baseball.'

It was an ongoing battle, but one aspect in which Beckham would have to concede temporary defeat was when it came to his chances for the international team. He had remained involved under Capello – even regaining the captaincy for a very temporary spell in a June friendly due to the inexperience in the squad – but the manager had made it clear that if he wanted to stay in the picture, he would have to be playing regularly. It was reported that Capello had told Beckham bluntly that he would not be considered for the friendly against Spain in February 2009 if he was not playing regularly. There were no guarantees of a recall after that. Now he had passed a century of caps, every appearance was significant, and as a player who took immense pride in representing his country, he could not afford to pass up any chance, or to be seen as taking it easy. That was one thing nobody would accuse David Beckham of doing, and it was a key factor in his continuing involvement which stood to be undermined.

The solution was a loan back to Europe, with the window for registration opening on 1 January. Front of the queue was Portsmouth manager Harry Redknapp, who attempted to pitch his case before Milan – another club rumoured to be interested – made their interest official. 'I would take him,' Redknapp said. 'I would definitely be interested in bringing him to Portsmouth. I haven't made an enquiry yet, but it has crossed my mind. He is a player you definitely think about, and no one will tell me that he wouldn't get in a load of crosses for Crouch and Defoe. He is a terrific player still, and maybe I will go for him. Who knows, you never can tell. He wants to play football, and he is still in great nick. If he wants to come to the Premier League, it would be fantastic for us to get him. But I am sure we would not be the only club after him. And I'm sure Beckham's missus would much prefer shopping in Portsmouth than Milan.'

She wouldn't; but Redknapp's own conviction was undermined by the fact that he quit Fratton Park days later to take over at Tottenham, where he once again tried to get Beckham's attention. By that time, however, it was too late – Milan had made their move and the wheels were in motion.

'I wasn't with the Galaxy then, but my opinion remained the same as it did when David signed, and we had talked about it then,' Alexi Lalas says.[2] 'I admired and shared the commitment he was showing his national team and understood why he felt he had to go to Milan. I thought it would be a good thing because David was still contracted to the Galaxy, and so it would show there was an MLS player doing well in Italy. It did rub me the wrong way that he felt – and rightfully so – that he wasn't going to be assessed in the same way because of the fact he was playing in MLS. There was nothing to me that said you can't be in the England team and playing in MLS. That he felt forced to do something like that was what irked me, not that he did it. That's our burden. That's the challenge for US soccer. To have an England player play for the Galaxy or even a team like the Columbus Crew and have them considered and picked for the national team and not even miss a beat.'

That time would have to wait. On 22 October, speaking at Milan's Malpensa airport, AC Milan vice president Adriano Galliani said, 'We are speaking with his agent, but we believe he will arrive for some months on a free loan. We shall register him for some months and then he will leave. Beckham has chosen Milan. Our squad is ultra-competitive and it will remain this way, but Beckham is something different and intriguing.'

---

2   These are Lalas's comments in 2020; he did, however, say that Beckham had made it 'very, very clear he doesn't want to be here' and predicted fans would boo him on his return because 'I don't think it's too much to ask from your players that they actually want to play for the club.' When asked if he expected to be booed, Beckham responded, 'I'm sure I will now after Alexi's comments … maybe he'll be one of them in the stands doing it!'

Milan manager Carlo Ancelotti was pleased with the addition. 'For me it will be a pleasure,' he said. 'Beckham is a great professional. If he is available for four months with us, we will be very happy.'

Vogue

'YOU SEE, if you ignore what Beckham does off the pitch, and forget what he cannot do on it, you are left with one fact: he can still deliver corners, free kicks and crosses better than any Englishman ever has,' Mick Dennis wrote in his *Express* column. 'There is another important fact. It is that, despite having more money than even his wife can ever spend, Beckham is still impelled by an insatiable compulsion to do his utmost best for his country – even if it means sitting, uncomplaining, on the bench for long periods and accepting a walk-on part instead of a starring role. That is why, while other England players put their clubs first and some would rather collect cars than caps, Beckham has put his reputation on the line in Milan. That is why, once he gets on the pitch, his selfless determination will win over the Milanese. That is why [Fabio] Capello will have to change his mind a third time about Beckham. I believe if the always-generous [Bobby] Moore were alive, he would lead the applause when Beckham equals and then passes his magnificent total of caps.'

David made his first appearance in a Milan shirt on 6 January 2009, in a friendly against Hamburg in Dubai. He played from the right in a midfield that featured Andrea Pirlo, Massimo

Ambrosini and Ronaldinho before being substituted at half-time. There was certainly a veteran feel to the legendary Italian club, even if the mind does play revisionist tricks – Pirlo was only 29 at the time, and Ronaldinho only 28. But the *Dad's Army* reputation came from the likes of Dida (35) in goal, Alessandro Nesta (32), Paolo Maldini (39, almost 40), Gianluca Zambrotta (31, almost 32), Pippo Inzaghi (35) and Clarence Seedorf (32, almost 33) to name just six further veterans.

The England star's official debut for Milan came on Saturday, 17 January against Fiorentina, where he started on the right-hand side of a midfield three in a 4–3–2–1 shape. Pato's early goal secured a comfortable 1–0 win; Beckham's contribution amounted to a 30th-minute caution before he was substituted to a fine reception nine minutes from time.

That game at the San Siro was watched by Victoria, who was joined by fashion legends Domenico Dolce and Stefano Gabbana. Victoria may well have been in her element, although she wasn't pictured with David the following day as he attended the Armani Menswear show at Milan Fashion Week alongside Roberta Armani. There, he told fashion industry 'bible' *Women's Wear Daily*: 'The club, players and fans have been amazing to me so far and have made me very welcome. It's rare I have time to make a show, so I enjoyed it … my priority, though, is working hard and playing well for AC Milan.'

Indulging in all that the city had to offer was all well and good; but now, more than ever, it was important for Beckham to make an impression on the pitch. The lifestyle of Milan was merely a pleasant coincidence.

Carlo Ancelotti's team had the experience already mentioned, but they were also inspired by the magnificence of Kaká, one of the greatest players in the world at the peak of his powers, and the highly rated youngster Pato. The Brazilians were in their majestic form in Bologna the following week, overturning an early deficit to lead 3–1 at half-time. On the hour mark, Pato played in Seedorf, who saw Beckham making the sort of overlapping run on the right-hand side that he had been making for 17 years; almost reminiscent of the position he took up in the 1996 FA Cup semi-final. Pato found him – this time, instead of going across the keeper, Beckham struck the ball with some power into the near top corner. This goal only rubber-stamped an already comfortable victory, but the popularity of the scorer was seen by the number of Milan players and substitutes who rushed to celebrate with him.

That 4–1 win was followed by a game with Genoa. In the 33rd minute, Milan were awarded a free kick to the left-hand side of their penalty area. It seemed much too narrow an angle for a shot, but there could be no disputing the purpose of Beckham's kick. The veteran was far too experienced for a cross to be mis-hit so badly, and on a second watch, it was easy to observe the brilliant and deliberate opportunism which he used to catch out the goalkeeper.

Despite that game ending 1–1, it had been a dream start for Beckham, who admitted, 'I am surprised at how quickly I have settled. I knew I'd enjoy myself, but I wasn't expecting to enjoy myself so much. I am learning Italian – an hour a day – and have been out for dinner a few times with my team-mates.'

He was asked by *Corriere Delle Sera* if he would consider moving permanently and, even though there is a definite tone of the politician in his response, one could imagine it would have been greeted with some discomfort back in Los Angeles. 'To play here is the dream of any player,' he said. 'But deciding is not easy. It's a situation that requires time. I am under contract and I have a lot of respect for Galaxy. But the possibility to play at Milan is something special. I knew I would have fun, but I didn't expect to have so much fun. In any case, I am a very respectful person. I have to admit that, having played in Europe, at times, it has been frustrating to take part in certain games [in the US]. But, once in a while, going from state to state, I have also had fun.'

Those comments were greeted with fury in the States. *Los Angeles Times* sports columnist T.J. Simers summed up the media's attitude to Beckham by calling him 'a fiasco, a flop, a fraud and a bloody awful investment'.

Clearly that attitude wasn't shared in Italy – although he was on a 'free' loan, they most certainly could not complain about value for money. Beckham was outstanding in a 3–0 win at Lazio, winning the man-of-the-match award and setting up the first two goals. Both Milan chief Adriano Galliani and Galaxy manager Bruce Arena spoke with some openness about the possibility of the move becoming permanent, but the objective of the temporary arrangement had been met already when Beckham was called into the England squad for the friendly against Spain. There, he came on as a substitute in Seville to equal Bobby Moore's record of 108 caps for an outfield player.

The game gave the English press a perfect opportunity to grab a few words, in which he insisted his family were still happy in LA. He was asked if the move had been a success. 'Off the field, yes,' he said. 'On the field? Well, we haven't even made the play-offs, so that's the tough part. I don't know if I have left any sort of legacy – we'll have to wait and see. But I do think the game will take off there.'

He confessed that his few weeks in Milan had already left an impression. 'When I made the decision to join Galaxy, Milan came in just that little bit too late,' he said. But I've always said I don't regret things, and I don't regret the two seasons at LA. They might have been disappointing, as we haven't won anything or even made the play-offs, but there are really good people at the club … I realised I wanted to stay with Milan pretty soon after I arrived, to be honest. I had expected to go there for a few months and then return to the Galaxy. It didn't really enter my mind when I made the loan decision to stay there, but after being there for a week and playing my first game, I realised I wanted to stay at that level.'

Milan had already made a £7m offer to make the move permanent, which had been rejected – it was suggested by some reports that Beckham might be willing to take a pay cut in order for the Italian club to afford a bigger fee. Some other reports, however, suggested that the offer had been closer to £2.1m, which would explain the angry reaction of Tim Leiweke.

'We are not close,' Leiweke said. 'Two weeks ago, Milan made a ridiculous offer, to which I replied "No" in a few seconds. With that figure, the Galaxy don't even cover the damages deriving from the shortfalls of not selling his shirts. Since then, no one has made any moves. There are no meetings arranged. I have decided to speak up because I have read too many inaccurate stories. After that ridiculous offer, Milan have not done anything. They have tried other people, from the commissioner of the league to David's representatives, but not us, who own his rights. If David doesn't return, who will replace him? Our transfer market is already closed. If Milan are so determined to keep him, why are they taking so long? Do they think that we will settle for less money? They are mistaken. What Milan don't understand is that behind this story, there are fans that are renouncing subscriptions, sponsors that want damages and rival teams that have the right to know if the Galaxy will play at their stadium with or without Beckham. David is an incredible professional and I am happy for him and for Milan that his Italian experience is going so well. This confirms that our choice to bring him to the United States was the right one.'

Leiweke was quick to point out that his frustration was with the club and not the player. 'David is a friend and asked me to listen to what Milan proposed,' he said. 'I have said "Yes" because of him. But I will not be taken for a ride and hence, on March

9, Beckham will be in Los Angeles and will work with the same seriousness and dedication as before. He already knows he doesn't have a choice, because the first option to come out of his contract is at the end of 2009. What really matters is that Milan make a real offer. I don't wish to talk about the offer, but the figures that I have read in the United States [around $15m] are close to what we want.'

There were a couple of setbacks – defeats in the Milan derby and against Sampdoria made hopes of a Serie A title unlikely. Under the terms of the agreement, these were the circumstances in which Beckham would be returning to the US to begin the MLS season, but hours after Bruce Arena had told press that he had only spoken 'once in 40 days' about the possibility of Beckham staying in Milan, it was announced that the loan spell would be extended until the end of the European season.

'I'm grateful to both clubs for allowing this dream to come true,' said Beckham. 'It will enable me to play for Milan and the Galaxy in the same season, with the possibility of being able to keep up my commitments with Major League Soccer and the development of soccer in the United States – something which I'm very passionate about.'

'I'm sorry that it had to go for so long, for him and for us and particularly for the fans,' Tim Leiweke told the *Los Angeles Times*, whilst the flat tone of Bruce Arena could comfortably be detected: 'I am confident that his presence will strengthen our roster in the last half of the season as we push for a play-off position.' The deal had been described as one which suited 'both clubs', but it did not seem ideal for the Galaxy, who were forced to cut ticket prices by 10 per cent to appease annoyed fans.

Beckham was moved into a new position – the 'Kaká' role behind the strikers – against Atalanta, and it was a successful transition as Inzaghi scored a hat-trick in a 3–0 win. In late March, he discussed how confident he was feeling, and admitted how his difficult end to 2006 had influenced his decisions. 'I didn't feel my legs had gone or that I didn't still have it when I decided to go to America,' he insisted. 'But confidence-wise I'd taken a few knocks. I've always been quite a confident person, and I've taken that on to the field. Maybe not having that at that time was the biggest reason why I decided to go there. I'd gone through a couple of down points in my career. Obviously being taken out of the England squad was a big one. That knocked my confidence a lot. It affected me. I didn't think I'd play for my country after being taken out the team by Steve McClaren. I assumed I wouldn't play for my country again, if I'm honest. At the time, when I was left out, the team were playing well. The first few games had gone so well, I just thought, "That's it." But I have no regrets. I wanted to try something different and start a new life. When I went to Milan, I didn't know whether I was going to play a game or whether I'd be able to keep up with the pace of some of the players in the team. But I surprised myself. The confidence is back. Form-wise, it has taken me to another level. Fitness-wise, it has definitely taken me to another level. Starting the Roma game was a big thing for me. Starting every other game has been huge, too. Playing at a club like Milan, and with the players we have there, has improved my confidence and my form. I'm playing pretty well at the moment. Fitness-wise, I'm definitely the best I've been for a long time. Maybe England will benefit. I'm still not going to have the pace I've never had. But I'm experienced, I'm playing well. I've always said that when my fitness is at a high level, I can perform.'

He continued to be one of Milan's better performers as the season concluded – they finished third, missing out on second place due to head-to-head results with Juventus – flourishing in that right-sided midfield role. England manager Fabio Capello (who, remember, had played him from the right at Madrid despite David having played exclusively through the middle there beforehand) suggested he could feature in this new position for his country. 'Beckham in the middle is one of the options,' said the national team manager. 'I saw some games that he played for Milan in this position, with three midfielders. I like it. It's not a problem for David.'

Beckham was only a substitute in a 4–0 win over Kazakhstan – coming on for the last 15 minutes – but he was back in the team from the start against Andorra, playing in that more central role. It was not the most influential display, but one of his free kicks did result in a goal in a 6–0 victory.

Carlo Ancelotti had moved from Milan to coach Chelsea, but Beckham doubted he would be following, despite enjoying such a new lease of life. 'I don't think that's a possibility,' he said. 'At the end of the day I'm still contracted to the Galaxy. I'll be coming back on July 11 to start training and then to finish the MLS season. But it's always nice to be wanted, and Carlo has been amazing to me since I've come to Milan, to play me in as many games as he has. I'm very thankful to him for that. Nothing has been signed yet for next season. Milan have already shown their interest in me coming back, so that's a good sign. But nothing concrete has been decided so far.'

* * *

Beckham's return to the US was preceded by a media storm not of his making, but still nonetheless about him. Journalist Grant Wahl had written a book entitled *The Beckham Experiment*, which was due to be published on 14 July 2009 and was already being serialised, with a large extract appearing in *Sports Illustrated*. The headline excerpts mainly featured the controversial remarks made by Landon Donovan, who had not held back in his criticism of the England star, including, in Wahl's words: '... that Beckham was a poor captain, that he wasn't fully committed to the Galaxy, and that he had become a bad team-mate during the second half of the 2008 season'.

Donovan – arguably the best American player – was clearly upset. 'Let's say he does stay here three more years,' the forward said. 'I'm not going to spend the next three years of my life doing it this way … If someone's paying you more than double anybody in the league, you should bust your ass every day. That hasn't happened.'

He was also said to have urged Bruce Arena: 'Hold him accountable. Bench him. Just say, "We're not going to play you. We don't think you're committed."'

Wahl later reported that 'Donovan's broadside set off a global media firestorm unlike anything Major League Soccer had seen since Beckham joined the league. Never before in Beckham's career had he been so harshly judged in public by another player, much less a current team-mate.'

Certainly, among some of the support, Wahl's book conveyed a certain image of Beckham which was not favourably received. David Garcia, a member of the Riot Squad supporters' group, said, 'When Beckham is actually here in LA, all he does is unsettle the team. He swans around rubbing shoulders with Hollywood stars. Landon was right to criticise his lack of leadership. That's what we expected from him, but we haven't seen much yet. He gives the impression he cares more about himself than he does the team.'

Beckham arrived back in Los Angeles on 10 July, and the following day he was at a community event in El Segundo when he told journalists he was disappointed with Donovan's comments: 'It's unprofessional, in my eyes. In every soccer player's eyes throughout the world, it would be unprofessional to speak out about a team-mate, especially in the press and not to your face … in 17 years I have played with the biggest teams in the world and the biggest players, and not once have I been criticised for my professionalism. It's important to get this cleared up, and I will be speaking to Landon either this evening or over the next couple of days.'

Donovan, perhaps anticipating the confrontation – or maybe even realising that his comments did not portray him in the best light – had told reporters that he had some regrets about how this had played out. 'I'm not going to apologise for the way I felt,' he said, but added, 'What I do feel badly about is that I should have been a man and told David how I felt, as opposed to telling a reporter. David and I will sit down when he comes back and talk it through.'

As they awaited the fall-out, the Galaxy players had an anxious few days in early July. 'There was tension to say the least,' Mike Magee recalls. 'The book that came out would have destroyed most teams. Most players would have left the team. But David isn't most players. He's a different level of class as a player and person.'

Magee insists that he understood David's decision to go to Europe. 'I was just worried he wouldn't come back. Thank God he did!'

Beckham was as good as his word and immediately sought out Donovan to settle any issues his team-mate had. That evening, the Galaxy were playing Chivas USA, and although David wasn't going to be in the team, he went into the dressing room to clear the air.

'Obviously, it was uncomfortable for both of us,' Donovan admitted later.

'David handled it better than anyone else on the planet would have,' Magee recalls. 'He dealt with it like a man and confronted people to their face.'

After the match, Arena held a meeting with Beckham and Donovan in his office, where Donovan apologised. 'I learned a lot, actually, from how David dealt with my apology, how he dealt with the whole situation, because if I put myself in his shoes I would have been really pissed off,' Donovan admitted. 'He might have been mad, but he was a man and he accepted my apology. And he didn't hold it against me. Anytime before this year I wouldn't have been the same way. I probably wouldn't have accepted it, and I would have held a grudge.'

Donovan, to his credit, publicly backed down and retracted some of the comments he had made, admitting he 'didn't even really mean' some of them. 'When I say he should have come in and done something monetarily for the guys, I don't really believe that,' he said. 'That's not his job. I just had these expectations of him that were unfair. I realised that he's a person just like everyone else.'

According to Alexi Lalas, the whole thing was blown out of proportion. 'I think that Landon felt that by contributing to the book he was participating in explaining a complex and nuanced type of situation,' Lalas says. 'He felt he was describing the realities and challenges that don't show up in the 90 minutes but still affect them. I'm sure that David could have looked at that as something of a betrayal. I can understand that. But they figured that out. That's where having Bruce Arena's leadership was crucial. He doesn't suffer fools. He will nip problems in the bud and put out fires, as he did, understanding they had different viewpoints but that he needed both of them. It was great relationship management. In the greater scheme of things, it wasn't that bad. I wouldn't look at it as incredible treachery. I think more was made out of it … I'm not saying that what Mike said, and the way they dealt with it, wasn't important. But winning fixes a lot of problems.'

The former president of the Galaxy believes that the relationship between the two best players at the club was not extraordinary: 'They eyed each other like two stars would. They had to come to an understanding of how they were going to function, because they are very different types of people. You don't have to be best friends – you don't have to necessarily like someone on your team, but you have to respect them. It doesn't always come immediately, sometimes it takes time. It's not resentment. We as American players naturally have a chip on our shoulder because of the way that we are often perceived or devalued. It's something that drives us and makes us incredibly competitive. That's a good thing. There was never any animosity. It just took time for them to get to know each other.'

Mike Magee says the matter was resolved, but wondered if the pair secretly still felt frustrated. 'On the field, yes [it was sorted], but off the field I don't know,' he says. 'They were both great pros and had the team's best interest at heart.'

Donovan had harboured suspicions about Beckham that preceded his arrival into the dressing room. He had allegedly told team-mates ahead of their first 'bonding meal' at a steakhouse that he would call David out if he didn't pick up the bill. David didn't – he just paid his share – but Donovan didn't confront him. The American had also questioned Beckham's form of leadership as captain, criticising him for not being as vocal as Donovan presumably would have preferred. In the interest of balance, we should recall Emile Heskey's observations of Beckham's generosity and instances in which he felt his skipper had been an excellent leader.

It is worthwhile considering another perspective from inside the Galaxy dressing room too. Bryan Jordan had joined the Galaxy in 2008, but was spending some time on loan throughout 2009; he missed the actual fall-out, but was familiar enough with the situation to give his opinion. Jordan agrees with elements of both what Lalas and Magee say.

'As a young guy on the team at the time, I tried to keep my nose mostly out of trouble, and a large portion of that first year I spent on loan back up in Portland for the Timbers, so I think I missed a bit,' Jordan explains. 'Although at times you could sense something was going on, I really didn't get to see any of the real negative things from it. But I can definitely understand the dynamic. I really do commend both of them for handling it the way they did, as it ultimately just proved to be just an obstacle on the way to the great things our team was going to accomplish. So I strongly agree with what Magee said … just to add, especially with some of the egos in sports, if they were different people this definitely could have ripped a team straight in two.'

Beckham was back in the middle next to Donovan in the following week's fixture against the New York Red Bulls in New Jersey. The England star was booed, but played well enough in a 3–1 win. Donovan scored an outrageous second goal which decided the game; as he celebrated, first on the scene was Beckham.

'It's to be expected,' David said of the reception. 'Sometimes it's nice to get the boos. It gives you inspiration, especially when we play like we did.'

Donovan enthusiastically talked up their combination play, describing their shared chemistry as 'fantastic', whilst Arena praised Beckham, saying, 'Given the issues and circumstances, he had a great game.'

All eyes would be on the next game at the Home Depot Center, though, where a truer reaction would be seen, particularly because this was a friendly match, ironically enough against AC Milan (arranged as part of the agreement to extend Beckham's loan). It was a sold-out game, and sure enough, Beckham was booed even before kick-off, with banners held up by the home fans which said, in the more polite ones, 'FRAUD' and to 'GO HOME'. Every single time he touched the ball, the midfielder was booed.

It was 1–1 at half-time. As the teams left the pitch, Beckham walked over to the most vociferous supporters and pointed a finger, apparently challenging them to come down and talk to him. The man he pointed a finger at, David Martinous, didn't, but Josh Paige, a supporter standing next to him, did. Paige was held on the ground by three security guards and escorted from the stadium. Another fan threw a replica 'Beckham 23' jersey at the player. 'It was surreal,' Paige later said. 'When David Beckham calls you out, you get on the field. In hindsight, I wish I didn't stoop to his level. I wish I was the bigger man.' Paige was initially banned for life but had that quickly rescinded.

Security guards escorted Beckham to the dressing room. He emerged to play the second period, and set up the Galaxy's second goal for Bryan Jordan in a 2–2 draw, after which he turned to the crowd, shrugged his shoulders and blew a kiss. He was substituted ten minutes later, and after the game, he insisted he had only wanted to shake the supporter's hand.

It was an eye-opening experience for Jordan, who, to his credit, could appreciate all sides of the problem. 'A person has aspirations, goals, and dreams, and you're going to set out each day to accomplish those things,' he says. 'Who knows, maybe a team mistreated you and you have something to prove, or any number of random things happen behind the scenes that fans don't see, that makes you want to do what you want to do. And I think David was doing exactly that. He came to fulfil his obligation in the States but [he] also wanted to go play back in Milan, so until someone puts their foot down and says, "No, you need to be in this one place" … he was just living life, trying to accomplish what he could. I can see how fans or press could see that in a bad way, especially if you felt he wasn't being loyal to us, and I can see how that could be frustrating on David. It was really kind of crazy to witness, at some of those games, how mad our fans were for a period of time, especially when it was supposed to be like a home game for him, you know? It was just really odd.'

Jordan's goal against the Italians was somewhat overshadowed, though he takes it in good humour. 'Against Milan, David served me up an amazing assist on a corner kick, and after I strongly buried that into the back of the net … while I did my celebration flip and ran over to the corner flag to him, I wasn't totally sure he was going to even celebrate with me … I'll tease David a little bit here … You know the kid was just trying to get a little shine, but I think his fight made even bigger news than my goal did,' he laughs. 'I'll never forget that goal, though – thanks for the service, my dude! A player always wants to do his best, no matter where he is, and he always wants the fans to back him and love him, so I'm sure he wasn't trying to upset anyone. He was just trying to live out his dreams, and the fans just didn't happen to like that one dream 'cause it didn't match up with their wants. It's similar to certain relationships if you think about it.'

Helene Elliott – the reporter who had spoken so glowingly of Beckham on his debut – now had a different tone in her coverage of the encounter for the *LA Times*. 'Many Galaxy fans see the multi-tattooed Englishman as an over-the-hill, overpaid superstar,' she wrote. 'On Sunday, they let him know how they felt in no uncertain terms.'

There was another row with a supporter the following week at Kansas City. A fan in the crowd – who was wearing an England shirt – got close enough to make insults about Victoria, when Beckham was about to take a throw-in. The midfielder turned around and exchanged angry words – he later told reporters: 'He shouldn't actually be wearing that shirt, because what he was saying about my wife was a disgrace.' (It was later reported that he had shaken hands with the culprit after he had calmed down.)

These were spats which would have made front-page news in the UK. Alexi Lalas is surprised by that. 'It's no Cantona, he wasn't jumping in the crowd,' he says, and attributes the abuse thus: 'Because the team wasn't winning and he was the focal point. Don't take the gig if you don't want that type of attention. I'm not trying to sound insensitive, it's just all relative to winning. Winning doesn't solve everything, but it solves a lot of things, and it enables you to gloss over a lot of things. Things that irk you become less significant when you're winning. They didn't win the MLS Cup, but they got to the final, and that was the sort of consistent existence that he had experienced at Manchester United and Real Madrid.'

The Galaxy's season was interrupted by one more friendly with a European team – Barcelona came to town, and went away with a 2–1 win, but Beckham left his own mark on the game with another wonderful free kick.

Back in the more serious business of MLS, Beckham notched his first official goal of the campaign with a sensational winner against Chivas USA at the end of August: the ball came to him around 17 yards out, having bounced once. He couldn't quite connect before the second bounce, but that made the technique for the finish all the more wonderful, as he fired a deadly accurate bullet in off the post. A couple of weeks later, Beckham got the first in a 2–0 win over Toronto – and though there were no further goals in the season, his contribution was felt as the Galaxy not only qualified for the MLS Cup play-offs, but then got through to the Western Conference Final against the Houston Dynamo. Whatever happened from now on, this was the team's best accomplishment since Beckham's arrival.

It was an eventful end to the year. England secured their place in the 2010 World Cup, with Beckham continuing his involvement, which suggested he could at least be sure he would be judged on his form to get a place in South Africa. He admitted that this was the only reason he had agreed to return to Italy for another loan spell in January. 'It's the only reason I am choosing to be away from my family,' he said. 'Being in the World Cup squad is not guaranteed, even if I go to Milan it is not guaranteed, but I need to do everything possible to give myself a chance. It's always a rollercoaster in my career, and it is going to be like that for the next six to eight months.'

First, he wanted to close out 2009 on a high. This had not quite been the character-restoring journey he had enjoyed in the past, but winning the MLS Cup might at least be seen as some redemption in the eyes of the fans who retained their reservations. A final place was secured, but it took a long time to get there. First of all, their game with Houston had to be stopped for 18 minutes in each half due to electricity cuts ordered by actor-turned-Governor of California, Arnold Schwarzenegger.

Beckham, who had made something of a career of his own out of saying 'I'll be back', had one of the crucial involvements in this game – creating the first goal, which finally came in extra time. The Galaxy eventually won 2–0. 'It was a crazy, stop-start match with the power blackouts and extra time,' David said afterwards. 'But I'm proud of the way we defended and stuck at it. I can't wait for that game [the final]. It means everything to me to win trophies with Galaxy.'

Real Salt Lake won the other semi-final on penalty kicks against the Chicago Fire. The final would be played in Seattle on 22 November. Because of Beckham's journey, there was still the narrative of redemption being somewhat prematurely played out in the media. If that seemed too soon, then it should be said that Bruce Arena was fairly measured in his analysis of Beckham's few months back in the US. It was fair to ask the coach if a player of lesser character might have buckled under the pressure Beckham had been subjected to since July. 'The reason it didn't happen is because he showed he cares about the LA Galaxy,' Arena said. 'His performances quietened his detractors. He's played with some of the biggest clubs in the world and has been through a lot. He has won over his team-mates and the supporters.'

There was a more pressing adversity in the days before the final. Beckham was forced to miss some training sessions because of a bruised right ankle which he required painkilling injections for. He was able to take to the field for the game; the Galaxy took a first-half lead through Magee, but conceded an equaliser midway through the second period. Goalkeeper Donovan Ricketts had actually broken his hand in the first minutes of the second half, but tried to play on before the Real Salt Lake goal went in. The game went all the way to penalties – Beckham taking and scoring the first one – with Real Salt Lake winning on sudden-death kicks.

'It's always tough losing, whether you lose on penalties or in normal play, but we can be proud of where we've come to,' Beckham said, after admitting he had taken three injections in his ankle that had worn off after 15 minutes. 'I wouldn't say it's tougher to lose on penalties, but it's Russian roulette. The people that step up are brave enough to step up and, if you score, great, and if you miss it's hard to take.'

For Beckham it was back to Europe, via South Africa, as he was attending the World Cup draw, which put England in the same group as the USA. Beyond repeating the same line as recently – that the move to Milan was not a guarantee of a place – Beckham was decidedly quiet due to the heartbreaking news that his grandfather Joe had passed away.

The reaction about the group draw came from Beckham's team-mates, starting with Donovan. 'Hopefully we'll both be there because a lot can happen between now and then, but if that's the case, it'll be fun,' the American said. 'There'll be a lot of talking before the first game. He won't be around with the Galaxy before the tournament starts, so it won't be as intense as it might be. We've just talked about being there and seeing each other there, but I don't think it entered our minds that we might be playing each other.'

Donovan had been in fine form through the year, scoring 15 goals, but was well placed to bring up the subject of the fickle hand of fate considering how he had missed one of the penalties in the MLS Cup Final.

Two weeks later there was another draw – this time for the Champions League second round. Beckham had claimed a reunion with Manchester United would be 'beautiful', but would still have been surprised to learn that AC Milan had indeed drawn his former club for clashes in February and March.

There had been a number of changes at Milan – not least the manager. As previously mentioned, Carlo Ancelotti had gone to Chelsea, and he was replaced by Leonardo. There had been a turnover of players, too. Paolo Maldini had retired, and Kaká had been bought by Real Madrid as the first of returning president Florentino Pérez's new collection of Galacticos.

Nonetheless, as soon as Beckham was in Italy, he was thrown straight into the team, and had a fantastic first game against Genoa as Milan won 5–2. He started at Juventus the following week, this time as the right-sided attacker in a 4–2–1–3. Here, he put in arguably his most impressive showing in Italy, creating all three goals in a resounding 3–0 win.

It was a strong return, and attention inevitably turned to United's visit in mid-February. This would be Beckham's first game against his former club since his sale; since when his replacement, Cristiano Ronaldo, had been signed and sold for a world record fee of £80m (the second of Pérez's new wave of glamour signings). Now the number 7 at Old Trafford was Michael Owen – a pure frugal gamble taken by Sir Alex Ferguson despite the England striker's poor injury record. Unlike Beckham, Owen had no realistic chance of going to the World Cup, and was instead acting as understudy to the player who had succeeded him in the England team, Wayne Rooney.

'When I was at Real Madrid it just never felt right to come back to Old Trafford,' Beckham told the *Express*. 'The thought of playing United always gives me that sick feeling because I missed the club so much. The first few years away were hard and there were a lot of things I missed. It was the club I always wanted to play for and I loved every minute of my time there. I always wish I was part of Manchester United, it's just in me. Even though I'm not there any more, I'm still a huge fan and watch every game where possible. I always want them to do well and be successful because the club still means so much to me. When the draw was made it just felt it was the right time to go back. There isn't one player I'm particularly looking forward to facing. I'm just looking forward to being a part of it all and savouring the atmosphere in both games. Returning to Old Trafford is going to be special and a very emotional night. I've spoken to Gary Neville since the draw and we both believe it's going to be a great tie.'

Sir Alex Ferguson spoke well of Beckham for the February edition of *Inside United*, although there was a sting in the tail which seemed to suggest, even seven years on, that the United boss was still insisting he was right to have sold him. 'I think I told him myself last year, when I saw him before our game against Inter, that he should be thinking about getting back to Europe if he wanted to go to the World Cup,' Ferguson said. 'And it looks like he might just get his wish now. He had a good spell with Milan last time, so it made sense to me to see him back there again. He's such a high-profile celebrity – not just a high-profile footballer. Our job is to concentrate on the football match and let the David Beckham media circus carry on.'

Before the first leg at the San Siro, Beckham discussed how anxious he had become thinking about the game, but insisted that was only due to playing against United and not the resurrection of any old battle with his former manager. 'There is no score to settle,' he said. 'Sir Alex Ferguson was always a father figure to me. He always has been and always will be, no matter what people have said in the past about our relationship. Whether it's been good times or bad times, the only times I remember are the good times. He was the man who gave me a chance of playing for a club I dreamed of. And we had so many successful times. Not one part of me blames him for forcing me out. It was my time to leave United in 2003, and I moved on. I definitely don't hold anything against the manager. He's an incredible man.'

Beckham was influential in the early stages, setting up a goal for Ronaldinho. But United responded, and in a familiar manner. Antonio Valencia was master creator from the right-hand side, creating chances at will, whilst Wayne Rooney helped himself to two as United won 3–2, but the former Old Trafford midfielder did emerge with credit. 'What you saw from Beckham – playing centrally and tidily for much of the time until he was substituted in the 71st minute – was the benefit of his years of playing abroad,' wrote John Dillon in the *Express*. 'He has a more highly developed sense of tactical discipline than most English players and he has always been one who is less prone to giving away possession than most.'

Dillon may have been right: certainly, there had been a long enough period of experience in the centre of the park for Beckham to have refined his short-ball game to be as economical as his delivery game.

It could equally be true that this was a case of not knowing what you've got until it's gone; certainly, there seemed to be a much greater argument to celebrate Beckham's relentless consistency – and therefore an acknowledgement of his enduring footballing intelligence – than there was to suggest there had been a remarkable Indian summer. The absent conversation – and surely the more likely truth – was that there had simply been far too many times that he had been written off prematurely.

Milan's form took a dip after the United defeat. Leonardo may have been obligated to stand by the agreement to bring Beckham back, but he did not have an obligation to start him, and was not as enamoured with the England star as Carlo Ancelotti had been. The midfielder was only named on the bench in a goalless draw in Rome, prompting Mick Dennis of the *Express* to describe the forthcoming return leg against United as a potential 'final audition' for the World Cup.

'He was only a substitute in Milan's goalless draw at Roma at the weekend,' Dennis wrote, a weekend after David had been an unused substitute against Fiorentina. 'There we have the Beckham conundrum – he is still worldwide news, but these days the hype and hope are seldom matched by reality. If Milan are not sure whether to pick him, what about England?'

Leonardo explained that he was exercising his right to rotate his squad, and would not guarantee that he would play at Old Trafford. 'Beckham is a very important player for our group,' he insisted. 'He has so much experience and has played so many big games. David is a key player for us. He is a big player, and we know we can call on him if necessary. Knowing him, and the attitude he has, he will be able to cope with the situation. For David, this match is something special. To have the opportunity to play against Manchester United, the team where he achieved so much, is amazing for him.'

This was not the greatest United side, but Ferguson had reorganised the team since Ronaldo's departure to play Rooney as a pure centre-forward. The formation had worked in the San Siro and it worked again at Old Trafford, with two goals killing the tie off. When, in the 59th minute, Park Ji-Sung took a brief breather from marking Andrea Pirlo out of the game to score a third on the night and a sixth on aggregate, the tie was over save for the sentiment. Five minutes later, Leonardo finally gave Old Trafford what it had been waiting for – the return of David Beckham. As is par for the course on such occasions, he was given a rapturous welcome on to the pitch, and then a boo just as loud when he took his first touch. United got a late fourth to rubber-stamp an emphatic win.

The testimonial feel to the conclusion of the game would have been just what Ferguson wanted. But he was given cause to reflect on the off-pitch attention given to Beckham that had played such a part in his departure from the club seven years prior, when the midfielder applauded the Stretford End after the final whistle. He went over to embrace supporters, and one handed him a scarf – a green and gold scarf, which at the time was representative of a protest against the club owners, the Glazer family, from United fans.

Images of him wearing the scarf around his neck were flashed all over the world. Some United supporters were excited about what this could mean for the public face of their protests, but they were left deflated when Beckham quickly confessed that he was not aware of the significance of the scarf's colours. 'I'm a Manchester United fan. When I saw the scarf I put it round my neck – it's the old colours of United,' he said. 'It's not my business. I'm a United fan and I support the club, I always will. It's nothing to do with me how it's run. That's to do with other people. I support the team. And I will always support the team.'

On the game itself, David was emotional, but disappointed from the point of view of a competitor. 'I keep saying it, but Wayne is such an exceptional talent,' he said. 'He's one of the best players, if not the best, in the world at the moment, along with Lionel Messi and Ronaldo. They don't come much better. I was happy with my form when I came on for the last 20 minutes … I was comfortable when I got on the pitch. It felt like home. It was nice to be back, but it was a disappointing night because we lost. Returning here is always special. The fans were unbelievable. I have to say thank you to all of them.'

It is worth taking a very minor diversion here to conclude the story between David Beckham and Manchester United. His father, Ted, remained a United fanatic, just as he had been in the years before David's birth. He travelled the country watching the team and in 2005 released his own book, entitled *My Son*. In promotion of it, Ted gave an interview to *Red News*, the fanzine edited by Barney Chilton – the pair obviously familiar with each other from the hundreds of games they'd seen each other at. Ted expressed his disappointment that a song for Cristiano Ronaldo had quickly been created which included the line '... makes Beckham look shite'. Ted admitted that he wished David was back at United, but conceded there was little chance of that happening. He also gave a very interesting insight into the biggest influences on David's career. 'I think it's got to be Cantona,' he said. 'The thing he said to me a few years ago was that he wanted to play with Mark Hughes and Bryan Robson. So he's done that. He's got so much respect for those two. Bryan Robson was his hero, but the most influential player was Eric Cantona.'

There were years in David's formative spell where he admitted that he felt influenced by those figures, and it could certainly be traced on to the pitch. The only one really missing had been Robson, but there was a certain emulation of him on the international stage, leading by example, if in a completely different way. Like Robson, Beckham would unfairly often be missing from the discussion of the greatest players of all time, his contribution hugely underrated and, at times, under-appreciated.

The convenient return to the UK had reintroduced David to the eyes of the British football journalists and therefore the back pages of the newspapers. Milan's trip to United would be the last opportunity many of them would get to see him live in Britain, certainly before South Africa, so as far as they were concerned this was, as Mike Dennis had put it, very much a final audition.

Beckham was asked if he felt the cameo appearance at Old Trafford had effectively secured his place in the World Cup squad, and he insisted there was still a long time to go. 'I am not guaranteed to go to South Africa,' he said. 'I have to work hard and hopefully win my place. There are a good few months left and plenty of games to play – but hopefully I can carry on playing well and get in the squad.'

He started against Chievo at the weekend. Ted had gone out to Italy to watch him play. Milan had tried and failed to find a way past their visitors, who were penned back looking to protect their point. In the 88th minute, Beckham received the ball in the centre circle and span his body around to open up the picture in front of him, the way he had done hundreds, if not thousands, of times in his career. This time, though, there was something different. As he went to strike the ball he immediately felt a strong discomfort.

He went to the sidelines and could only watch as Clarence Seedorf struck a fine late winner; according to Leonardo, Beckham knew there was a serious problem straight away.

'David understood immediately that he had torn his Achilles tendon … he felt the muscle begin to come up, which is a typical symptom when you break an Achilles tendon,' the Milan coach told Sky Italia. 'It's a real blow. Beckham's injury makes us feel terrible. He is an extraordinary guy and today's game proves it yet again. I cannot enjoy this evening considering this serious injury.'

He may have been considered a peripheral figure to the extent that his mere inclusion in the World Cup squad was a matter of controversy, but images of Beckham on the floor in agony were on the front pages of some British newspapers as it was clear he would not achieve an ambition of becoming the first Englishman to play in four World Cups.

Back at Milan, there was an outpouring of sympathy and emotion. 'He'll probably be out for five or six months,' AC Milan vice president Adriano Galliani said. 'I saw him really suffering. In the changing room, I hugged him and told him that if he wants he can join us next year, too.'

Defender Gianluca Zambrotta gave an indication of how popular David had become in such a short spell with his Milan team-mates. 'He came here because he wanted to help Milan return to the top, and he was looking to get a shirt for the national team and participate in the World Cup,' he said. 'If other victories come, there will surely be a dedication for David Beckham.'

Sentiment aside, there was the cruel reality for Beckham to face – that at the age of 34, it was not only his World Cup, but even his career that could be at risk. 'David was absolutely devastated,' a source told the *Daily Star*. 'Poor old Ted spent much of the night consoling him. David was very tearful and convinced his career was over.'

Beckham immediately flew to Finland for surgery – Dr Sakari Orava, operating, said the tendon was 'totally torn' but that the procedure was a success.

The day after the surgery, David's team issued a statement on his behalf: 'I'm feeling positive and now concentrating on getting back to full fitness over the coming months. The operation was a success and I'd like to thank Dr Sakari Orava and all the medical staff who looked after me during my time in Finland. I'd like to take this opportunity to thank everyone for their messages of support. They mean a lot to me.'

Fabio Capello had made an emotionally supportive call to Beckham which echoed that of Galliani, suggesting that the European Championship in two years' time could be an achievable goal. The sobering reality of this situation was that even for a man who had overcome varying degrees of adversity, this challenge in his football career was likely to be his final one.

The Beckham Redemption

AFTER FEELING that he had rushed recovery from injuries earlier in his stint in America, David Beckham was keen to not only give himself every chance of a proper recovery, but to prove to those who had invested in him that he was dedicating his time to a serious return. That meant coming back to the country as soon as he'd had an operation, and giving positive soundbites to local press. 'I won't be running for another three months, so I will be playing again in, probably, November,' he told ABC television in late April. 'My mentality is to kind of push it and get moving and running as soon as possible. But it's an injury that has to take time to heal.'

New LA Galaxy head coach Bruce Arena had not needed David to get off to a flying start. The team had an arrangement with Brazilian club São Paulo where they took three promising talents on initial loan deals – Leonardo, Juninho and Alex Cazumba. There had been sensible squad additions such as Jovan Kirovski, the experienced forward who had spent some time at Manchester United with Beckham in the 90s, and Mike Magee, a reliable goalscoring attacking midfielder.

The Galaxy started their MLS season with ten wins and two draws from their first 12 games. Their summer form was again mixed – but even a rocky spell of five defeats in ten games wasn't enough to take them out of top spot in both Western Conference and overall standings.

Beckham had been working hard through the year and, after originally being ruled out for the entire year and then admitting himself that he wasn't likely to play until November, was given a prospective date of 1 October as a return after he resumed light training on 13 August.

It was a boost that he needed after a double blow in the summer. Milan had confessed they were unlikely to bring him back, despite Adriano Galliani's promise.

And Fabio Capello had delivered a rather poorly timed swipe after his team had defeated Hungary in a friendly at Wembley. England had suffered another poor tournament and were in another rebuilding phase, with this restart featuring Theo Walcott and Adam Johnson on the wings. Capello was asked if he would consider picking David for the next competitive game once he was fit, and replied: 'No, I need to change it. David is a fantastic player, but I think we need new players for the future.' Capello admitted he had not discussed this with the player and, anticipating the criticism he might face for the way he had apparently called time on an international career, quickly added: 'If he is fit, I hope we will play one more game here at Wembley so the fans can say goodbye.'

Given that Beckham had been welcomed as part of Capello's coaching set-up for the World Cup, it seemed poor form to have not discussed the matter privately beforehand.

Beckham's representatives issued a short statement in response: 'For your information, there has been no discussion of retirement. He will always be available for his country, when fit and if needed he will be there.'

He was more keen than ever to get back on to the pitch, and it was rumoured that he might even return to the Galaxy team in mid-September. 'A few people are [surprised], but I'm not. I expected to push myself to the limit and I have,' he told the Galaxy's official website. 'In my own head I could have been back a month ago. The doctors said October 1, but hopefully it will be a few weeks before that … The focus is the team and repairing my tendon. That's the biggest thing to me. I've been hitting it so hard the last two years, every month, all year round is obviously tough on my body. It's about getting back this season as soon as possible, playing the rest of the season and then taking the time to get the rest in and repair my body and being ready for next season. I never feel as if I can push myself enough. I will know personally when I am ready. Obviously I have to listen to the advice of the doctors, but in the end, it will be me knowing whether I'm ready or not.'

On 2 September, Beckham revealed he had targeted the game against the Columbus Crew on the 11th as the day he would be returning.

'I'll keep my fingers crossed and hopefully will play in part of the game against Columbus,' he said. 'I'll be on the bench and hopefully I'll get on the field for 15–20 minutes.'

Beckham's dedication to get back to playing at the age of 35 was more than just commendable, according to his team-mates. 'It was bizarre to see the amount of work he put into his rehab at that point in his career,' Mike Magee says. 'Risking everything to come back early. A setback would have ended him, but he didn't care. He has worked his ass off, rushed back and I think what he accomplished at that age after that injury isn't spoken about enough.'

David was indeed back for the game against Columbus, coming on in the 70th minute with his team leading 3–0, and wasting no time in showing that he was ready to get stuck in by picking up a booking just four minutes after arriving on the pitch. The Galaxy were sure to make the play-offs, so the goal for Beckham was to ensure he was ready to start in those games. He was in fact back in the first eleven when the New York Red Bulls travelled to the Home Depot Center on 25 September. And in the following game, against Chivas USA on 4 October, he demonstrated that he was back and in business in classic Beckham style, scoring a brilliant long-range free kick which decided the game.

He may well have been more satisfied with his strike on the last day of the regular season: Donovan tigerishly competed for the ball and won it back before laying it off to Beckham on the edge of the area. A rare open-play opportunity presented itself, and the English midfielder drilled it into the corner – the equaliser in a 2–1 win over FC Dallas. However, the Texas team returned to the Home Depot Center three weeks later in the Western Conference play-off final, and exacted revenge with a crushing 3–0 victory.

For the second year in succession, a redemption arc had conveniently laid itself at the feet of David Beckham, but the general and marked improvement in the team had not been reflected in their achievement. There was one thing that the Galaxy could count on, though, and that was the dedication of their star name to make the team the number-one side in North America by the time he had gone. That would include complete attention – and although he returned to England to train in the winter, and entertained discussion of a temporary move, this time those conversations were held with the condition that he would be returning to Los Angeles for the start of the MLS season rather than spending the remainder of the European season with a loan club. Despite those injury concerns of the prior year, and despite his veteran status, three of England's top clubs were vying for his attention.

Everton – coached by David Moyes, who was assisted by Beckham's friend Phil Neville – were interested. 'If David wanted to pick up the phone and say he wants to come to Everton, we would be here for him,' said Moyes in November. 'I played in the same team as David at Preston. I made his bad crosses look OK and scored from one of his corners once. If David wanted to come back to the Premier League, he would only need to pick up the phone to me or Phil.'

But when David did arrive in England, he stayed in London, and first spent some time with Arsenal, as he had done a couple of years earlier. 'Of course I would consider signing Beckham,' Arsene Wenger admitted. 'I love David Beckham, and when he was here he was a fantastic example on the professional side. He was the first in and the last out.'

Harry Redknapp, still at Spurs and overseeing something of a revolution at White Hart Lane, made the most serious move and convinced Beckham to train with his club with a view to a short-term loan.

'It can't go on too long or it'd be a waste of time,' Redknapp said on the prospect of deliberating over the negotiation. 'By the time David comes here and settles in, if it's four, five or six weeks, then it's a waste. I was looking at three months really. Suddenly we're talking nine weeks, or nine or ten games, and it's getting less and less. I'm not cooling on the idea, but if it's only a very short-term deal, it can be a problem, as much as I like him. I can't start leaving people out then mess around with the team again when David goes back. It's a difficult one if it's for that short period. It just depends how it all goes. He's never going to be short of somewhere to go. David would be good around the place. He knows how to win games and he would be good for us on the pitch. He has a lot to offer. Players like Aaron Lennon could learn an awful lot just being around him. They are different players, but it would be interesting. Beckham's delivery and making goals is what it comes down to. The end product. But they're complete opposites really. It is not definite, but if the deal is done by then, there is a chance he will be there. This is good for Tottenham. It isn't doing us any harm, is it? And he's been around this most of his life, so it isn't going to affect him either.'

It wasn't doing the Galaxy any harm for Redknapp to be so openly, and urgently, coveting their main man. It would have been music to the ears of Bruce Arena and Philip Anschutz to hear Redknapp explain what a boost it had been just to be linked to Beckham. 'It says a lot about Spurs' stature in the game now,' he boasted. 'He has been with Manchester United, Real Madrid and AC Milan – and he could be coming to Tottenham. He looked at the club, likes the way we play and try to play the game. He can come here and play with Luka Modrić and Rafael van der Vaart … I don't just see David coming off the bench. He can play in a midfield role. It will all depend on circumstances.'

Talks dragged on, with all parties willing to agree to a short-term deal that would conclude in mid-March, but Spurs hit a problem with their insurance and couldn't resolve it in time for the player to be registered by the transfer deadline. They agreed he could train with them until he went back to America, with Redknapp conceding that he would look at striking a deal at the end of the year, when Beckham's contract in the US was due to expire. 'You would love to have him at your club,' he said. 'I love the way he plays. He has looked great in training. He has been fantastic and is a top-class bloke. He comes in and works hard every day. He has been great around the place. He's welcome back here any time.'

On his last morning before going home, Beckham treated Spurs staff at their Waltham Abbey training complex to pie and mash, a traditional London dish.

Under Bruce Arena, the Galaxy had built a side that was most definitely more competitive than it had been previously, but it was also clear that further steps were necessary to bridge the gap from also-rans to MLS champions. The attempt at doing so was made with the acquisition of Juan Pablo Ángel, the former Aston Villa player who had enjoyed a very good spell with the New York Red Bulls. The move was not a success. Ángel scored just three goals in 22 games for the Galaxy, his first coming in a miserable 4–1 defeat at Real Salt Lake early in the season. Arena realised that the move wasn't working, and it wasn't until Ángel was taken out of the side that the form began to improve to the standards of the previous year. The Galaxy, still hunting for a goalscorer, found one in the shape of Robbie Keane, who arrived in August before play-off season.

Beckham, too, took a while to get going, collecting yellow cards quicker than assists, and waiting until the middle of May to get his first goal of the year. When it duly arrived, it was a blockbusting free kick as one would expect; but, coming as it did in the dying minutes of a comfortable victory over Sporting Kansas City, it gave cause for some to question how significant his contribution was. Of course, that was merely the traditional time for Beckham's true worth to reveal itself.

'He remained underrated, but not to his team-mates,' Magee says. 'He's clever and two plays ahead. The American fan base was one step behind. Most of his greatness was unnoticed. He was brilliant. Most players couldn't see what he wanted to do … I could. When he would get the ball, I'd just run to the most dangerous place on the field that he could play it, because I knew he'd get it there quickly.'

Magee insists that Beckham's determination never diminished: 'He fought like a bastard every day. He never slowed down. I saw it every day in training, so his brilliance was normal to me.'

According to Alexi Lalas, Bruce Arena deserves some credit for using David in a deeper midfield role and being smart with his deployment (Beckham was also suffering from back issues throughout the year). 'He came back from his injury as a valuable, viable player,' Lalas explains. 'He changed, as all players do when they get older. He got smarter, he became more efficient. I think Bruce Arena recognised what David was good at and what he wasn't, and he put him in positions to succeed. That applies to everybody in the team, though. From a physical perspective, his recovery was not a problem because of his attitude to training. David was certainly a major influence. He wouldn't hurt teams in the same way that Landon or Robbie would, but the reason they would be able to is because David would consistently find those guys in good places. His ability to serve a ball never changed over the course of his career. His understanding of angles, his capability of striking and curling the ball, did not diminish. Those skills never dissipated.'

In some respects, you could liken the last two years or so in MLS to Beckham's breakthrough years in the Premier League. He was more experienced now, but there was something fantastic in his prowling of the midfield area and his capability of scoring long-range goals from open play, which was reminiscent of the younger days, before he was so predominantly regarded as a relentless production line based almost exclusively on the right touchline.

The appreciation from his team-mates was also now found from the fans in the stands. Lalas believes that Beckham's very public refocusing not only worked to rebuild a relationship, but also started to re-energise the feeling around the Galaxy, so much so that all of those initial hopes for the transfer were finally beginning to blossom, and even to exceed those first aspirations of how it might take off.

Did starting the season in America help? 'I think so,' Lalas says. 'I think he enjoyed his time in California and in the United States. Once the soccer part of it started to go better, and he didn't have to worry about that so much. I wasn't surprised that he stayed so many years. In a certain sense of the best of all worlds. From a business perspective, we know he was able to expand that brand. To this day, when we look at the history of American soccer, the importance and value of David Beckham is going to be rightfully honoured and praised. As far as seminal moments are concerned, there is before David Beckham and after David Beckham. The number of people who tasted soccer as a consequence of his involvement was amazing. The transcendence that he had and the importance of that … I was amazed, perhaps I shouldn't have been, at the number of people who before didn't care, suddenly did because of David. And that's what we wanted.'

It is curious, then, to observe the repeating of a pattern which was followed at Real Madrid, and one can't help but feel Magee's assessment is on the money. Perhaps it was no coincidence that early perceptions of Beckham's move had been more critical because of the expectation (although those first two or three years in the US were not a runaway success by anybody's definition). That is not to say that Beckham failed to meet expectations, just that what people thought they were getting was not in fact what arrived. Maybe they didn't know themselves. No one with more than a passing interest in football would proclaim Beckham to be something that he wasn't. It was clear to see that his talents laid in the more unsung areas of the game, such as his accuracy and consistency of delivery. This could be appreciated by team-mates and even opponents, but it was not going to electrify supporters in the same way that a dribbler or regular goalscorer might. He was known as a free-kick wizard – averaging three or four goals from these situations a year was probably par for what might be expected, but their relative scarcity in comparison to other goals might well be perceived as inconsistency to those unfamiliar with him.

Beckham never changed, not when it came to his style of play. He may have become more efficient and economical, whether that came with experience and maturity or with the help of astute coaching; but, aside from the refining of those existing abilities, there were no new tricks, so to speak. Therefore, for attitudes towards him to change in such a dramatic fashion, one or both of two things had to happen. The first was some major incident in which David could be seen as the protagonist, and someone to rally behind in adversity. The second was an evolution of the consumer, the general soccer fan, whose appreciation for the mechanics of the game might grow. This does not exclude long-term diehard soccer fans: sometimes those who have watched the game for all of their life can take a while to fully appreciate the qualities of a certain player, and when there is a certain public projection of that individual, those misunderstandings are reasonable. Both elements of this equation combined with an upturn in the Galaxy's success on the field, and even though Lalas's previous observation about greater talent surrounding Donovan and Beckham was completely accurate, the fact that the team and the league were now beginning to see the English star controlling games in the way he could do for his national side meant that he was now finally perceived as something like value for money and hype. Arena had Beckham playing deep in the middle and the Galaxy were purring.

The 4–1 win over Kansas City was the first of eight in a run of 12 games unbeaten. Beckham's next goal came in a man-of-the-match performance against Chicago in July. His set pieces had already been causing havoc before he finally created the opening goal for Donovan in the 58th minute. 'The best right foot in Major League Soccer … the service is incredible … world class,' exclaimed the announcer for the Fox Soccer Channel – but this was merely the type of cross he had delivered thousands of times in his career. His 15 assists this season would see him ranked second in MLS.

Chicago hit back within minutes, but so did the Galaxy with a retaliation of their own. This time, the accuracy of Beckham's set piece was so on point that his corner kick went straight into the Chicago goal. The image of six defenders watching as the ball curled in and bounced through the goalkeeper's legs and into the net was iconic.

Arena's team were certs for the play-offs, but added a little security in August with the blockbuster signing of Robbie Keane. At the age of 31, and still representing the Republic of Ireland with distinction, this was another coup – a transfer that most certainly would not have occurred without Beckham paving the way.[3] The Galaxy topped the Western Conference and overall standings for the second year in succession. Juan Pablo Ángel had once observed, early in his time in MLS, how he felt the way soccer competitions were run in America was unfair, as they didn't seem to give a reward for achievements in the regular season, with everything coming down to the play-offs. It wasn't a matter of fairness, though – these were the rules of the competition, and teams were judged by their success or failure.

The Galaxy's first opponents in the play-offs were the Red Bulls, who themselves had a former Premier League star in their attack in Thierry Henry. It was a standard-setter for the US game with so many decorated individuals, but it was Beckham's star which shone the brightest, with the sort of controlling and patrolling midfield display he had so often dreamed of putting on. It was a shame that his creativity was only rewarded with a 1–0 win in the first leg at the Red Bull Arena, but it was fitting that he created the game's goal for Mike Magee.

In the return leg three days later, the Red Bulls played a more physical game in their attempts to get back into the tie. They restored parity with a fourth-minute goal and looked as if they might have gained an even bigger boost when Beckham collapsed in agony after an aerial challenge with Dane Richards. David's back appeared to give out, but it was not serious enough for him to be substituted. Soon after his return to the pitch, he

---

3   The respective local profile of the pair, though, was best summarised by a gaffe made by a photographer who took a picture of both Beckham and Keane with Russell Brand at a Los Angeles Lakers game in October 2012, with the description given to Reuters of Keane as an 'unidentified fan'. By that point Keane had done more than enough to cement his own place in Galaxy folklore, but not enough, clearly, to transcend the game and move into the local celebrity scene.

took a corner from the left and it was met with deadly accuracy by a delighted Magee. New York were deflated by the goal, and Landon Donovan's late penalty – won after Beckham had been scythed down in the box – added some conviction to the scoreline.

The Galaxy were now entering the territory of past heartbreaks, but in their Conference Final against Real Salt Lake, it was Beckham's creativity making the difference again: they were 1–0 down after the first half, but early in the second, one of those brilliant curling crosses was headed in by Magee, whose navigation system had been so in sync with that of his colleague in recent games.

'I led the team in play-off goals ... I believe every goal I scored he assisted on, so I loved playing with him,' Magee laughs. Magee, of course, had not known what to expect, and his opinion had been formed from seeing David in MLS. 'He was a good-looking fucker,' he says of his first impression of the former Manchester United star. 'He was kind. Normal. It was weird. He'd ask me if I wanted an espresso or how my family was. He'd constantly ask how my little princess Keira, my daughter, was doing. I know that's how people are supposed to be, but he has no reason to be so down to earth. But he was. He tricked me into thinking him and I were the same. But he is one of a kind in the history of the game. David is a different level of competitor. He will always have to prove people wrong. He will always win. I don't care how successful he is, and neither does he.'

Magee gives a glowing assessment of Beckham's level of quality after returning from injury: 'Well, he signed with PSG three years after that injury. Every other team in the world wanted him. That says it all.'

The Beckham–Magee connection had been the functional dynamic on which Galaxy's play-offs were building, but the Donovan–Keane combination also came into good effect, bringing a third goal to add security to the result.

There was an experienced and clinical edge to Arena's team, a feature they would need in the MLS Cup Final against the Houston Dynamo. The Galaxy were heavily favoured to win, and so the narrative in the build-up included much discussion about the penalty shoot-out defeat to Real Salt Lake two years earlier. For Beckham, there was the welcome familiarity of rain and cooler temperatures at the Home Depot Center, making it feel more like Manchester than Los Angeles. There was the unwelcome familiarity of an injury in the build-up. A hamstring strain caused him to sit out some of the training sessions in the week before the game, but there was no way he was going to miss it. The five-year deal he had signed at the start of 2007 would effectively expire at the end of this game.

The English midfielder had been described as the 'point guard' of his team: a basketball reference which effectively translates as the leader of the side and the player who orchestrates the attacks. To those more familiar with straightforward soccer parlance, he excelled in his role as deep-lying playmaker, with his passes frequently causing issues for the Dynamo. When the breakthrough finally came in the 72nd minute, Beckham was involved, but not in his usual fashion: he flicked on a pass with his head to Keane, who found Donovan, who found the net. This was justice served, as 15 minutes earlier the linesman's flag had incorrectly gone up just as Keane had put the ball into the net from a Beckham pass.

The Galaxy had been accused of becoming too excited defensively with their conceding of goals earlier in the play-offs, but this time – at just the right time – they held firm. Houston's approach had been to counter-attack, but when the time came to take the impetus, they lacked a cutting edge. The Galaxy secured a win that was more emphatic and controlled than the 1–0 result suggested.

'When David Beckham joined the Los Angeles Galaxy in 2007, he made it clear that he had two overriding objectives,' wrote John Godfrey of the *New York Times*. 'He wanted to help raise the profile of Major League Soccer, and he wanted to bring a championship to the Galaxy. The first of these two goals were achieved the instant the Beckham celebrity machine arrived in Los Angeles. The second took a bit longer, but Beckham delivered in dramatic fashion Sunday night, leading the Galaxy past the Houston Dynamo, 1–0, in a stirring M.L.S. Cup final.'

Many believed this was the culmination of his five-year journey, but Beckham insisted he was only thinking about the moment and not the future. 'I've loved it here,' he said. 'The fans have been unbelievable, the owners, the players ... every one of them are heroes tonight. They've been incredible all season, and this has capped it off. People were talking about if we didn't win tonight it was going to be a disappointment and an unsuccessful five years. It's quietened a few people, which is always nice.'

It quietened the criticism, but not the speculation. The 36-year-old David Beckham was the hottest free agent in world football. The most serious contenders appeared to be Paris Saint-Germain, who had been taken over in June 2011 by Qatar Sports Investment and were keen on making David their first headline capture. Writing this in 2020, with all that has been achieved by PSG and by Manchester City after an earlier similar takeover, rejecting that move may seem like a strange decision – but it's worth remembering that as recently as late 2011 there was some doubt about the credibility or even success of City's approach, and consequently there was some concern over the project in Paris too. Things looked very different just one year down the line.

However, before the proposed move to Paris collapsed, Zinedine Zidane had given a glowing summary of the former team-mate he had once dismissed as 'gold paint on a Bentley': 'I don't know how he manages to be so at ease outwardly on the pitch. He is almost a pop star. I couldn't do that. It is incredible, especially given that he is as timid as me ... His arrival at Real made it possible to share the roles. I had less responsibility. In any case, that is the feeling I had. When he came to Real, he was worried about what the team thought of him. In his integration, he worried about everything that was said about him in the media, and that it would constitute a problem for his performances. But on the pitch, he has great technique and shows the combativeness typical of English players.'

Beckham insisted he would not be rushed into a decision. A further spanner had been thrown into the works with the United Kingdom hosting the Olympic Games the following year, 2012. Great Britain would have a football team, coached by Stuart Pearce; and, considering that Beckham had been used as a political figure to help the country get the Games, it was expected that he would be selected to represent 'Team GB'.

'I have got a big decision to make now,' he admitted in early December. 'I said I wanted to wait until the end of the season, and it is the end of the season now, so I need to take some downtime and decide what I need to do next. I'd have to decide in the next few weeks, maybe before Christmas, maybe just after. But I'm going to take my time. It's a big decision. I've had other offers [besides PSG], which is nice, especially when you're 36, some people would say towards the end of my career. I've got options and offers, but I'm still a Galaxy player right now and that might not change. I hope to be part of the Great Britain team,' he said. 'Everyone knows how passionate I am about playing for my country, and to represent my country in an Olympics would be pretty incredible, especially as the Olympics is in a part of London where I grew up as a kid.'

David revealed that the Galaxy had put the offer of a new contract on the table, and he again said that he had enjoyed his time there. 'It's been such a great experience on and off the field,' he said. 'Off the field, I accomplished everything I wanted to accomplish. I wanted to be part of a league that was growing,

I wanted to see the interest grow and we've seen that in the last five years. I wanted to be successful on the field, whether it's my last year or not, and we won the championship, which was nice. I knew that this league and this sport could grow in this country, but I didn't expect it to grow as it has in the last few years. I've seen the interest levels go up. Now the MLS is talked about around the whole world, which it wasn't before, so it's been nice to see the growth.'

The Sequel

IN TRUE Hollywood fashion, when one story is so successful and has an incredible ending, the demand for a sequel is just too impossible to resist.

On 18 January 2012, the LA Galaxy announced that they had re-signed David Beckham to a two-year contract.

'This was an important decision for me,' David said. 'I had many offers from clubs from around the world; however, I'm still passionate about playing in America and winning trophies with the Galaxy. I've seen first-hand how popular soccer is now in the States, and I'm as committed as ever to growing the game here. My family and I are incredibly happy and settled in America, and we look forward to spending many more years here.'

Bruce Arena was delighted to retain the services of his midfielder. 'I am thrilled that David has chosen to rejoin the Galaxy, especially as he had numerous options where he could continue his career,' the coach told the club's official website. 'I felt that he was one of the best players in all of MLS last season, and we could not have achieved the success that we did without him. We look forward to trying to replicate that success this season with David once again in a Galaxy uniform.'

Arena was experienced enough to know it would not all be about Beckham, or even Beckham, Robbie Keane and Landon Donovan. His squad underwent a huge post-season transition, with six players in and 11 out, before the MLS season got underway. The results were – predictably – underwhelming. The highlight of a poor start to the season came with a 3–1 win over the Portland Timbers, in which Beckham scored his first goal of the campaign, a wonderful 25-yard shot into the top corner.

Another fine goal followed – a free kick this time, in Montreal's Olympic Stadium, to earn a 1–1 draw – but the Galaxy's chances of topping either the Western or overall standings were in tatters by only the 13th game of the season. A 2–1 loss at Houston (who were claiming their own revenge from the previous year) was their eighth of the campaign so far. Yes, the turnover of players had played some part, but from the players who remained, the performance overall had been flat, as if the triumph of the previous season was the final accolade.

That said, if any player could be said to be maintaining standards, it was most definitely Beckham, who was in no comfort zone: indeed, he was, at the age of 37, given a renewed sense of purpose with someone to prove wrong after he had, to the shock of the UK, not been included in the Olympic squad – this after he had carried the Olympic flame after it arrived there in May from Greece.

'It's been an incredible week to be with the team in Athens and to bring the flame home, and it's a very proud moment for everybody,' he had said. 'I mean, it's amazing and the team have done an incredible job, and to be a part of the team – not just bringing it to London, but to the East End, where I grew up. We are going to have an amazing couple of months.'

But Stuart Pearce instead selected Ryan Giggs, Craig Bellamy and Micah Richards as his three over-age players. 'There's no doubt David had a burning ambition to be part of this,' Pearce said with some sympathy. 'The other 18 players had the same burning ambition, the three over-age players especially, they have been absolutely desperate to be part of this. We mustn't be sidetracked to think that David is a stand-alone professional who is desperate to play in the Olympics above anyone else who is on this sheet of paper. That isn't the case. I do enough hours watching matches, and I think I've done due diligence on all the players here. And in regard to ticket sales and merchandise, I'm a football man and I pick solely on football ability.'

This was a bitter blow for Beckham, who had also not been given the farewell from the international team which had been proposed by Fabio Capello in 2010. His England career had ended on 115 caps with the substitute appearance in the 3–0 win over Belarus in October 2009: a 32-minute display which saw him pick up the man-of-the-match award. It would be a fair statement to say his contribution had not been treated with the respect it deserved, both with the England team and the Olympic side. Team GB gave a mixed performance in 2012, losing on penalties to South Korea in the quarter-finals.

In the circumstances, with such a heavy feeling of anti-climax, one could have forgiven Beckham for going through the motions. He had nothing left to really prove, but it was to his enduring credit that he felt a responsibility to do so anyway. He would not get a recall to the England team, and there were no other unique international opportunities for him, but he still took personal responsibility to turn around the season for the LA Galaxy. Beckham put in another good display (and scored another free kick) in a combative 4–3 loss at San Jose. There were sparks of life, but the Galaxy needed a genuine boost to turn things around. It finally came in Oregon against the Portland Timbers on 14 July. Arena's team conceded an early goal, but refused to feel sorry for themselves and hit back in spectacular fashion. Donovan and Beckham in particular took responsibility, as leaders would. In the 19th minute, Donovan did well on the ball and Beckham found himself 30 yards from goal with room to set himself. He took one touch, and the entire Galaxy bench jumped up in anticipation. No, Beckham was not the type to excite a crowd with an exquisite dribble, but he was of a rare breed capable of scoring a spectacular long-range goal, as he did here. This was typical Beckham, a goal seen so often as to become almost monotonous if it was not so brilliant. And yet, having scored with such a stamp of individuality, his celebration – arms out, soaking in the applause – was undeniably reminiscent of his hero Eric Cantona.

Four minutes later, there was another quintessential Beckham moment to add to the collection, this time yet another free kick. He had personally turned the game upside down, and the Galaxy continued to punish their vulnerable opponents in the 26th minute when they were awarded a penalty. Landon Donovan assumed seniority over Beckham, denying his colleague a chance of a hat-trick, but scored Panenka-style to ensure he wouldn't be criticised. Before the game even reached the 30-minute mark, it was four. Beckham showed relentless tenacity to win the ball back, Donovan found Keane and it was game over. The Galaxy eventually won 5–3, but it was the earlier nine-minute spell of spectacular football which remained in the memory.

The team won nine games out of 12 – a run of fixtures which featured one more Beckham free kick, in a 2–0 win over Vancouver – and whilst this transformation wasn't quite enough to top the Western Conference, it was enough to get the Galaxy into the play-offs. Their journey to the Conference Final was straightforward: Vancouver and San Jose were put to the sword with some ease, and then the hard work was done in the first leg of the final against Seattle to set up another MLS Cup encounter with the Houston Dynamo.

As soon as qualification for that match was secured, Beckham issued a press release. The next game would be his last for the Galaxy, as he sought to end his career elsewhere. 'I've had an incredibly special time playing for the LA Galaxy; however, I wanted to experience one last challenge before the end of my playing career,' he said. 'I don't see this as the end of my relationship with the league, as my ambition is to be part of the ownership structure in the future. In my time here, I have seen the popularity of the game grow every year. I've been fortunate to win trophies, but more important to me has been the fantastic reception I've had from fans in LA and across the States. Soccer's potential has no limits in this wonderful country, and I want to always be part of growing it.'

As a reflection of that growth, all three teams that the Galaxy had faced in the play-offs had not even been in MLS prior to his arrival. When he came to the US in 2007, only five of MLS's 13 teams had stadiums solely dedicated to soccer; in 2012, that number was 15 out of 19.

Before the game against Houston, the Galaxy 'Riot Squad' held up a banner which read: 'This is Los Angeles. We win trophies. Get used to it.'

Beckham's departure, and the confidence of the home crowd (the game was again held at the Home Depot Center – this time because the Galaxy had the highest points total in the regular season, whereas a predetermined venue had been used in previous years), gave a celebratory air to the occasion. Houston briefly threatened to dampen the day by taking a half-time lead, but the Galaxy's recovery in the second half was the most professional job. Omar Gonzalez, a key defender, levelled things up before a Donovan penalty – as regular as Beckham free kicks in 2012 – gave the Galaxy the lead. Bruce Arena's side put in a containment job just as effective as in the previous year and, with the game deep into injury time, were waiting for the ball to be put out of play so Beckham could be brought off for acknowledgement from the crowd.

There was one more act, though: Mike Magee clipped in a ball over the top and Robbie Keane followed it, only to be brought down by the goalkeeper. Keane was permitted to take the kick by Donovan – no sentiment from the Irishman towards Beckham – and the 'unidentified fan' ensured people would remember his name by making the game secure.

After the goal celebrations, Arena did indeed bring off Beckham, who did indeed get that standing ovation as he gave almost every one of his team-mates a hug.

As the team were awarded the MLS Cup, David ensured each of his children got a chance to hold the trophy (Brooklyn and Romeo had been joined by another son, Cruz, and a daughter, Harper); the location of the triumph making it an even sweeter farewell.

It had been a long time – 12 years – since Beckham first made wearing a beanie hat famous. It had been a long time since he had made the news for having a markedly different haircut, come to that. He had no need to grab attention, but it was nonetheless a good piece of PR to wear a beanie with 'LA Galaxy – MLS Cup 2012' on it at the post-match press conference.

'It's what we set ourselves as a goal at the start of the season,' he said. 'I've spoken about it before. You always want to win a championship at the end of the year. Last year we were amazing and we did it. This year we didn't start very well, but we came good when it was the important time. So today's a special day for us, to win another championship in front of our own fans in our home in front of our friends and our family – it's very special, so today's a good day. Winning a championship in my last game at Manchester United, winning a championship in my last game at Real Madrid, even though I was only on the field for 68 minutes, I think it was … and then winning a championship here in my last game … it never gets old. I'm 37, and I've been lucky to play in finals and championship games. I still love it like when I won my first.'

He was hopeful it wouldn't be his last.

One Last Challenge

IT WAS speculated – as you might expect – that David Beckham would finish his career in England. Manchester United manager Sir Alex Ferguson admitted he had been asked once or twice by reporters, but said in his book *My Autobiography* that there was 'no point going down that road'. Once United were off the table – and you have to say that with a midfield of Michael Carrick, Anderson, Tom Cleverley and a close-to-retirement Paul Scholes, Beckham wouldn't have looked out of place – it was unlikely he would go back home.

If there was even the slightest temptation, due to Mark Hughes's status as a childhood hero, to go to Queens Park Rangers (as Hughes had indicated he would explore upon the news that David would leave Los Angeles), then that move was dead in the water when Hughes was sacked before November was out. Harry Redknapp succeeded him, and despite their shared experience on the Spurs training pitch, Beckham would not go to London.

There was a keen plea from Australia. Emile Heskey and Alessandro Del Piero were among the recognisable names to make recent moves down under, and the A-League hoped that Beckham might do for them what he had done for MLS.

'We're putting forward an offer,' said Melbourne Heat chief executive Scott Munn. 'It's compelling, and the opportunity is here for him to come here. That is absolutely legitimate. Let's let David get through next week, play the final of the MLS, and hopefully he'll have a win. Then I'm sure he'll assess every offer.'

A Central Coast Mariners spokesman claimed that they were involved in discussions: 'There's stuff going on behind the scenes. We're definitely putting our hand up. He would fill the stadium and change the game up here.'

As a free agent, David could relax a little – his expired registration meant he didn't have the deadline of 31 January which European clubs have to make transfers. Nonetheless, it was the 31st when his final move was made official. David would be moving to Paris. It was not only a move which made sense, but really, the only move which did, considering the previous negotiations, and the fact that Paris Saint-Germain were coached by Carlo Ancelotti and had Leonardo as their technical director.

There was a hugely positive feeling around the move – Beckham announced that he would be playing without salary (a nominal fee of around £2,000 per month would be paid, with the reported £175,000-a-week salary he would have got being donated to charity in its entirety).

'I was lucky to work with Carlo and Leonardo for a few months,' Beckham said about the move. 'Carlo was one of the best managers I've played for, so it's exciting on a number of levels. Zlatan Ibrahimović is one of the players I'm excited to play alongside. Ibra was someone I've watched for many years, in my early days playing for England against Sweden, and I always felt he could be one of the best players in the world. I watched a lot of games last year and a lot of games this season. There's a lot of talent in this team.'

David had not yet decided if this would indeed be his last club: 'I don't know. People have been speculating about that for a number of years, but I continue to play and sign contracts. I will see how I feel, but I want to play as long as possible. My passion is football. It always has been. When I play football, it is not about the biggest contract.'

Hiring Ancelotti had been the first eye-catching move from PSG after they had been taken over from Qatar Sports Investment in October 2011. At the start of the 2012/13 season, they had commenced their campaign to recruit and spend heavily (a figure of £250m already committed before Beckham arrived), with intentions of dominating French football and hopefully European football in the future. Thiago Motta, Ezequiel Lavezzi and Marco Veratti had all joined, whilst the more legendary figures of Thiago Silva and Ibrahimović added some stardust. In the week before Beckham's arrival, PSG had won two consecutive games to claim top place in Ligue 1 – a position they would not relinquish for the rest of the season.

David's first game would come against Marseille on 24 February, almost a month after signing. 'No substitute has ever been given quite so much attention by the world's paparazzi during a warm-up,' wrote Ben Smith for the BBC, 'and before kick-off the former England captain was given the freedom of the stadium to lap up the adulation PSG has been waiting almost a month to show him.'

Beckham came on in the 76th minute with the score 1–0 to his team; he was involved in the move for the late goal which secured the victory. 'There was a bit of nerves, but I enjoyed coming on,' Beckham said after the game. 'Mind you, I couldn't feel my feet for the first two or three passes. They were frozen from sitting on the bench. The atmosphere in the stadium and the reception I got was pretty incredible.'

This was the first of two clashes with Marseille in a matter of days (the second coming in the French Cup), which meant head-to-head clashes with fellow English midfielder Joey Barton.

Barton, however, had an extremely controversial past which made Beckham's look like playtime in comparison – the players were depicted on the cover of that week's *France Football* magazine as 'Ange Et Démon' – Beckham, of course, the angel.

It seemed unlikely that these combustible elements could coincide for two matches without some form of explosion, and it came in the second game. Barton, however, was not the culprit. Alaixys Romao committed a bad foul on Beckham, which provoked a good old-fashioned 'melee' between the teams. PSG won 2–0, with Beckham's only notable contribution to proceedings a second-half booking, but Ancelotti still felt the midfielder had done well in the middle of the park. 'He made a very good performance,' the manager said. 'He made good passes as usual, he was well positioned on the pitch alongside Blaise Matuidi. He was very solid.'

Beckham was used sparingly in the following weeks, coming on as a substitute until he was given his first start in Saint-Étienne. It was his first visit here since he was sent off at the 1998 World Cup; he gave a measured performance, despite the attentions of opponent Brandão, making 114 passes – the most of any player. PSG led 2–0, but came away with only a point; two minutes from time, Beckham had the opportunity to win the game with a free kick, but fired just wide.

Ancelotti caught everyone by surprise by picking Beckham from the start in the Champions League quarter-final against Barcelona. The former United star said before the game that he hoped to catch the attention of Roy Hodgson, now England manager.

'One of the reasons why I've never retired from the England team is because if there's ever an opportunity to play for them again, then I'm available,' he said. 'If there is any chance of me ever playing for my country again, I would never turn that down. I'm almost 38 years old, so the chances are very slight, but you never know.'

Hodgson, though, had already given his verdict in February, and it wasn't positive. 'I'm pleased for him,' he said. But when did he last play for England? 2009? About four years ago. It seems that for four years he's actually been prepared to play his football [for the LA Galaxy] and not think too much about Europe. But if he is at Wembley on Wednesday night [for a friendly where England faced Brazil] and says "I'm off to Paris and I'm going to play well there, so keep me in mind," I'll say, "Fine, David. I'd love to do that." But I don't think that's going to happen, to be frank.'

David was selected to face Barcelona from the start, and was trusted to do an energetic but disciplined job against the most heralded midfield in the world; he did just that, and PSG emerged with a creditable 2–2 draw. They also achieved a draw in the second leg – Beckham came on for the last 15 minutes at the Nou Camp – but the 1–1 scoreline saw PSG eliminated on away goals.

Just as he had done at Milan, David had made an instant impression in Paris. In 2009 and 2010, that had been more to do with his performances on the pitch. In France, his mere presence had lifted PSG, giving them an air of credibility they were desperate for, and desperate to keep. Club president Nasser al-Khelaifi said, 'He is very happy in Paris. Frankly, we want to keep him with us for next season. We will talk about it with him. He's fantastic on and off the pitch. Sometimes you can make bad choices. But recruiting David was one of my best decisions. As a man, player, ambassador, he is exceptional. He creates something in this group. Everyone loves it.'

Beckham played a few minutes as a substitute in a 1–0 win at Troyes, and was asked to do the same at Évian with the scoreline the same. Veratti had been sent off in the 81st minute, so the veteran had been tasked with calming things down; however, the game was bubbling away, and Beckham too was sent off in injury time for what was deemed to be a dangerous lunge on Youssef Adnane. PSG held on for the victory, but after the final whistle,

Évian striker Saber Khalifa and PSG goalkeeper Sirigu were also given red cards. The ugly scenes undermined the significance of the result – PSG had a nine-point cushion at the top of the league with just four games remaining.

Beckham was suspended, then, for the following game against Valenciennes, but was back in the squad for the trip to Lyon on 12 May. This was the title decider – even though there was a suggestion that the club may be deducted two points following another disciplinary incident in that game against Valenciennes, where director Leonardo had been accused of barging a referee.

The third consecutive 1–0 win on the road secured the first league title for the club since 1994. Beckham had come on in the last minute of injury time for the goalscorer, Jérémy Ménez: a token appearance with a significant consequence, as he became the first English player to win a championship in four different countries.

'I'm going to enjoy tonight and that's the important thing,' he said, dodging questions on his own future in the mixed zone after the game, although it was reported by *The Guardian* that he was 'hoping to be offered another year's contract at the French club'.

The following week was clearly one of contemplation for Beckham, and an apt time. In England the previous week, Sir Alex Ferguson had announced that he would be retiring as manager of Manchester United. Perhaps this final success had given Beckham cause to reflect that it was unlikely to get any better than this – another league title in France, maybe, but it would not mean as much as the history-making first. Despite PSG repeating their offer of an extra year, on 16 May, David announced that he would be retiring as a player at the end of the current season.

'I'm thankful to PSG for giving me the opportunity to continue, but I feel now is the right time to finish my career, playing at the highest level,' he said in a statement. 'If you had told me as a young boy, I would have played for and won trophies with my boyhood club Manchester United, proudly captained and played for my country over one hundred times and lined up for some of the biggest clubs in the world, I would have told you it was a fantasy. I'm fortunate to have realised those dreams. To this day, one of my proudest achievements is captaining my country. I knew every time I wore the Three Lions shirt, I was not only following in a long line of great players, I was also representing every fan that cared passionately about their country. I'm honoured to represent England both on and off the pitch. I want people to see me as a hard-working footballer – someone who, when he steps on the pitch, gives everything he's got. When I look back on my career, that is how I look back on it, and that is how I hope people have seen me. I want to thank all my team-mates, the great managers that I had the pleasure of learning from. I also want to thank the fans who have all supported me and given me the strength to succeed. I wouldn't have achieved what I have done today without my family. I'm grateful for my parents' sacrifice, which made me realise my dreams. I owe everything to Victoria and the kids, who have given me the inspiration and support to play at the highest level for such a long period.'

The news was met with the same mix of shock and acceptance as Ferguson's own announcement; it was also met with an equal amount of fanfare. These tributes came in droves from former team-mates, but it is worth selecting a few of note.

'David Beckham has been an outstanding footballer throughout his career,' said UK prime minister David Cameron. 'Not only that – he has been a brilliant ambassador for this country, not least if we remember all the work he did in helping us win London 2012.'

Erstwhile England manager Sven-Göran Eriksson could not speak highly enough of his former skipper. 'A fantastic football player, a fantastic man, probably the biggest sports personality in the world,' he said. 'If you talk about David Beckham, all over the world they know who that is. I don't think there is any other football player more popular than him. I remember all the matches with England and all the travelling – airports, hotels – and it was all about Beckham all the time. I rank him very, very highly. I never had any doubts about picking him.'

Former Galaxy coach Bruce Arena said: 'We were honoured to have him here. He did wonderful things for our club and our league. He is a global icon and a terrific ambassador for the game.'

And even FIFA president Sepp Blatter made a comment on the news. 'David Beckham, one of the most iconic figures in global football, is retiring from playing,' he said. 'It's the end of a chapter of an amazing story. David grew up as a football-loving child and achieved his dreams, and unquestionably inspired millions of boys and girls to try and do the same. Whatever he chooses to do next, I'm sure he'll approach with the same dedication and good grace he displayed the last 21 years. Good luck!'

Whilst the accolades from former team-mates, colleagues and opponents are almost too plentiful to mention, it is impossible to omit the remark of former rival Diego Simeone, whose Machiavellian act in Saint-Étienne in 1998 arguably contributed as much as anything to the birth of this celebrity sporting career which was coming to an end in the country it was created. 'He's a great professional,' said the Argentine. 'An extraordinary player, and had success wherever he went. I wish him all the best in what he does, and I am sure he will be successful because he is very capable, and above all very intelligent.'

Perhaps it was contrived or engineered; but there was still that suggestion of romance and fate in the way Beckham's career was concluding. John Dillon of the *Express* penned a wonderful career obituary for the former England captain: 'The current phrase is "game-changer". It is used about footballers who shape the course of matches. David Beckham changed the whole sport. What the hell, he changed the whole nation. Not always for the best, but mostly for the good. Mostly with success. Mostly as a good story rather than a bad one. He won't be finished yet, either. With a striking sense of serendipity, his playing career is going to come to an end in nine days' time at Lorient, a short drive along the southern coast of Brittany from where it could be said all the fuss really got started. You might almost think he planned it that way. You might almost think he planned the whole tale if it wasn't quite so remarkable.'

There were two matches left of PSG's season – but it was decided that Beckham's final curtain would be drawn in the penultimate game, against Brest at the Parc des Princes. The Brest match was at home; it was the night of the trophy celebration. There would be no better night to bow out on. There were no special criteria to meet to qualify for a league title medal – he had achieved that status simply by playing one game.

Ancelotti gave Beckham a start, and also the captain's armband. 'The manager called me in and said, "We've spoken to the players, it's the players' idea – we want to make you captain,"' Beckham recalled. 'It's really special for an Englishman to be captain of PSG – especially on a night that meant so much to the club and the players. It was an amazing gesture and one I'll always be thankful for.'

This was a routine victory over Brest; a game treated as a testimonial by the home crowd, who didn't have a long association with their new man, but gave him a celebration as if he had played there for the entirety of his professional career. Beckham was involved in the early build-up for Ibrahimović's fifth-minute goal and had a more familiar and direct involvement with the team's second. His corner was met by Blaise Matuidi, who performed an excellent scooped volley that went into the top corner.

In the 36th minute, PSG were awarded a free kick in prime territory for Beckham to strike it. But Ibrahimović did, and the ball flew into the net – a changing-of-the-guard moment, with David, as he always was, the first on the scene to celebrate with the immodest Swede. Ibrahimović performed an almost Cantona-esque, arms-out celebration.

With a reputation for being outspoken and confident, Ibrahimović had reportedly asked David Lagercrantz, the ghostwriter of his 2011 autobiography, 'Who the fuck is Beckham?' when Lagercrantz told him he had found the former England captain's books 'boring'. But Zlatan was certainly appreciative of Beckham being well known when he arrived in Paris. 'I think it's good for me that Beckham came so he gets more attention than me, so they leave me a little bit alone,' Ibrahimović told CNN in April 2013. 'Since I came here, everybody said don't worry, as a football player you can walk in the city and nobody will disturb you because as a football player it is not like it is in Italy. But since the day I came here, it's been totally stressful. Everybody is chasing me with their scooters. I don't even walk in the streets. So when David came, he got more of the media. That's good, because he takes care of that and I can play football and focus on football.'

The forward had conceded that Beckham had been more important for PSG than his number of minutes on the pitch suggested: 'I think he has been very important for us. The club has been changing from a normal club to a top club, and Beckham gives you some kind of confidence. He has a quality, big quality. He has a touch that I haven't seen many players have. And he is very elegant when he plays.'

His final performance had been one to enjoy. Sky Sports described Beckham 'rolling back the years' with a 'vintage' display 'worthy of his peak years'. Brest scored a consolation goal in the 81st minute; an opportune break in the game for Carlo Ancelotti to give the entire stadium an opportunity to say farewell to a legend.

Beckham was tearful as he realised this was the moment his playing career was to end, acknowledging the standing ovation of the entire crowd – many of whom were chanting 'Reste, David, reste' ('Stay, David, stay') as he walked off the pitch one final time.

After the game, as the team celebrated with the league trophy, Beckham addressed the crowd: 'I want to say thank you to everybody in Paris – to my team-mates, to the staff, to the fans. It's been very special to finish my career here. It could not have been any more special. I just feel that it's the right time. I feel that I've achieved everything that I could in my career. I wanted to go out as a champion. I've finished my career in a team that has treated me like I've been here for ten years. After 22 years of playing football, I'm going to take a few months to enjoy time with my family.'

After the game, Beckham explained why he wouldn't be starting in the final game. 'There's a plastic pitch next weekend. I ruptured my Achilles a few years ago, so it's not great for it,' he told Sky Sports. 'Like I said, tonight was very special. I'll be part of the team next week. Whether I play or not, who knows?'

He didn't – but nobody could disagree that he had already experienced the final farewell. A career that saw 719 club appearances, 115 international appearances, ten league championships and countless more accolades – one of the most famous football careers of all time – was finally at an end.

Reinventing the Wheel

CONSIDERING IT was such a dominating aspect of Beckham's post-Old Trafford career, it is no surprise that his spell in the United States remains the most fascinating, even above that at Real Madrid. In Spain, Beckham was one of a number of genuine superstars, and the only surprise was that the league title he won there took so long to arrive. There were challenges involved – the most impressive coming in the final season – but it was nothing compared to the size of the challenge he embraced when he decided to move to MLS. There, he was effectively tasked to individually transform the reputation of an entire league. More than that, he was asked to do this on an internal and external scale – he had to seduce a nation into loving soccer, and convince the rest of the world it was competitive and credible. Soccer in the US had suffered severe damage to its reputation after the collapse of the NASL in the 1980s. There were genuine intentions behind some of the more high-profile moves of those halcyon years. Perhaps because of the demise of the league, it had ultimately been seen as what many cynically felt it was: a graveyard for over-the-hill footballers looking for a payday.

There is no doubt that North American soccer fans reminisce fondly about the fact that Johan Cruyff, George Best, Pelé and others spent some time in their country, as they rightly should, but those tenures were always perceived as 'gimmicky' by the Europeans in particular. Best's career, for example, is seen almost exclusively as spent with Manchester United before an early retirement, with his time with the Los Angeles Aztecs and Fort Lauderdale Strikers as merely a depressing postscript.

This demeaned all the positive work done, some of which influenced the British game, before it all went wrong. There was, for instance, a promising set-up where some English clubs would send their young talent to American clubs – Gordon Hill, mentioned earlier in this book, was a prime example. At the age of 21, Millwall loaned Hill to the Chicago Sting, where he enjoyed tremendous success under the tutelage of former Manchester United defender Bill Foulkes. Foulkes tipped United off about Hill, and the rest was history.

Gordon Jago – mentioned much earlier in this book due to his connections with the Dallas Cup youth tournament – had an even earlier involvement with the North American game as he spent time coaching the Baltimore Bays in the late 1960s. If it sounds like this writer is trying to assert that most positive influences on the American game had British origins, that could not be further from the truth. Jago was so enthused by his experience in Baltimore that when he went back to coach in England, he was a champion for dramatic changes in the way that media accessed the players. His methods had mixed success – introducing reporters into the dressing room after games, for example, as he had experienced in the US – but the fundamental takeaway point was that there were aspects of the North American game, in its original format, which were positive contributions to the worldwide sport.

The matters of the death of the NASL and how the game was resurrected with the World Cup and MLS are for another record; suffice it to say that the North American game David Beckham joined in 2007 was self-conscious, cautious and – rightly or wrongly – still observed cynically as a whole by Europeans.

In some respects, David Beckham as the choice to improve the reputation of US soccer was as confusing as it was perfect. After all, one of the battles he fought all through his career was to be truly appreciated for the qualities he had. Despite all the battles he won, that was one which would continue to divide opinion long after his retirement.

Furthermore, he had carried around one of Sir Alex Ferguson's most infamous criticisms on his shoulders ever since he left Old Trafford. Ferguson's description of the 'circus' was as iconic as it was difficult for the midfielder. In their battle for credibility and legitimacy, one would think that bringing in a player with such a description would be the last thing MLS needed.

It is surprising therefore to hear Lalas candidly embrace Ferguson's classic line.

'I loved it,' he says. 'I *loved* the circus. Just because there's a circus, just because there's confetti, music and bright lights, and pomp and circumstance, doesn't mean that he can't be beautiful, genuine, authentic, real and passionate and emotional … and of high quality. I want the show. I *prefer* the show. David brought the show, and it was wonderful to have been a small part of it. We wanted the circus, we paid for the circus and we used it to great effect and impact. The whole thing was about getting people into the soccer tent. We knew not everybody is going to stay there, but this was always about getting as many people into the tent as possible. Nobody got them in in greater numbers, or faster, than David. A lot of them stayed [after Beckham left].'

If your takeaway from those comments was a concession that MLS in fact needed the hullabaloo around the player, it wouldn't be completely unfair. It seems to this writer, though, that Lalas was taking a pragmatic view of how likely the soccer public and the non-soccer public were to take to Beckham, and how much more easily that connection would be created because of the traits he possessed which would endear him to those people much more quickly than they might do otherwise.

Ferguson might have fumed at the idea of a major cup final being all about the departure of one player in the way that the MLS Cup in 2012 seemed to be. To Lalas, this was a welcome opportunity, a spotlight shining on the event in a way that it might not have been, and a chance for the Beckham story to have a conclusion fitting for its location.

By the end of Beckham's time with LA, the generally understated attributes of his game were the more appreciated. In that respect, Los Angeles was no different to Madrid. There was a common thread. In truth, his story in the last two years – player returns from injury to win supporters around and then win trophies – was hardly unique in football history. But it needed David's stardust, and possibly even that of the Galaxy too, to be the catalysts who could help the American public connect.

In 2019, a statue of Beckham was erected and unveiled outside the Home Depot Center. By that point, some of English football's most famous names had followed him to the Galaxy, although it has to be said that they were closer to the back end of their careers than Beckham had been. Robbie Keane became a legend by the time he left, with 104 goals in 165 games. Steven Gerrard spent two relatively unsuccessful years there in 2015 and 2016, and Ashley Cole followed him, playing from 2016 to 2018. Zlatan Ibrahimović went from Old Trafford to Los Angeles and was the first to assume the same sort of profile as Beckham; though, in keeping with the Swede's personality, this was more to do with a personal ego than it was a marketing brand.

In order for Beckham's story to have any resonance, for his spell to have any meaning, there needed to be elements of success on the many fronts on which the credibility of the transfer was challenged. There were enough personal moments to justify his quality. The consistency of his free kicks and set-piece delivery remained as strong in his last year as the reputation he had brought with him to the country. There were two MLS Cups. There was a definite marked and tracked progression of the team he played in and the players he played with.

By sheer force of nature and perseverance and a single-minded refusal to give in, by the middle of his spell there, he had made what was arguably his greatest breakthrough of all, which was to make it possible that a player could play in MLS and be considered for the England national team. In doing so, by the time he left to go to Paris Saint-Germain, there was a growing acceptance that MLS was now competitive enough to be treated seriously in Europe – crucially, the league itself was seen as a serious competition. Of course, the quality of the league in that five-year spell had a lot to do with it – this was not solely a David Beckham rescue mission – but it is unquestionable that without him, the scale of that credibility would have been comparatively negligible.

'David wasn't the best player in MLS, not even on his own team, yet he will be remembered because of who he was, what he did and for how he fundamentally changed the sport and the league,' Lalas says. 'That will sound like a back-handed compliment, but it's not. So he wasn't the best, maybe not even in the top 20. What I'm really saying is I have an incredible amount of respect and appreciation for someone who wasn't the best player and yet rose to be considered one of the greats of the game. That's wonderful. The way that he did it was a tribute to the talent that he does have, and no one ever suggested he wasn't talented. He knew what he was good at, he knew what he wasn't good at, he knew the power and leverage that he possessed, and he turned it not only into an incredible career, but also an incredible brand. He certainly expanded his brand. He was a big fish in a big pond. Los Angeles is the home of celebrity and entertainment, but he was still a big fish. Sometimes in America we speak about these things in detached and unemotional ways, and we refer to them as "products", "brands" and "customers" and all that stuff. That doesn't mean that we *can't* be romantic and that we *can't* see beauty. It was a saga. You had the initial wide-eyed potential. You have the moments of despair and failure and challenges you had overcome. And the other side of it, the triumph and the victory, the moment in the light. It finished incredibly and with a tremendous amount of joy and success. When you are looking at somebody who has come to represent the Galaxy, and the impact that goes well beyond the goals, the championships that were won, that's why the statue is there. Of those players who were better, nobody had an impact that was even close to what David had.'

One could argue that Lalas's assessment is a little unfair – dismissing Beckham as out of the top 20 seems harsh – but that is merely reflective of the ongoing conversation that will probably always surround the player. David is not alone in that regard. Even the greatest players – even his heroes – remain subject to the same debates. How good would Bryan Robson have been without injuries? Did Eric Cantona's ineffectual European performances damage his legacy? It is better to concentrate – as Lalas does, to his credit – on the positive impact that is beyond question.

Beckham's transformative impact on the North American game is something that continues to this day and has been felt in every corner of the sport, according to Mike Magee. 'Every day since the day he got to MLS, the league has gotten better,' Magee says. 'We were in a bit of a holding pattern before … Now, the popularity of our league is due to him. Salaries went up because of him. Every game I played in was sold out because of him. The world saw me score goals because of him.'

Bryan Jordan, another team-mate, provides a little more balance in terms of appreciating David's quality as well as his influence. 'David was one of the best I've ever played with for sure,' he says. 'There are certain players that just really have that class and skill on the ball. I definitely learned a ton playing alongside him and watching him at training … ultimately I think we can only be thankful. It really was a special time for MLS, I think, to have a player like him really open the floodgates with bigger players coming over and getting us television contracts. I'd question anyone who didn't think his contributions weren't huge. I mean, our team was pretty damn good as it was, but having a guy like that just puts you over the top. We made it to the final three times in those five years, losing one and winning two. And even my personal life, with all the travel we did with teams or sponsors that wanted to see him play, I got to see a lot of the world, probably in a big part because of him, so it's always something I truly appreciated. I do have a view or a question I'd be interested to hear his response to, though. I'm curious if there are players like myself who are always fighting for those starting spots and if a lot of these big Europeans coming over, and are taking some valuable playing time from young American players, I wonder what that means for our overall national team and US soccer. I mean, as you can tell, I'm obviously thankful for him, and I know it's a competitive sport, it's business, and our league needs to put people in the seats and continue to grow, but it's always something I've thought about … just as far as the development of US soccer players. There's no time like on the field in big games time.'

Jordan displays some prescience with such an observation. It brings to mind the same argument in the English Premier League – when it commenced in 1992, most teams had a foreign player or two, but it was still a relative novelty. On 26 December 1999, Chelsea became the first English team to field an all-foreign starting eleven, prompting one journalist to quote Yeats in his match report: 'All changed, changed utterly: A terrible beauty is born.'

England were one of the powerhouses of European soccer, though. It was always discussed how necessary and how beneficial the foreign influx was. In future times, Jordan's concern for how the American game could be shaped may have some genuine grounding, and at that time it may be deemed that Beckham's transfer was the start of that terrible beauty. In 2020, though, if that was an issue at all, it was so minor as to be considered collateral damage worth risking in the short term. There was almost no aspect of the transfer from which MLS and US soccer did not benefit.

Beckham gained from it too. From a marketing perspective, the brand exposure and operation had been a colossal success. The transition from soccer star to nationally known celebrity had been as relatively smooth in the US as it had been in England. In early 2020, his position as the 'most-followed' UK individual on social media network Instagram was strengthened when he passed 60 million followers (in fact, of current soccer players as of the time of print, only Cristiano Ronaldo, Lionel Messi and Neymar have more). He is as likely to make appearances on Jimmy Fallon's *Tonight Show* on NBC as he is on *The Jonathan Ross Show* – if not more. In 2020, he featured in the final season of the show *Modern Family* playing himself – one of a number of small such roles. As immensely popular as he was and is, it is difficult to imagine that 'Brand Beckham' would be anywhere near as famous without the spell in Los Angeles.

It had come at a cost, however small. The academies in London and Los Angeles closed in 2009 with just about the lowest profile you could expect to find for something associated with David Beckham. And, though he has always insisted it wasn't his intention, it would be practically impossible for him to be a manager, primarily because of his existing profile. Since retirement, as well as acting as an ambassador for numerous good causes and business ventures, Beckham has retained an interest in football. He and his 'class of '92' colleagues became part owners of English non-league club Salford City in 2019, and in 2020 his club Inter Miami finally made its MLS debut.

Beckham had announced in February 2014 that he intended to exercise his option to buy an MLS 'expansion team', and spent the following years working on building an 18,000-capacity stadium in Fort Lauderdale as well as building the club.

'The team in Miami is often referred to, and rightly so, as "David Beckham's Inter Miami",' Lalas says. 'That's the power that he wields. I love the fact that he's still involved, that he's an owner. It's great for MLS. There will be a whole generation of MLS fans who never saw David play: they will see him as an owner and an iconic type of figure. He will have expectation, some of it unrealistic, but he will take that pressure and see it as opportunity, I'm sure.'

Lalas – involved in those exploratory conversations to bring Beckham to the United States when large financial figures were thrown around – feels the financial 'experiment', such that it was, has effectively been a bargain: 'I would say the Beckham transfer has yielded incredibly successful and long-lasting results, even beyond our wildest expectations. The impact and the ultimate success doesn't happen without everything included, the problems and the challenges, the failures along the way – they're all part of the story, and it's all part of the ultimate labelling of it being a success. We all learn along the way. I certainly did. I don't regret any of it. I was privileged to be a part of it.'

Certainly, it seems as if Beckham's involvement with the American game will continue for many years to come.

How his contribution as a player will be seen in history is a story still unfolding.

In the Galaxy's pre-arrival charm offensive, both Tim Leiweke and Alexi Lalas had made bold predictions – Leiweke that Beckham would 'have a greater impact on soccer in

America than any athlete has ever had on a sport globally', and Lalas that the sustainability of the transfer would have more beneficial long-term effects than Pelé's spell had on the country's 'soccer culture'. Naturally, this was misreported as Lalas saying Beckham would be 'bigger than Pelé' – prompting Ron Newman, the former Portsmouth forward who was involved in the NASL, to tell soccer publication *The Blizzard*: 'That was not a clever statement.'

It feels somewhat reductive to narrow the discussion to two players – particularly when one is widely regarded as one of the best of all time, and the other faces consistent questions about how good he actually was. It is also a skewed argument, considering that in the modern day, it was the LA Galaxy by themselves making a bold move. Pelé was brought to the US by the Cosmos. Johan Cruyff and George Best by the Los Angeles Aztecs. Gerd Muller by the Fort Lauderdale Strikers. It was an all-out assault by the franchise owners across the board.

Results were mixed – and ultimately fatal for this inception of the professional game – but there is a strong enough sample size for us to observe some trends. Pelé's peak of influence came in his retirement year of 1977, when the Cosmos drew an average home gate of 34,142. That only tells part of the story. For example, only 13,527 turned up to watch a game against the Dallas Tornado, but 57,191 packed into Giants Stadium to watch the Cosmos defeat the LA Aztecs 5–2. League averages reveal more of an insight. Pelé's arrival brought a spike from 7,642 to 10,295. By the time he retired, that had risen to an average of 13,558, and at the peak, in 1980, the NASL's average attendance was 14,440.

The Soccer Bowl of 1978 drew a record crowd of 74,901 for the game between the Cosmos and the Tampa Bay Rowdies – more than double the attendance of the previous year (35,548), and still comfortably higher than the games in 1979 and 1980, which both drew just over 50,000.

'Alexi's statement is maybe unfair in that David was not a great individual player – he wouldn't dribble past players – but he made other players good with his passing ability,' Gordon Jago explains. 'His arrival gave the league some status. The Galaxy at that time was probably the best team in the league, so they were an attraction. But the NASL for a number of years was a very good league, with a host of big names who brought out the fans in big numbers. You had Pelé, Best, Moore, Beckenbauer, Chinaglia, Carlos Alberto, Cruyff, Hunt, Tueart and Marsh, so many top players spread around the league, and it did make for a great league. Unfortunately, to do that, it cost a lot of money in fees and high salaries. Many overspent trying to compete with the Cosmos, and so the decline started. I prefer to look at the positives and see that the NASL created an interest for young players and youth soccer which developed around the country. Those youngsters became the fans and the players of the MLS. When David came, he added an interest to the MLS, which, in comparison, did not have too many star players. I would say that even today the standard of play is nowhere near that of the NASL.'

David's move to MLS did not encourage an en masse movement in 2007, but we can say with some certainty that without him, the likes of Zlatan Ibrahimović, Thierry Henry, Frank Lampard, Cole, Gerrard and certainly Keane (who was enthralled by Beckham's conversations about the lifestyle when he was on one of his winter training sabbaticals in London) would not have followed. Crucially, Lalas says, the negotiations for the Beckham transfer gave them the experience of the mechanics involved in pulling off such a transfer. And, having worked with Beckham and all that his brand entailed, subsequent transfers were straightforward.

When Zlatan 'came and conquered', he did so on a record salary of $7.2m. The lowest base annual salary in MLS in 2019 was around $56,000, a jump from around $10,000 when Beckham arrived. In status, MLS could be compared with the English second tier, the Championship. A player in England's League Two – two leagues lower than that – could expect to earn £78,000 (around $96,000 in mid-2020).

The Los Angeles Galaxy's acquisition of David Beckham came at a time when they were already the team drawing the highest average crowds. The size and capacity of the Home Depot Center (27,000) means it is difficult to come to a dramatic conclusion as to Beckham's impact. Their 2006 average crowd was 20,814, which was down from 24,204 the year before. Clearly, the signing was part of a strategy to turn that around, and it was successful in the short term, with averages of 24,252 in 2007 and 26,008 in 2008. However, this declined in the following years to around 22,000, even when the Galaxy were winning MLS Cups – it is a level they have stayed at since Beckham's departure, although it is significant to note that the average ticket price in 2007 at the Galaxy was $32.50, and when he left it was $89.47.

Attendances across the league rose by 8 per cent in 2007; declines of 1.8 per cent the following year, and 2.6 per cent the year after that, indicated that the boost had been temporary, but Beckham's own turnaround was reflected in percentage increases of 4, 7.2 and 5 in his last three years. The league average went from 15,504 before his arrival to 18,807 as he left. In subsequent years, that has continued to rise. In 2019 the average was 21,305 (there had been a peak of 22,113 in 2017) and a total attendance of 8,676,109, which was the most in an MLS season ever.

Tracing Beckham's influence in all that, and attempting to define it as significant, is not easy. Trends change. The clearest takeaway is that there was a lull in MLS before his arrival and there has been a definite upwards trajectory ever since. The peaks are not quite as high as they were in the NASL, but the MLS model appears to be sustainable for the long term.

There is, however, a certain importance in Beckham's involvement when it comes to the fact that ticket prices effectively trebled at the Galaxy in his time, and attendances continued to improve. That can be reflected in the average value of MLS teams across the board from 2007 to 2012 – from $33m to $105m.

It brings to mind a study undertaken by this writer on the impact Eric Cantona had on Manchester United as a financial entity. In 1991 – the year before he went to Old Trafford – the club's value was £47m. In 1998 – the year after Cantona retired – BSkyB attempted to buy United for £623m. United were perfectly placed to capitalise on the money pouring into the game from broadcasters. Beckham's numbers are not quite as big, but they are probably even more impressive when you consider that he *was* the change, and that not only was the impact felt over an entire league, but also that the league was in North America, and that there was an established resistance and scepticism both inside and outside of the US – it is possibly an even more remarkable achievement. Breaking the stranglehold of the 'hand' games, as Jose Mourinho put it, was never likely to happen in just five years, but, as Lalas says, the transfer was always about striving for relevancy in the global world of soccer. The Beckham circus was a critical element in that advance.

The generational gap and the evolution of the sport since the rebirth makes it a fool's errand to attempt to draw a genuine comparison based on the legacy of the players in their respective scenarios. It is, however, reasonable to compare Beckham to his peers – and in that respect, it is probably fair to give Lalas the final word, in 2020, some 13 years after he had made those projections: 'Is he the best player to play in MLS? I would say no, absolutely not. It's not even close. Is he the most influential? Absolutely. His value cannot be overstated when it comes to how important he was.'

Epilogue

THROUGHOUT HIS career, it was often said of David Beckham that his place in either his club team or his national team was awarded on the basis of reputation and profile instead of any special talent. Surely, though, all of the evidence suggests that his reputation and profile impacted his playing career in the opposite manner. This is not to say that he suffered any genuine hardship on this score, but it is incontrovertible that he suffered spells out of his teams because of perceptions associated with his life away from football. At the height of his fame and his brand, at the points in his career where the financial figures involved would mean he had nothing to prove if he did not have a sporting motivation, a common and recurring theme is that Beckham was the most dedicated, the most professional and the most hard-working.

His profile made him a convenient target when coaches wanted to make a statement. Without fail, the consequences of axing David Beckham never produced a positive result for the coach in question. Steve McClaren came back to him. So did Fabio Capello. Sir Alex Ferguson didn't – and furthermore, would never include Beckham on his small list of mistakes – but Manchester

United were crying out for that consistent delivery in the two or three years after David was sold. There is a fair argument that the vacated space on the right facilitated the arrival and development of Cristiano Ronaldo, but a look at the players who played in the centre of the park for that period would not convince anyone that United wouldn't have been better off with David in that area instead.

Beckham is such an interesting case study for so many reasons, another being that he is the polar opposite to Ryan Giggs in terms of media profile and accessibility. Sir Alex Ferguson's post-managerial book *Leading* is a manual on the importance of control. It is clear that he was able to control that side of Giggs's career, and whilst one would never use the word 'submissive' to describe the Welshman, it has been obvious by his longevity that he was certainly more agreeable to the United manager's theory of what was the right thing to do. Giggs grew up against a backdrop of comparisons to George Best, who was accused of wasting his potential and never fulfilling the greatness many had hoped for.

Beckham's footballing education had been different. He was gifted, certainly. In his precocious years, even as the most gifted player in his junior teams, he was also the hardest-working. This was not done to compensate. It was done to give him an edge. That dedication, present throughout his career, was there so that nobody could ever say David Beckham did not make the most of what he had.

It is easier for people to digest smaller ideas and, especially when the propensity for resentment was so high, it was much more palatable for people to believe that Beckham was more popular than he was talented or hard-working. That may even have been true. But along the way the issues became confused and the matter of his popularity became a self-fulfilling prophecy, regardless of how unfair it was or how many times he had to prove those opinions wrong. It was more difficult to stomach that because someone had been talented and they worked hard, they had become popular. In some ways, it feels like that work ethic (which, it ought to be said, was only ever questioned once, and that was by Ferguson in the months before the move to Madrid) was Beckham's greatest sin, because the football world is littered with popular and talented players who provoke nowhere near the same amount of vitriol and jealousy.

These are merely the observations of a supporter and a writer. You can't change the tide. You can only present facts and theories and hope that some come away with a greater appreciation for David Beckham the footballer. One hope I had when planning this book was that I would be able to make a more overwhelming case for this, but it has proven impossible – he is such a polarising figure that almost every single observation about him, whether it comes from someone who watched him, played with or against him, or worked with him, has an opinion which is affected by the entire package of what David Beckham came to represent.

Sometimes it is easy to forget how this all started – a little boy who dreamed of nothing more than playing for Manchester United, and a father hoping that he would do just that.

One more theory, then, if you'll indulge me. One that isn't affected by any of that – one that isn't even affected by David Beckham at all, really. Sir Matt Busby and Jimmy Murphy, the two men responsible for the enduring identity of Manchester United, once spoke in detail of the qualities they sought in their perfect United midfielder and winger.

'Wingers – these are the match-winners in football today,' Murphy said in his 1968 book *Matt ... United ... and Me.* 'There was a time when a team could have a frail player on the wing, not now. I look for a strong, direct type of player with the speed and ability to go storming past the back. As a general rule the winger is next to the last man to receive the ball – the last man to get the ball should be the one who has a crack at goal – and therefore it is obvious the winger must be able to cross a ball at speed and above all he must be accurate. There is no point having a modern [Stanley] Matthews out there on the touchline practising his soccer sorcery if, when he crosses the ball, he miscues and either hits it too far, or not far enough, or straight to an opponent. If he does, all the careful build up is completely and utterly wasted. There must be an end product: either a goal, or at least an attempt on goal. In modern football I think the wingers need courage more than ever before. If he loses possession he cannot stand still and put himself out of the game. He must double back and challenge, or at least place himself in a position where he is facing the ball again and marking his opponent. Not long ago a winger wasn't in the game until the ball was rolled to his feet, these days he must mark the opposing full back as much as the backs mark him. Therefore when I check on a wingman, I look for speed, courage, accuracy when centring, and the guts, speed and stamina to chase back and do a job in defence when his own team has lost possession.'

And now the words of Sir Matt Busby, describing the perfect midfielder, and the importance of such a player: 'For real success the middle men, the creators, are the ones who really shape the game, the ones from whom most blessings flow. Deep-lying inside-forwards and wing-halves used to do the job, so there is nothing actually new about middle men ... these are the men predominantly who start things. They have to have vision, imagination to hold the ball or pass it if passing it is "on", and ability to beat a man, which is the hard way, used if a pass that will do the same work for him more swiftly and economically is not on. But the middle man has also to be able to win the ball, so he has to be able to tackle, read, or smell when an interception is going to present itself.'

Of course, he achieved his dream of playing for Manchester United with some distinction. He surpassed his father's wildest dreams by becoming more successful than his own hero. Arguably the greatest tribute to give David Beckham, considering the words of Busby and Murphy, is that he was the perfect prototype and example of what a Manchester United player should be, going back to their ideals when they arrived at Old Trafford in the 1940s.

Busby struggled with the fame of George Best; it was a contributory factor to his own retirement. Ferguson and Beckham could not co-exist, at least in the manager's eyes, if he wanted to retain the iron fist in the dressing room; although it is almost certain that if Beckham, bells and whistles included, had played for any other club, he was exactly the sort of player Manchester United would have moved heaven and earth to sign. But he belonged to Manchester, and then he belonged to the world, out there as England captain and flag-waver for the 'Golden Generation'.

Once his post-World Cup '98 recovery was complete, David was also a willing political figure used by the English FA whenever their need arose. They were unable to capitalise on his presence to win the hosting of a World Cup, and on the pitch, David could have perceived England's inability to win a trophy as a failure. As far as his personal contribution was concerned, though, his performance in major tournaments matched that of any England player over the duration of his career. When it mattered, Beckham would usually be there delivering from a cross, corner, free kick or penalty. It would not stop criticism at the time, but a journey back over those contributions with the benefit of hindsight reveals the truth. He was a true England great: 'Goldenballs' was, at least, the most golden from the generation that ultimately failed to shine.

His moves to Spain and the USA were successes for reasons already discussed at some length. By the time he was playing his last couple of years in Los Angeles, they too had become so used to the things he was brilliant at consistently, that a whole list of spectacular moments went relatively unappreciated. Take his last full season, for example, where almost all of his eight goals were goal of the season contenders – a real throwback to his breakthrough season at United, where he consistently scored long-range spectaculars. As a veteran, there was an experienced touch of class to these goals – how could it be that someone capable of such extraordinary feats was so often categorised as ordinary? Surely we should be flipping that argument around, celebrating the product of all that hard work and dedication, and asking if David was the best there has ever been when it comes to set-piece consistency? Has there ever been a player who could cross so beautifully and so economically? He made the functional aspects of the game fashionable, and did so with such inexorable consistency that it was, in the end, taken for granted.

Beckham's brilliance – and it is important to describe it for what it was – is notable by the absence of an equivalent in today's game. The closest there has been for years is Kevin De Bruyne, and he is a player who, on song, has often been described as the best player in the Premier League. There is no hidden secret to David's quality, and yet it remains a testament to how hard he worked and how committed he was that only one player in top-level English football has even come close to replicating the quality and range of his crossing.

As Alexi Lalas, and others, observed, though, the modern professional trains harder, has a diet more conducive to athletic development, and seeks every edge. So, by the time Beckham retired, there was no longer a case to say he worked distinctively harder than a team-mate or was more dedicated to self-improvement than the average professional; and yet the average professional can still not do the things David did to an expert level. Maybe, then, it's time to admit that David Beckham was a special talent, after all.

Acknowledgements

I AM so grateful to the following for their help in writing this book: Gordon Jago, Gordon Hill, Paul Parker, Martin Edwards, Danny Higginbotham, Ben Thornley, John O'Kane, Kevin Pilkington, Emile Heskey, Alexi Lalas, Mike Magee, Bryan Jordan and Luke Chadwick. I would also like to thank Paddy Barclay for being such a fantastic role model, and also Rob Smyth, Ian Herbert, James Robson, Bill Rice, David McDonnell and Simon Mullock.

Thanks as always to Jane Camillin and all the team at Pitch Publishing, Duncan Olner for his work on the cover and Graham Hughes for his copy-editing – it is a pleasure to work with you all.

To my friends and family, Dan, Kim and Alex Burdett, Hayley, Elfyn and Gruff Roberts, Gemma and Steve, Mikiel and Phil Gatt, Tony Bil, Tom Warren, Stan Chow, Matt Beadle, Alan Monger, Luke Smalley, Mike Pieri, Stel Stylianou, Matt Galea, Oyvind Enger, Barney Chilton, Chris Culkin, Ben Allen, Tyler Dunne, Steve Crabtree, Roy Canavagh, Jon Wilson, Bjarte Valen, John Gubba, Deiniol Graham, Pat McGibbon, Gary Thompson. Ben Greenwood, Ben McManus, Nipun Chopra and, as always,

ACKNOWLEDGEMENTS

Eifion Evans. A special thank you to Kerry Rutkin. All of you have supported and encouraged, and I am so grateful for that.

Thanks also:
To Pete Yorn, and to Charlie and the family for their support and friendship. To the most important person in any book, Dave Murphy; and that paragon of patience, Caroline, and the rest of the Murphy clan. To my in-laws: I love you, and I'm so grateful for all of you. To my brilliant nephews Freddy and Noah, who I love with all my heart – playing football with you is the only thing better than writing about it. To my mum, for never believing any dream is too unrealistic. And finally, my wife, my biggest champion, whose support and love I could not live without – I love you, and thank you; for pushing and inspiring me, for listening, for giving me confidence, and for taking this journey with me.

Also available at all good book stores

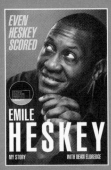

9781785315008

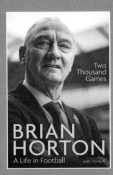

9781785316685

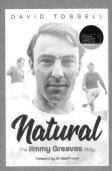

9781785314902

9781785314995

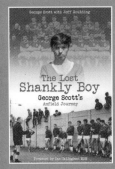

9781785316784

9781785316524

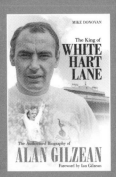

9781785315510

9781785316333

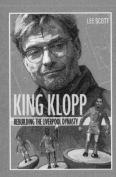

9781785316500